To Ellen
With love,
Grandma Louise.

Comox, B.C.
August 30. 05'

Mackenzie King
Friends & Lovers

Also by Louise Reynolds

Agnes: The Biography of Lady Macdonald
- Samuel-Stevens, Toronto, 1979
- Carleton University Press Inc., Ottawa, 1990
as the second book in their Women's Experience Series.

MACKENZIE KING
Friends & Lovers

BY

LOUISE REYNOLDS

Louise Reynolds.

Mackenzie King
Friends & Lovers

by Louise Reynolds

© **Copyright 2005 Louise Reynolds** All rights reserved.

Book Design & Cover illustration by David Dalton of **onedesign**
onedesigngraphics@yahoo.ca

No part of this publication may be reproduced, stored in a retrieval system, or transmitted, in any form or by any means, electronic, mechanical, photocopying, recording, or otherwise, without the written prior permission of the author.

Note for Librarians: a cataloguing record for this book that includes Dewey Decimal Classification and US Library of Congress numbers is available from the Library and Archives Canada. The complete cataloguing record can be obtained from their online database at:
www.collectionscanada.ca/amicus/index-e.html
ISBN 1-4120-5985-2

Printed in Victoria, BC, Canada
Offices in Canada, USA, Ireland, UK and Spain

TRAFFORD

This book was published on-demand in cooperation with Trafford Publishing. On-demand publishing is a unique process and service of making a book available for retail sale to the public taking advantage of on-demand manufacturing and Internet marketing. On-demand publishing includes promotions, retail sales, manufacturing, order fulfilment, accounting and collecting royalties on behalf of the author.

Book sales for North America and international:
Trafford Publishing, 6E–2333 Government St.,
Victoria, BC V8T 4P4 CANADA
phone 250 383 6864   toll-free   1 888 232 4444
fax   250 383 6804;   email to   orders@trafford.com
Order online at: www.trafford.com/robots/05-0886.html
10 9 8 7 6 5 4 3 2 1

This book is dedicated
to the memory
of my
husband

Ralph Edward Reynolds
1920 - 1994

Table of Contents

Preface xi

Introduction xix

Chapter One — Mathilde Grossert 1

Chapter Two — Bert Harper 23

Chapter Three — Marjorie Herridge 47

Chapter Four — Violet Markham 71

Chapter Five — The Governors-General 99

Chapter Six — Rockefeller 141

Chapter Seven — Joan Patteson 169

Acknowledgements

Sources

Index

Preface

"But what about King, the man?" This was the question that came up during a conference arranged by the History Department of the University of Waterloo on 17 December 1974. The gathering, which marked the hundredth anniversary of Mackenzie King's birth, was basically an academic critique of King, the politician. One of the organizers, however, recognized this as an opportunity to record the reminiscences of some of the distinguished participants who had worked closely with King. What he was looking for was some insight into King's personality, which seemed to be as much of a puzzle as ever a quarter century after his death. The result was hardly enlightening: King was variously described as being verbose and dull, but could be wonderful company in private; he was not charismatic or lovable but was sentimental; could be vindictive and working for him was 'all industry and no humanity'; had a particular sense of humour and told good stories; had few friends but was a gracious host. It all added up to seeing King as a complex man whose personality was very hard to pin down. Of those interviewed, Charles Ritchie, who had a way with words, expressed it best:

> Well, he was too evasive and elusive to sum up in a few words. . . . There was no kind of dead center to him, you know. The minute you thought that this was a definition of him, it shifted; he seemed to be able to finesse with the basis of his intellect in the most uncanny fashion. . . . [He was] rather like a conjuror, you know, pull him out of the sleeve and then suddenly the hat and there was the rabbit and they all vanished.

By the time of this conference, there was no shortage of books or articles of a scholarly nature about King; three had already appeared before his death in 1950. The first of these, *Mackenzie King* by Norman Rogers,* was politically motivated and King, himself, had a hand doing the revisions and reading proof. The end product, however, disappointed him except for the sections on his background and home, parts which he presumably wrote himself. It was an American publisher who set the ball rolling in the right direction in 1943 in search of someone to write a full-scale biography. Three possible writers were suggested only to be dismissed by King. One of them he considered to be "too old & wd only be able to treat of political, not personal side-too racy in style & not the understanding of inner life or point of view." Another was rejected as being "too indolent & unconcerned with others than himself, wd be all right to revise & rewrite in certain style but wd be hopeless re research." King was unfamiliar with the third person suggested but the idea of a biography was acceptable to him, provided it was done along the right lines and he felt he knew who could do this. Emil Ludwig, the German biographer, had recently approached him about doing a portrait sketch. At first King demurred, saying that "[Ludwig] is too great a man & too busy & in the eyes of the public today I am too insignificant to merit such a biographer." Despite these protestations, the work was undertaken with King in the role of research assistant. The result was a little booklet of some fifty pages and, in King's eyes, it was "far from being adequate or balanced. . . . it reminds me of a half-finished plastic model [and] does justice neither to him or to me." The author, too, recognized its short-comings and complained that "[There is the] hope that professional excavators may some day bring his doings to the light of posterity. Those with whom he shares his confidence most fully are not allowed to do this."

The first full-length biography, *Mackenzie King of Canada*, was published in 1949. Written by H. Reginald Hardy, a member of the Ottawa Press Club, this book, too, had its critics. The most that a reviewer of it could say was that it was written by a newspaper man who had an eye for detail and the human interest slant but his complaint was that King, as a statesman, was not yet given proper treatment. King took the opposite stance, finding it "On the whole good when on public issues" and "I felt moved at the close to

---

*Norman Rogers was one of King's secretaries in the 1920's. The other three possible writers were J. W. Dafoe, editor of the *Winnipeg Free Press*, L.W. Brockington, broadcaster and special assistant to King, 1939-42 and Bruce Hutchison, journalist. Others suggested were Gregory Clark, B.K. Sandwell and Charles Stacey.

think so good a story . . . had come from the press gallery."

As someone remarked, 'Dead men tell the most interesting tales' and, certainly, King could be placed high on that list. After his death it looked as if he had been preparing to be better known than in life. All the clues were there—in his diaries from 1893 to 1950 and in his massive collections of letters and papers. The earlier writers did not have the advantage of access to this treasure trove but after the two million or so pages of documents were sorted out and the diary transcribed, there was plenty of ready material for 'professional excavators'. The use of this material was the responsibility of King's Literary Executors[*] who chose R. MacGregor Dawson, a Professor of Political Economy, as the official biographer. Dawson began work in 1951, with the sorting out of King's archives keeping only a short step ahead of him. When the book was published in 1958, its title, *William Lyon Mackenzie King: A Political Biography,* (1874-1932), defines its focus although there was a surprising amount of detail about King, the man. There was not yet enough to answer the question posed at the University of Waterloo conference, but some reviewers seemed to be quite interested in what it showed of King's personality, as well as his political side. Professor Dawson died before this book was published and the writing was carried on by Professor H. Blair Neatby whose scholarly and objective work brought the story up to 1939 in two volumes, *The Lonely Heights* (1924-1932) and *The Prism of Unity* (1932-1939). The final years of King's political life, 1939 to 1948, are told in his own words in *The Mackenzie King Record*, four large volumes of extracts from his diaries which were prepared by J. W. Pickersgill. As well, all of the King diaries were available on microfiche by 1973.

At the same time as Professor Dawson was writing, another King biography was in the works. This one was written by Bruce Hutchison, one of the three writers who had been spurned by King in 1943. His book, *The Incredible Canadian*, was written without access to any of King's papers and while it purported to be 'A Candid Portrait of Mackenzie King', it was an arm's length one, dependent, as the author said, on "many persons who were as close to him as any man could be, who knew all the facts but differed sharply in their conclusions. I doubt that King would be satisfied with the resulting portrait."

[*]The executors were King's former secretary and later assistant, Fred McGregor; Dominion Archivist, W.K. Lamb; PMO secretary, J.W. Pickersgill and Norman A. Robertson, Clerk of the Privy Council and Secretary to the Cabinet.

What *would* King have wanted written about himself? When talk of a biography was first raised, King stated that he would like to write his own memoirs but not until the timing was right, possibly waiting until he was out of office. Over the next few years, the idea stayed with him and "Indeed it is only because of it", he wrote, "that I am keeping the record of day to day experiences in the form that I am." His plan was predictably high-minded: "There is some great message to be given to the world if I am spared to be able to give it. The purpose is to give significance to the truths I may be able to experience, in relation to life and power here and life hereafter." He would, he said, go back to the family sources which had given him whatever he possessed of good and with that as a base he envisioned a Book of Memoirs, consisting of his relations with different people. "My friendship with Ludwig", "Relations with Sovereigns of Britain", "Mr. Rockefeller and our relations" would be typical chapters.

It is interesting to speculate on what might have been learned about Mackenzie King's personal life had he written his autobiography. In 1947, he had referred to writing about 'life, power here and life hereafter' but in 1949, he resented Hardy's mention of spiritualism and 'the personal incident side' saying "the individual private life parts…a man should write himself." He had earlier stated his intention to do this: "Better no biography at all than one that would miss the secret of a life….shld write my own memoir when the right time comes, not lay bare my soul before others." Had he written, it would surely have been a heavily self-censored story. It is difficult to believe that he would have told the reader of his 'storms of passion' or of his sessions at the little table. Eventually all of this was told by others, sometimes in a distorted manner. In his retirement years, however, he simply ran out of energy to do anything more than sort out a few of his papers, burn a few letters and wish that "he had realized one could be writing Memoirs and doing ones day to day work at the same time, enjoying also the opportunities of reading and of meeting with ones friends and the public instead of being so completely a slave to routine."

There were other books written about King aside from the ones previously mentioned. One that appeared in 1955 covered King's life up to 1919 when he became leader of the Liberal party. This book, *The Age of Mackenzie King* by H. S. Ferns and B. Ostry, was looked at with suspicion by the reviewers who felt there was a hidden motive behind the writers' hostile approach which damned King on all counts as merely 'an inflated human ego, an unprincipled self-seeker'. Another book, *The Fall and Rise of Mackenzie King: 1911-1919* deals with the years when King was out of political office and working for the Rockefeller Foundation. Written by Fred McGregor who had been in King's office from 1909 and who remained with him during this period, this book is revealing as to the personality of both King and his employer, J. D. Rockefeller, Jr. , who became one of his closest friends.

"This is an age of sensation & vulgarity", King had remarked when he found a few references to his personal life in Hardy's book. "It does seem most unfair that one cannot enjoy one's own privacy, or some privacy." Words would have been inadequate to express his feelings had he known what was to be written later. In 1976, there was little the reading public did not learn about him when *A Very Double Life: The Private World of Mackenzie King* burst on the scene. When the military historian, C. P. Stacey, was researching other topics, he was given access to King's diaries (open up to 1946 at that time) by the literary executors and he realized he was on to some startling information. He was bowled over to learn about the ladies in King's life, the dogs, the mediums, the seances, facts which had been largely left out of the official biography or mentioned discreetly. What is now out in the open was all there in King's own words and Stacey felt compelled to write about it. It would be more financially rewarding than his usual writing and, for some reason, he thought he could do this more 'acceptably' than others. This turned out to be another hostile look at King and here the axe to grind was in the hands of a military man opposed to King's stand on conscription during World War II. A reviewer of this book asked what was the point of publishing the 'private world' parts separately from the rest of King's story and suggested that what Stacey had done was to take an excursion 'on the margin of the biographical lake' which was not very rewarding.

In writing of this book, Stacey remarked that "This volume is far from being the last word on the subject. I am sure that various investigators.... will find in the Papers material to occupy them for generations to come." Dr. Joy E. Esberey took up the challenge in 1981 with the publication of her psychobiography, *Knight of the Holy Spirit*. This was a formal study of King in which the author concentrated on his complicated personality traits. Putting him under the microscope, she found him to be a complex, insecure and neurotic man but she refuted some of Stacey's charges such as King's dependence on spiritualism in his political life and his unproven consorting with prostitutes. King, if he had written about himself, would have gone back to his family roots to show the source of whatever was good in himself. Esberey went back, too, but to show the result of being raised by a manipulative mother and a father who was not influential in that role.

By this time, King was a lively topic and, as such, was appealing to the media. Two television biographies were done by the CBC, one in 1960 which left the impression that King was a crackpot, an evil genius and half of the program was taken up by his interest in spiritualism. Then in 1988, there was a massive three-part, six-hour saga, *The King Chronicle*, a docudrama without adequate documentation and lacking in drama. King was portrayed as "an eccentric tea cosy of a man, a fussy, old, asexual nutcake who seems to trip pigeon-toed through history like a dear maiden aunt." In between the presentation of these two programs a play, *Rexy!*,* ran on the Toronto stage. Purporting to be a serious work, it drifted into comedy with King as a buffoon, seeking resolution to political problems from the ghosts of his grandfather and his mother. Obviously what one would hear of King's personality in any of these three presentations depended on the stance taken by the producers interested, naturally, in headlines and ticket sales. Nor was Heather Robertson's, *Willie: A Romance*, the right place to look. In this novel, the first in a trilogy called *The King Years*, it was impossible for the average reader to know where fiction and real narrative merged. Predictably, it was attacked by historians and others who had been grappling with the King psyche over the years and who were now presented with a person as unknowable as ever.

Two later books of note are *Mackenzie King: His Life and World* by J. L. Granatstein and *Right Honourable Men* by Michael Bliss. In the former book, King takes his place in the history of the first half of this century. Drawn into politics, it demonstrates that he succeeded despite carrying the baggage of being the grandson of 'The Rebel'. In the latter book the author takes a long look at King who, warts and all, comes through not as a 'fussy, old asexual fruitcake' but that "King's life is not a Jekyll-and-Hyde epic. Willie King did a good job both as a politician and a human being."

---

*King had acquired the nickname 'Rex' when a freshman at the University of Toronto. The nickname stuck and 'Rex' (Latin for 'King') was what he was called by close friends thereafter.

More has been written about King than about any other Canadian politician. However, one of those persons interviewed at the Waterloo conference in 1974 suggested that, as far as King was concerned, it was not a case of biography being about chaps " 'but biography is about gaps'. The gaps between private and public, person and legend, reality and image, body and soul." In Mackenzie King's case, he felt that these were 'unusually disconnected'. In the intervening years some of these gaps have been closed and, although King, 'the politician', is never very far away, there is a lot to be learned about him, what you find when you 'pull him out of the sleeve' as it were.

Introduction

William Lyon Mackenzie King

Sat in the middle and played with string

And loved his mother like any thing

William Lyon Mackenzie King

This little nursery rhyme by Dennis Lee expresses how some Canadians felt about Mackenzie King. It is true that, politically, he often 'sat in the middle' and that he doted on his mother. He also, they said, consulted psychics and when seated at the 'little table', discussed matters of importance with his mother and others who had 'gone before'. He even 'talked' by this means with his little departed Irish terriers. It was said that he kept a close watch on the hands of the clock to see that they were properly aligned before he made some decision or other. In fact, he was an old fuddy-duddy, a strange, aloof man.

The general public who found it easy to make him the butt of jokes has given Mackenzie King a hard time over the years. He was summed up once as being "A steady, colorless man with too much honor and intellect to be a demagogue, too little fire to be an orator, too little hair and too few mannerisms to be spectacular." With much of this King, himself, would have agreed especially regarding his personal appearance. "I never had anything to boast of in features or looks; I confess to a feeling of discouragement at my own appearance, the loathsome opposite of all I would like to be" and "This has been a part of the bane of my life." The words 'too little fire to be an orator' would have been denied by Mathilde Grossert, his first great love, who told him that his voice was like that of 'a master in Israel'. A member of the Ottawa Press Gallery, on the other hand, declared that "his speeches were as heavy as a flight of crows on a November day." As for character faults, he was very self-critical and his diaries reflect this from their start in 1893 until the end of his days. Other critics might grudgingly concede that he was great at a wedding or a wake but he did not give himself even that credit.

Obviously the electorate was not put off by King's dull image. They voted him in time after time; he was Leader of the Liberal Party for 29 years and Prime Minister for 21 of those years, setting an unexcelled Canadian record. His political accomplishments have been the subject of many biographies. Some of these books were written years ago while he was still active, others shortly after his death in 1950. Some were very respectful of his private life, others less so. At one time he was determined to write his autobiography and it would have been a book, he said, combining both the biographical and the historical, but time and energy ran out for him.

There was so much to tell—more than anyone expected and the picture of King that began to emerge seemed hardly credible. In *A Very Double Life: The Private World of Mackenzie King*, the reading public was told by Charles Stacey that King had, indeed, been into 'table-rapping', that he had consulted psychics, that he was rather too close to some of his married lady friends and, moreover, that he had made forays into the seamy side of life. What had been only rumour before or known to a few loyal and discreet people was now there in black and white, according to this author. King would have to admit that some of this was true. What started as a passing interest in psychic phenomena became an important facet of his life in the 1930s when he began to consult mediums. In his desire to communicate with departed family members and others, he also used the ouija board or the 'little table' at times of crisis when he sought reassurance that he had made the right decisions. He was not alone in this interest; it was one that was shared by many during the 20s and 30s but few, perhaps, went to the lengths that King did in keeping records of these experiences. Had they done so, King's activities would not stand out the way they do. As for his closeness to some of his married lady friends, it is evident that he did not handle these relationships very wisely nor did they. The phrase, 'A Very Double Life', was King's own, taken from his diaries as were many of the quotes in this book but it is the interpretation of them that is ambiguous. A reading of these diaries when he was a student in Toronto, especially, tells of his evening strolls

*Four King children
Jennie, Bella, Mackenzie & Dougal*

'on the dark side of the world', strolls followed by self-flagellation for what it is not clear. In his struggle to come to terms with his own sexuality, a struggle that went on through most of his adult life, he was the victim of his Victorian upbringing with its emphasis on the seven deadly sins, one of them being lust.

King's diaries are a natural source for anyone writing about him. They began on 6 September 1893, with the caveat that they should "contain a very brief sketch of the events, actions, feelings and thoughts of my daily life. . . . It must above all be a true and faithful account." The final diary entry was made just a few days before his death on 22 July 1950. While the diaries remained 'a true and faithful account', they did not keep to being brief sketches but, instead, they became his one true confidant, thus revealing those inner torments that plagued him so.

As well as the diaries, there are masses of personal letters in the Library and Archives Canada in Ottawa, letters exchanged with friends, which will be used here to bring to life some close associations. There are also family letters and memorabilia to which one must turn for a look at King's formative years. His early days were spent in Berlin, (now Kitchener), Ontario. He was born there on 17 December 1874, the eldest son of Isabel and John King. There was already a sister, Bella, just thirteen months older. Another sister, Jennie, was born in 1876 and two years later, the birth of Dougall Macdougall (always to be known as Max) completed the family.

When King was twelve years old they moved from a small house in downtown Berlin to Woodside, a property on the outskirts. This was the perfect setting for bringing up a family, a large, rambling ten-roomed house set in extensive grounds. In the autumn of 1947, over seventy years later, King revisited his old home. Both the house and grounds had suffered badly from neglect but, as a gesture to him and what he had accomplished in Canadian politics, restoration of the property was about to be undertaken and King had been asked to come and see what was planned. His impressions were recorded in his diary thus:

> *I recognized at once the familiar contours of the hills and fields . . . and then Woodside itself. We drove up the old avenue. . . a winding avenue. I was delighted to see in front of the house there was still the appearance of the old lawn. The grass, of course, was overgrown . . . and I walked through some of it to the spot where, as children, we all mourned the loss and burial of the little dog Fanny. I recalled many of the incidents related to Old Bill, our horse, thought of the days we played cricket on the lawn, of sliding down the hill in winter and of my brother Max sliding down on one or two occasions in a barrel. I walked up the old lover's lane . . . and also up the hill where we used to camp at times and spend Sunday evening. One could still recall and trace the path which made a short cut home across the field at the end of a day at school.*

Later, he went inside and there, too, signs of neglect were evident but "one can see there, the charms of the upper rooms. I could see them, of course, in terms of how the place looked in my father's and mother's day."

By the time the King family moved out to Woodside, John King's law practice had grown and although they were not wealthy, there was money enough, at that time, to provide for a comfortable living. Isabel King had help in the house and there was a man to look after the grounds and Old Bill, the horse. The children all had their little chores to do and King particularly liked working in the garden. Once when his father was away on a business trip, King wrote to him that

> *I cleaned the lawn in front of the door and around at the side. We then cleared out all the orchard and made a terrible large fire of all the limbs and all the rubbish in the yard. Thomas says that he needs my help all week so as to get all the seeds in.*

On his return visit in 1947, one of the first things King did was to try to locate where the flower beds had been and to look around for the old trees. By then, of course, he had built his own gardens at Kingsmere, in the Gatineau hills outside Ottawa, and had made his own 'terrible large fire' when clearing the ground.

In all, King spent only five full years of his life at Woodside, the years between twelve and seventeen. By 1891, he was ready to enter the University of Toronto. All of his schooling up to that time had been in Berlin where he was remembered by a former teacher as having been an average student with the energy and high spirits that made him a bit of a mischief. "Ringing doorbells, playing hookey to go swimming in the Grand River and stealing apples and plums from local orchards were all a part of the day's routine." King agreed that he was just an average, normal young boy when later discussing his early days. He was a sturdy young man who got rid of some of his animal spirits on the playing fields and in the gym. He swam; he played football with greater enthusiasm than skill; he made the soccer team once and he was no stranger to the cricket pitch. In the classroom, he was not a top-notch scholar but he did well in English and History and was making a name for himself by his debating skills. It was said that "He distinguished himself by his precocious platform manner and his fine command of language, both of which placed him head and shoulders above his classmates."

Although King spent only a comparatively short time at Woodside, he always considered these years to have been the formative ones. When he went back in 1947 he spoke of those days, saying that many happy memories came to mind and made him realize how strong were the influences of childhood and youth. "Those of home are generally the strongest and most enduring. For most of us, fortunately, it would be difficult to think of home apart from school and church and their associations."

The home in which King was brought up was typically Victorian in its values and, as he remarked, school and church were prominently featured. Children were expected to do well in school and to attend church regularly. The Kings, as a family, went to the local Presbyterian Church. It was told of King that his schoolboy penchant for getting into mischief sometimes spilled over into the church. A too-long sermon could have him "sending [his sisters] into fits of suppressed giggles over some detail of the sermon or other occurrence which tickled his sense of humour." Then there would be a stern look directed at the girls by their mother while young 'Billy' or 'Willy', as he was variously called, assumed a pious air. The children went to Sunday School, as well, memorizing the little Biblical texts of the day. It seems that there, too, King got into mischief. Ladies wore bustles on the backs of their dresses at that time, some of these bustles being detachable. This was too much of a temptation to King and, on one occasion when a teacher was wearing a particularly flamboyant one, he managed to tie it to the back of her chair with predictable results. The children's religious education was supplemented at home by daily Bible readings. This activity became an important part of King's adult life and a day did not pass without his making time to read some part of the book. He knew it well, knew where to look in it for solace and strength and he often quoted from it in his diary.

The King family read other books as well. They would gather out on the verandah in the summer or near the fire in winter, reading aloud from books of politics or novels or romantic poetry. This latter would bring Isabel King to the point of tears just as it would strongly affect other women in King's life. There were evenings also given over to music, with the whole family gathered around the piano. King's mother or one of his sisters would play while John King sometimes kept time on castanets and they all sang. King's voice was never very good as he, himself, admitted when he was, nonetheless, a member of the Glee Club at university. "I sang with the 2nd basses (tho my voice is not much good for singing)" was his assessment. But this did not stop him then or later. Towards the end of 1949, just a few months before his death, he spent an evening with his old friends, Godfroy and Joan Patteson, and with his cracked old voice he joined Joan in singing "old darkey minstrel songs, Afton Water and hymns for about an hour." It was the hymns that pleased him most and a Sunday evening without its hymn-sing was rare. One of those hymns, O God of Bethel, became, in fact, his Battle Cry and he sang it, perhaps superstitiously, before each new session of Parliament opened.

The King parents did not neglect the social side of their children's upbringing, either. Their position as one of the leading families in Berlin meant that they

King with his parents (Sept. 1911)

entertained often, thus exposing their children to that side of life. In the years after he left Woodside, and especially after he moved to Ottawa, King developed a strictly ambivalent attitude towards social life. While he began to look on socializing as a cross that he had to bear, he often admitted to his diary that when he did accept invitations, he enjoyed himself more than he thought he should. This bothered him and, although he knew it would not be easy, he determined to, at least, observe the Lenten fasting period each year. In 1928, he promised himself that

> *I must renounce the things of sense, Lent now approaching. I have kept my self-imposed vow not to touch wine or liquor. I shall hold to that thro' Lent. I shall give up dancing as well & seek to keep my thoughts on a high plane.*

In the judgment of an early biographer of King,

> *[The Kings] formed a social unit in a very real sense. They stood staunchly together, fought one and another's battles, gave support when and where it was needed, rejoiced in victories and extended consolation in defeat. [While] all members of the family must have had a share…it is clear that little would have been possible without the constant vigilance of the parents who furnished both the inspiration and the example.*

What about this latter assertion? Were Isabel and John King such paragons as parents? According to the writer of a psychobiography of King, they were quite the opposite. Had the term 'dysfunctional' been used in the late 19th century, it would have been applied to the King family. Neither parent filled the role as glowingly as set out by this early biographer, Isabel King being self-centred and, in many ways, an immature person and John King was unequal to the task of providing for their shared social aspirations, especially after the family later moved to Toronto.

Of the four children, Bella, the eldest, was the most serious. She looked at things from the standpoint of a practising Christian and tried to make a life for herself in that mold. Her motto was 'Try to do good deeds' and this was the message she passed along to King one evening in 1936 by means of the 'little table'. In recalling her life, she reminded him that

Long ago I went to the Institute in Toronto.
The girls I helped are here beside me.
Long ago I tried to help poor people in trouble.
They are here beside me.
Long ago I had a girls' club at Lake Simcoe.

There was no mention here of what had been her dream. For years she had wished to care for the sick and in 1898 she sought to train as a nurse in Toronto. Her indifferent health at this particular time and her father's well-known antipathy to this profession for one of his daughters put a temporary end to the plan. A few months later, however, she was allowed to go to Boston where King was at Harvard and she began training in a hospital there, safely away from the society in which the Kings moved back home. Sadly, her health was not good enough to withstand the rigorous training and she returned to Toronto where she took various courses which she hoped might lead to work to help the family in their precarious financial situation. As she told King that evening at the 'little table', "Long ago I tried to earn some money in the Bank of Commerce. Long ago I tried to help Mother and Father." Faithful to the end in her Christian beliefs and to what she saw as her duty to her parents, Bella died, unmarried, in 1915 at the age of 42.

Jennie, like her elder sister, was expected to carry her share of family responsibilities and to make whatever sacrifices were necessary to ensure that both her brothers had university educations. She was more outgoing than Bella and seems to have enjoyed the social activities available to her. In this she was encouraged by King up to a point:

I am glad [Jennie] had such a good time at the Osgoode Hall dance. And the Institute next morning! That's right. Get all the joy the world can give you but turn your face where its beauty may be reflected into darkened corners. . . . In the ballroom and in the slum with the same heart. There are very few who can do it but . . . this I believe both my sisters [can].

Jennie's attendance at social functions was determined by whether or not her father was able to get tickets 'other than by paying out hard cash'. Her social calendar was more likely to be filled with teas, luncheons and making calls. While there was opposition to Bella becoming a nurse, there was no such reaction to Jennie's being a paid companion to the prominent Mulock family for a year. Except for this one break, Jennie remained at home, a dutiful and caring daughter, until her marriage at the age of 30 to Harry Lay, a banker. He was a widower with a three-year old son, Nelson. Four children were born to the Lays- John, Jean, Harry and Rosabelle. They recall that as an uncle to small children, King was not the kind to produce candies from his pockets but when they lived in Barrie, Ontario, they had meals in his private railway car as it sat overnight on a siding during an electioneering tour. There they enjoyed 'the best ice cream in the world'. They remember, too, that after their father died in 1945, King supported their mother generously for the rest of her life. Both they and Max's children were often visitors at both Kingsmere and Laurier House; it was only the pressure of work that dictated how much time their Uncle Willie could spend with them.

Max, as the youngest of the King children, was the focus of the family's attention as a boy. For a time, however, he stood in the shadow of his brother's accomplishments but, as he matured, he developed confidence in his own abilities. Medicine was his chosen field and for a few years he practised in Ottawa. His promising career was cut short by illness and in 1914, he was forced to move to the drier climate of Denver, Colorado. Despite this, his health continued to fail and in 1922, he died, leaving a wife and nine-year old twin sons, Arthur and William Lyon Mackenzie King II. King sent generous gifts of money on birthdays and at Christmas to the boys and also to help their mother. Lyon followed his father in the career of medicine and he was serving on a Canadian ship in 1943 when it was torpedoed and sunk.

Arthur King spoke for both boys when recalling his uncle's role in their upbringing:

He was very strong in his advice as to our progress and as to the role that we should play in society and how we should acquire ability and power ourselves as individuals. I used to listen with quite some interest to his advice in letters and through mother. [But there were limits]: I early learned to regard his advice as regards women or girls as totally unrealistic and to discount it and pay no attention to it. . . . He made it quite clear that you do not consider taking a girl out unless you were ready to assume strict moral regard for her wellbeing and as to how she would get along in the future as having been influenced by you.

Of the four King children, only Mackenzie King carried scars into his adult years. One clue to that may be found in looking at his full given names: William Lyon Mackenzie. King's mother, Isabel, was the youngest daughter of this man for whom her first son was named. Mackenzie, or 'the Rebel', as he was commonly called, came to prominence as the leader of the abortive 1837 Rebellion in Upper Canada (now Ontario). After its failure, he escaped with his family to the United States and lived there, an impoverished exile, until he was granted a pardon. He returned to Canada in 1851 and lived in Toronto. By then the once rambunctious rebel was an embittered man who was subject to frequent black moods. He died in the summer of 1861 by which time he had become a virtual recluse.

It seems that hard though the circumstances had been while the Mackenzies lived in exile, the parents had "struggled to keep their children well-dressed and to send them to schools which satisfied their father's high educational standards, even if, at times, the family was living without adequate food or fuel or necessary household furnishings." Perhaps Mackenzie's high standards were the best gift that the children could have been given and one that made up, in part, for what they otherwise had to endure during their early years. The daughters all came out of this period with many of the graces and accomplishments of better-off young ladies. This stood them in good stead in the years following Mackenzie's death when they were able to help their mother make a living by giving lessons in music and dancing to girls from well-to-do families in Toronto. An early biographer of King's wrote about Isabel Mackenzie as having come through this period of straightened circumstances quite well. "Happily, adversity seems to have had little effect on her spirits or disposition, and one of her friends remembered her at this period as 'a sprightly girl, taken with the lighter things of life'." She had, however, inherited her father's high-strung temperament and her entire life was a series of highs and lows. Her nervous nature would lead her to fling herself into a frenzy of activity which would be followed by a period of bed rest and then the cycle would repeat itself. Although it might appear that Isabel was frail and helpless, she had a will of iron and usually managed to get her own way. One of her grandsons, who could not have been more than four or five years old at the time, remembers her as having been tiny, vivacious and rather charming. Another grandson who was a few years older agreed but felt there was just something about her which did not allow him to be fond of her as children are supposed to be of their grandmothers.

John King's nature, on the other hand, was quite different. His background and upbringing had none of the intense drama and turmoil that the Mackenzies had suffered. He has been described as having "a friendly manner which consorted well with an easy-going nature." Since his university days he was well-known as an after-dinner speaker and a writer of articles for law journals. It seems that his competence in those fields was more pronounced than in the practice of law. King wrote of his father that there was 'goodness and gentleness in his face'. Certainly, his children loved him and turned to him for help in their small problems. What is to be regretted is that, by his nature, he was not a dominant force in their lives but was more like a friend to them.

King, unfortunately, became disillusioned with his father in later years. This stemmed largely from John King's lack of success in his profession after the family moved to Toronto in 1893. What had been looked forward to with great expectations proved to be very disappointing. No one was more aware of why this should be so than John King, himself. "If I had coarser feelings and a harder nature, careless of riding roughshod over everything and everybody, I would have been better off today." During those years King was trying to chart his own future and the situation at home made its imprint on his thinking. "While I have a longing to be better, nobler and to rise higher, [he wrote], still I have not had a definite personal ideal man, as it were, before me. We should have an ideal for our daily acts, etc., as well as for our life work."

If King did not have this ideal in his father, was there anyone to whom he could turn? At times it seemed obvious that William Lyon Mackenzie, the grandfather whose name he bore, might fill this perceived lack. The King children had been brought up on tales told them by their mother of the difficulties she had experienced as a child. Of the four children, King seems to have been the only one who was deeply affected by these stories. After reading a biography of Mackenzie he noted in his diary that "I imagined I could feel his blood coursing through my veins." As he read on, his feelings deepened and he "became a greater admirer of [Mackenzie] than ever, prouder of my own mother and the race from which I am sprung." From there, it was only a small mental jump to come to the conclusion that he was meant to accomplish something great in his life.

> *The thought occurred to me why should this man escape the many, many attempts to end his life, suffer imprisonment, experience poverty in its worst forms, be exiled from his native country, that to him a young child [Isabel] should be born, the 13th & youngest of a large family, who should bare of [a] son to inherit the name of his grandfather.*

While this determination on King's part must have been pleasing to his mother, there is no indication that she ever did more than attempt to have King vindicate his grandfather's name. The last thing she wished was to have another 'Rebel' in the family but she was convinced that something should be done to atone for all the suffering and deprivation. It was clear by now that John King was not the sort of person who would rise to prominence so she turned to her children for help. King was the eldest, he bore the name and he seemed to have all the necessary traits. When he fell in love and expressed a wish to be married while still a graduate student, she was distraught for here was a real threat to her hopes.

The story of King and the girl in question, Mathilde Grossert, is told in Chapter 1 and there one reads of his reaction to a letter from his mother during that time. "She speaks of me forsaking her ... she speaks as tho' all at home had been resting on me and as though I had been selfish, forgetful and never thought of them all." It took only a little more pressure along those lines and King's romance was a thing of the past but he was left an emotional mess, full of guilt for what he had contemplated and what the effects might have been on the family. Then and later, when he might have formed a normal happy relationship, the ghost of his mother appeared and he was convinced that "I see Mother love, my love for Mother controls me absolutely, that whatever disappoints or wounds or runs counter to that love provokes the most violent reaction." While he recognized this, still he was never able to free himself from the invisible but strong bonds that bound him forever to his mother: "dear, dear Mother, my guardian angel, my most dearly beloved of any known on earth or in Heaven."

This thwarted love affair of King's youth did nothing to dampen his interest in the opposite sex. He desperately wished to have a wife—and there were women who were only too eager to marry him but, sadly, it never worked out. Although he was not successful in finding the right person to marry, this is not to imply that he lacked female companionship. He developed many close friendships over the years, two of them being

Mackenzie King 1910

with Ottawa women. Marjorie Herridge, the wife of a Presbyterian Minister, filled this role during King's early days in Ottawa and Joan Patteson, whose husband was a local banker, was close to him for over thirty years. In each case, the relationship became more involved than one might have expected but they were more or less open secrets with little gossip being heard. Only occasionally were King and these two lady friends a bit careful of appearances. During the 1930 election campaign King wrote in his diary that "I can see they [the Tories] will try to make something yet of my friendship for Joan. I shall have to be circumspect in that particular." When corresponding with either Marjorie or Joan a code was sometimes used but otherwise everything pointed to normal friendships. Undoubtedly people looked at Mackenzie King as being less than a romantic figure. Another association that spanned many years was with an English lady, Violet Markham, and this was a case of a pure and simple friendship for, as she herself said, they had never been in love.

Of King's male friendships, one in particular stands out. This was with Bert Harper who had been at university with King and, later, they worked together in Ottawa. Sadly, King lost this companion through Harper's untimely death by drowning in 1901 and no one ever took his place. Another man whose friendship he cherished was John D. Rockefeller, Jr. Their acquaintance developed after King spent some time as an employee of the Rockefeller Foundation in 1914-18 and it extended to other members of the Rockefeller family, as well. King owed much to J. D. R., Jr. both with regard to his friendship and to financial help in his retirement.

Being at the centre of power in Ottawa as King was from his move there in 1900, it was natural that he should see a great deal of the various Governors-General who lived at Rideau Hall. He got along well enough with most of them and with some he was able to share an interest in psychic matters both when they were in Ottawa and later. His greatest disappointment was that he did not have the expected close relationship with John Buchan whom he knew and admired. This King felt was because Buchan's personality had changed on having been elevated to the peerage before taking up his position. King had a problem with titles but he had a greater one with what he saw in Buchan as

> that infernal 'tranquil consciousness of effortless superiority' which Asquith noted in the people of the British Isles, and which makes them so misunderstood and often disliked when they go abroad. . . . Perhaps knowing their background so well is what makes it more difficult at the present time.

As far as the general public was concerned, King remained an enigma with one newspaper referring to him, in 1947, as being 'just a cold fish'. "Not so", said a writer in the now defunct *Ottawa Morning Journal*. "Mr. King is not cold in his private and ordinary human relationships . . . meet him anywhere, alone or in a gathering, and he is the personification of warmth, gay, genial, humorous, whimsical." The writer expressed the hope that someday, someone would "give us something of the real man . . . whatever his shortcomings. Such a portrait, if it ever comes . . . will not present 'a cold fish'."

In spite of all the books about Mackenzie King, no one has written about him simply as a person, as a man with ordinary weaknesses, strengths, ideals, shortcomings, and imperfections. No one has written about him simply as a friend, as a family member, as a young man in love, as an old man with an old man's concerns. It is the present writer's wish that the following chapters will enlighten readers on King's personality as seen in his relationship with these, his closest friends. For that reason, politics, although always present in his life, is not the primary interest here and is only mentioned as a peg on which to hang some moments in time. Each chapter stands on its own and except for the one on Bert Harper, each ends with King's death; nor is there much interplay from one chapter to the other. This was in keeping with King's philosophy that 'one at a time is best'.

Mathilde Grossert

At first glance it seemed a strange thing to come across in a box which otherwise holds an assortment of Mackenzie King papers in the Library and Archives Canada. It is a small dainty case made out of a scrap of blue silk and some bateese lace with the monogram 'K' handworked on the inside of it. It encloses a folded card on which there are lines from a German poem, which mean, in translation,

Say, what has fate in store for us?
Say, how did it bind us so perfectly together?

Then, there are the words, "Mathilde, 1915", and it all began to make sense. She was the love of Mackenzie King's life for a brief period in the late 1890's and this was obviously a gift to King from her. By 1915, however, the sentiment expressed in these lines of poetry (likely from the German poet, Goethe, who was a favourite of Mathilde's), did not have the same meaning as it would have had when their relationship was new and in such turmoil. On the surface, an answer to these questions had been found long before 1915.

The intervening years brought many changes to the lives of both Mathilde and King. They met in 1897 when he was a graduate student at the University of Chicago and she, then Mathilde Grossert, was a student nurse at St. Luke's Hospital in that city. Their paths probably would not have crossed except that he became ill with typhoid fever in March and was hospitalized for three weeks. During his stay at St. Luke's he recorded in his diary that "It would be hard to express the unbounded admiration that one has for those nurses. I have seen here what is noblest and best in woman." By the time he left the hospital, his comments became more personal: "I like Miss Grossert exceedingly. She is a very heroic character."

King was in Chicago until June and during that spring he and Mathilde spent some time together, enough for him to be impressed by "the nobility of character I find in her. She is much the type of woman I long to know well & be associated with." But, while on the one hand, King was prone to put those women whom he considered to have 'pure Christian hearts' on a pedestal, there were the other women, the women of the streets, who were proving to be a real temptation to him. They were the source of such self-accusatory entries as "I wandered about and again rather forgot the narrow path although I returned home safely, somewhat ashamed of my weakness. Will I ever overcome this devil?" Whether in Chicago or back home in Toronto it was the same story. "How the chains of Hell pull a man when he is tired! Got home alright," and he admitted to feeling that he sometimes led a double life: "I fear I am much like Peter, I deny my Lord when the maid smiles at me."

Mathilde Grossert

King spent the summer of 1897 in Toronto trying to earn some money and making plans for further studies, this time, as it turned out, at Harvard. In his diary that summer, he wrote "I could not help admiring her. In truth I cannot help loving her. She has such a pure Christian heart." But he was not writing of Mathilde who seems to have been temporarily put aside in favour of Helen, a summer romance.

Mathilde, however, had not forgotten him and in August he had a letter from her. Unfortunately it is not available but her enthusiasm for opening a correspondence should, by rights, have been dampened by his reply, a part of which is extant. In it he expressed the hope that

> *your life [may] appear to many as it has appeared to me a precious star of hope and love, commissioned by Heaven to point men's hearts ever toward the Master's throne, a light to dispel the gloom of earth's sufferings and distresses, a comforter of much affliction and a bearer of much happiness and peace.*

Her reaction to such a lofty response obviously did not discourage her and their correspondence continued after he went to Harvard in September.

King's letters to Mathilde over the winter months grew in intensity and a paper romance began to develop. Early on, he still thought of her as his "ideal woman, in her love for others, her life of devot'n to the helpless, her constant aim, her purity, and noble mind." But Mackenzie King was falling in love for the first time in his life and it caught him by surprise. By February 1898 he knew that "I love the girl with all my heart and yet I don't know what to think about it all." Separated as they were by the miles and letters being their only contact, it was natural that in his reflective moments King did wonder about his situation. How did Mathilde really feel about him? She seemed a little distant in her letters where, in keeping with late Victorian formality, she often addressed him as 'Mr. King'. But there were times when the salutation was 'Meine liebes Kind'—My Dear Child. Was that how she saw him? He wondered if possibly she was older than he? In fact, Mathilde was born in January 1873 and there was thus less than two years difference in their ages. In his fevered mind he imagined her to be much older. Certainly, she was the more mature of the two. Her letters, which he had now tied together with a blue ribbon, were read over and over as he searched in them for signs of her feelings towards him.

This must have been a very confusing time for Mathilde. The King whom she got to know slightly in the spring of 1897 was a sober young man who had recently been thinking of dedicating his own life to the betterment of conditions for the poor and down-trodden of this world. Since going to Chicago, however, things had not worked out as he had expected. A little practical experience of living in a settlement house* in one of the worst slums in the city left him disillusioned and convinced him that he had not yet found his real calling. It worried him, too, that he had given so much time to the idea that, as a result, his studies had suffered. Over and above this, he was far away from his family for the first time and felt a great loneliness, with no one around who was interested in him.

At the end of December 1897, he looked back over the past year, with his usual self-critical feelings of having left much undone, but also with satisfaction that the disappointments he encountered in Chicago had been

---

*Toynbee Hall, London, England was the first settlement house. After its founding in 1884, others followed including Hull House in Chicago. These were essentially community centres where people of different backgrounds might be helped with improving their living conditions and environment.

replaced by his present success at Harvard. He could also say that

"I have struggled hard towards a purer life, it has been an almost hourly struggle but the battle has been better fought, I think, than in former years." There was one more thing: "I must not forget the hospital in Chicago & my taste of love for the little nurse." Over the Christmas holidays in Toronto, he told his friend, Bert Harper, about his love for Mathilde "for I must call it love. She has more true character than any woman I have met as yet." King also had a confidant at Harvard. John George, who had been a colleague in Chicago, had also come east to study and it was to him that King turned in his hour of need. "I told him of my love for Miss Grossert & read him parts of her letters which certainly were gems. She is a splendid woman. Does she care for me?" This was King's dilemma. He was not sure of his own feelings nor of hers: "I have thought much of Miss Grossert all day. Does the girl love me? Do I love her? Ought I to love her more????" By the end of January he was no further ahead. Mathilde hadn't committed herself and King came to the conclusion that "She probably doesn't care a rap for me," and this is where his selfishness comes to the fore: "I believe that if I felt some one really loved me I could work to better effect." From the beginning of their relationship King had looked on Mathilde as one who could be an influence for good, someone who would help in his struggle to live a better life. Suddenly in February 1898, this question became academic. King was deeply in love. No longer was he idealizing Mathilde but he was loving her for herself. Soon he could write to her saying

> *I love you with all my heart. I have spoken of friendship and admiration but I have never felt words so hollow before. It is not friendship, it is love deep deep love, deep and true. It is not admiration. It is love, true, true love, and it is all love of you, Mathilde Hedwig Grossert, you I love and with all my heart.*

There followed a very difficult time for both King and Mathilde. No sooner had he posted the letter than doubts began to creep in. Had he acted too rashly? He found he had practically proposed! Had he any hope of winning Mathilde? Patience was one thing King did not possess at this time and while waiting for her reply, he composed several more letters to her. In one of them, a long, earnest dissertation, a whole morning's work, he again dwelt on her greatness and goodness:

You are the only woman with whom it has ever seemed to me that the ocean of life might be crossed in perfect happiness & peace. . . . It is the thought that if together, our lives, might each be doubly blessed & a double blessing to those around us that has made me unfold my heart to you & beg of you to accept it all.

In another part of this letter he, again, became the impassioned lover, writing:

Oh, my little girl, I love you & God knows with what a deep & tender love. My dear Miss Grossert, I cannot help the words & now that they are down I cannot strike them out. Surely we can be children once again, only for one bright Summer's day, loving & being loved in perfect confidence and trust.

His letters to her during this time, obviously, could not help her come to any conclusion but the world finally seemed to open up for King a few days later when he recorded in his diary that he had had an encouraging reply to his latest pleas. His relief was tempered with the knowledge that this was only a step along the way to complete happiness: "A cloud fell off, a heavy, heavy cloud but there are others there and the storm has only just begun."

King was quite right. The storm had already begun. By a pathetic coincidence, the next entry in his diary was that, on that very day, he had received letters from his family in Toronto which were to have long-lasting effects on the lives of both Mathilde and her 'liebes Kind'. It had been impossible for King to hide his love for Mathilde from his family. There were veiled hints in his letters to them, which caused them to wonder at his sudden abundant enthusiasm and confidence, feelings that he had credited solely to it being springtime. Eventually he did tell them about Mathilde—not that things had gone so far—but enough to prompt his father, mother and sister, Jennie, to respond immediately and in no uncertain terms. The family, especially his parents, had been concerned earlier about King's actions when he was in Chicago. When he moved into the settlement house and considered devoting his life to social causes following the example of his grandfather, the Rebel, they looked on this as a threat that he would not fulfill their career expectations of him. Now there was a new worry and one that might be harder to resolve. The first letter came from King's mother, Isabel, and she did not spare the whip.

Only part of this letter remains and in it she says:

> Billy, . . . I would be the last one to tell you to live the lonely life of an old bachelor [but] I would tell you to consider before you step into matrimony. I have built castles without number for you. Are all these dreams but to end in dreams? I am getting old now, Willie, and disappointment wearies and the heart grows sick. Sometimes when I hear you talk so much of what you would do for those that suffer I think charity begins at home and as you do so shall it be done unto you. I am not grasping for myself but I do feel for your sisters and I know you who has got such a big heart will not forsake me. I am afraid those Harvard young men have contaminated you but when you come to your senses and will look at all things in the light we do . . . I have waited till the dawn will break to write to you and I trust an answer will come that will relieve my mind. I am very wearied but that is nothing new for Mother. [It] is only one more lesson not to put your trust in anything under the sun. Goodbye may every blessing attend

By the same mail, he had a letter from his sister, Jennie, questioning his judgment and putting a few plain home truths to him:

> If I really thought you were in love with the girl I should feel sorry for you but it seems rather weak when you say she is the only girl you have ever loved or are ever likely to love. If a fellow, thinking himself in love with me, expressed such a sentiment, I would send him on his way in a hurry. It needs a vast amount of love to carry you through married life and it doesn't strike any of us you have the genuine article. Then suppose you really are in love, you pay a girl a very poor compliment when you start off to propose to her without money enough to buy her a ring let alone anything else. . . . You had better know how you are going to keep a wife before you get one.

Then she abandoned that approach for another one:

> It seems a pity for you to ruin your career for the sake of a fancy. . . . Are all your chances of Oxford and Old Country life to be sacrificed because you fancy it is time you were engaged? Where is all your talk of the marvelous companionship of books gone! Do you think yours is the only nature that is not understood? As for a lonely nature, you are no

more lonely than anyone else and ought not to be as lonely, you were not, either, until you got this notion in your head.

And there was more:

But, Willie, Father and Mother deserve to be considered. Poor little Mother!... Why did Mother do without a servant all last year and do the work herself? Simply because by so doing we saved [money]. You ought to think of all these things and remember that by helping your parents you are doing what will be a blessing to you for all of your life.

The letter, which King received from his father, a few days later touched on the same points as the other two letters had done. Obviously, there had been a family conference and a battle plan had been drawn up:

Your letter has astonished every one of us more than I can describe, myself not the least by any means....Your honesty and straightforwardness has been a redeeming feature; if you had not done so and had entangled yourself with a foolish and imprudent engagement...we should have been pained beyond expression. You are but a boy with foolish fancies....You have had a training, a home, and chances and opportunities and assistance that I never had when I was a young man....Frankly speaking, and I say it all in kindness, I think your first duty is to those at home....Come to us and be guided by what we shall all conclude is best under such trying circumstances. I am really too upset to write anything more.

Harsh though all these letters were, there was a grain of truth in them. King, himself, had wondered if he had acted too rashly: his family was certain of it. As Jennie rightly pointed out to him, at present, he could not afford to even buy an engagement ring, let alone support a wife. But if King had had the courage of his convictions, his prospects were good. In discussing his situation with one of his professors, he was told that within two years he could have a good position and that it would be well for him to stand by Mathilde in spite of family opposition. Although Jennie did not think it fair to ask Mathilde to enter into a long engagement, this might have been a viable solution, but King seems not to have given it much thought. Indeed, at this time, he was not capable of such a thing as rational thought, beset as he was by suggestions from home that he was just a young, selfish boy who was letting a fancy run away with him. Over the next little while, King was driven nearly to distraction by his family's attitude. At first, he adopted an air of bravado, saying: "Here is something that can only be resolved by myself." But that was succeeded by bouts of self-reproach and worry. There were a few happier moments such as when he actually made an attempt to take charge by writing home and "telling distinctly that I could not break my love for [Miss Grossert], that it was as real to me as my love for home, and praying that the two might not be brought in conflict as they would lead to infidelity or despair."

Eager though King was to get back to Chicago, Mathilde had to wait her turn. During the Easter holidays, King went first to Toronto as he had been bidden to do. "A sadder journey I never remember. I was tired and careworn, my thoughts were dark & cloudy." During this visit, King would have been able to tell his family about Mathilde's background, something that should have been of interest to them, at least. Not surprisingly, during his precipitous falling in love, he had not paused to find out very much about Mathilde. What little he did know was that she had been born and was brought up near Wurtemburg in the Black Forest area of Germany. Her mother was now dead but her sister and her father, a retired military man, still lived there. Mathilde, herself, had left Germany a few years earlier, moving to England with the family of her uncle, a medical doctor. When they decided to live in United States, she came with them but later left to gain her own livelihood by training as a nurse in Chicago. Whatever the King family thought of Mathilde's background is not known. Obviously, King was the centre of their attention, a perplexed and agitated King who must have guessed that his romance did not stand a chance once he was back in the bosom of the family. On Easter Sunday afternoon, "I talked with Mother & Father in reference to my love affair....Father thinks it would be a terrible mistake for me to become engaged, that it would cramp me in every way, it wd. be unfair to the girl, etc. etc. I see the truth of much of this now but is it not too late. I cannot be dishonourable, I cannot now retract." Obviously, King was swayed by his parents' arguments and he began to look for a way out of the whole desperate situation. "My prayer is that [Mathilde] may not love me or if she does that she may or we may be led to see whether or not it is well for us to become engaged. I promised that I would not become engaged but I would not promise not to love the girl or not to engage myself at a later time to her."

He was like a beaten man when he went on to Chicago a few days later.

"My poor heart has been so crushed. I have been told so much of my folly and worthlessness that I am like a hunted stag, that fears everything." As was to be expected, given this frame of mind, the visit did not go well. The situation they found themselves in seemed totally unreal. King was quite ambivalent at this time, one minute deeply in love with Mathilde, the next doubting this love. What King could not bring himself to tell Mathilde, he confessed to his diary:

> *Where is the love that was so beautiful and strong in me, what are these feelings of pain and anguish that now fill my breast. . . . I did not have the thoughts I longed to have. . . . Nor was I carried as I had hoped I might be to other worlds. I was more of the earth earthy . . . what sort of man am I. We talked together, we had dinner together. I felt more like crying than eating. We walked together to the Lake shore drive. She was not altogether happy, nor was I. There was not enough reality in it all, or perhaps to [sic] much.*

There was to be one more meeting before King went back to Harvard, a meeting that King felt he needed in order to tell Mathilde 'all':

> *[We] met, we took a cab and drove along Michigan Ave. We stopped near a light and I read her some back pages of my diary showing my love for her. I then told her the last few weeks had destroyed so much. We each really wanted the same thing. We wanted to know that we loved each other but no engagement yet. We agreed to go back to where we were in our writing before words of love were spoken of and learn whether we were each in love or not. We are neither of us ready for an engagement yet and both are too sensible to trifle in the matter.*

On the train going back east, King started out quite composed, full of 'new resolve' and 'new determination'. He was also reading a book, ironically entitled *The Ships That Pass in the Night* which he found 'absolutely worthless'. ["I only finish it because I do not like to leave a task undone."] For him, his immediate personal task had been undertaken and solved: he had gone to see Mathilde and had come away from that visit feeling that: "I have kept faith with those at home, with [Mathilde] & myself & I am happy." King, the future conciliator, had just worked out a compromise solution to a very vexing affair. Back at his studies, he came to the conclusion that "I must keep quiet for the next few years, study hard, watch every day, be careful of the steps I take. I am apt to rush too quickly into action of one sort or another." It was one thing to have this resolution, another to take his own advice. Keeping quiet, mentally, was impossible for him and at times he felt he was going insane as a procession of worries nagged at him. His diary shows the lengths to which his imagination drove him. In his over-taxed state, he laid some blame for his confusion on Mathilde's being in Chicago, in the West. "I do not like the west. I am very fond of the east. The people and their country are alike different taken as a whole." But it was not just the fact that Mathilde lived in the west but that she was a professional woman who happened to be working there. "I have wished with such a heart that [Mathilde] were in a home in the east. I do not like her in an institution in the west." This sounds like an idea that was implanted by his parents who would certainly have preferred that, when he eventually married, it would have been to someone of their own social circle or its equivalent. In his irrational state, he totally ignored the fact that he had earlier idealized Mathilde because of her dedication to the sick and the poor. Now he wrote, "If she had been in a home instead of an institut'n she would have been the most beautiful and loving of girls. Oh, it is a mistake – this new woman, worldly freedom idea." 'New women are a perversion' was his summation.

Back in Chicago, Mathilde scarcely knew what to think or do. Without any family nearby to consult, she had paid a visit to a Doctor Knudson whom she knew, going not as a patient but as a friend, to ask for his advice. He already had the story from King's point of view and after he had talked with Mathilde, he wrote frankly to King. His first comment was that "I did not expect you to 'storm the fort' in such a heroic manner. King, you cannot conquer a woman the way Dewey did Manila." His advice was good, but perhaps not what King wanted to hear because it was so rational. "Now just have a little pity on the poor girl and give her time to think.... She has not thought about this near as long as you have although she has thought of what may be from your letters." Dr. Knudson also stressed the importance that Mathilde placed on her work as a nurse. "You must stop to think that she was getting as much engrossed in the life work as you and do you think it would be easy to turn you from your life plans?" King derived some hope from the letter when he read that "She admires you, and I believe, loves you when she has time to think it out in her own mind....the poor girl is not able to do anything."

In late June 1898, King's colleague, John George, went back to Chicago for a short visit during which time he acted as emissary on King's behalf. It was just after her graduation reception that he met with Mathilde and was instantly captivated by her, "A woman altogether lovely and beautiful". Her immediate question of him was 'And how is Das Kind?' "I told her that when I left . . . that his last words to me were to be sure to give Miss Grossert his best love." Mathilde had a further question: "Did Das Kind not send any other message for me? Did he not tell you to tell me more about himself?" To this, George reported that "I told her of your career at Harvard and how well you had succeeded and how you were regarded by the authorities at Harvard. Of all this she seemed very proud. In short, King, I told her all that you wanted me to, and was most happy of my own accord to add a good deal more about your manly qualities and your high purposes."

Mathilde, in turn, talked of her own aspirations saying that "when she made her life plans she never dreamed that the question of love would come into her life. 'But', she said, 'love has come into my life and has come to stay....I love him and he loves me, and we cannot help it'." John George came away from his talk with Mathilde calling her "...one of the most beautiful souls I have ever met. Beautiful! Beautiful!! Beautiful!!!.... A divine woman devoted to a divine purpose in life....And this woman, King, loves you and is yours." But there was the warning for King that "You must be patient....She is not trifling with you ever. It is simply the old contest 'twixt love and duty'....After a while when her rush is over, and she has had a little vacation I feel sure that another visit would be profitable to you both."

Towards the end of this conversation Mathilde had a message for King: "You must tell him not to worry about me. He must not do that." George's response was that "But you are the one who must tell him that, and I am sure he will not worry when he knows you love him. To this last she replied as sweetly as anything I ever heard 'He knows I love him. I have given him sufficient reason to assure him of that'." But nothing, it seems, had any effect on King that summer. He remained in Boston, working on a project during which time he was much alone, the other students having gone their various summer ways. This solitary life did nothing to relieve his troubled mental condition. "In fact my mind at times seems diseased. I am in a morbid condition all the time....I am wearing out my mind & life & I must have these clouds lifted somehow." But there did not seem to be anyone around to turn to in his distress. He debated writing home and telling them how he felt but he knew that would be foolish.

There was, in the end, only one thing to do and that was to go back to Chicago and see Mathilde once more. It seems that advice given by friends and the information they passed on did nothing to help matters. King, in his irrational state, had talked himself into suspecting that Mathilde might even have tried to entrap him, especially if she was older than he, possibly much older. They were simply not communicating well even now and, as for the past, "I made the greatest mistake that I have ever made, I took a great step too hastily. I knew nothing of her, had heard but a few words from her life, know really nothing of her now. Still I loved her....But I have learned a lesson in this my first love experience which I will never forget." With thoughts like these going through his mind before he returned to Chicago, it seemed evident that there could not be any rapprochement: "I see that it will be impossible for us to come to any understanding other than that we must at least be friends, and this I pray we may be with all my heart." King left for Chicago on 23 August and spent a week there. What happened during this period is not known; his diary for that time is mute. Nothing more was written in it until 3 September when he made the brief note: "Returned home at 9 o'clock. Was truly thankful."

After a summer spent partly in Toronto, partly in Muskoka with friends, King returned to Harvard in the autumn. There, he was again obsessed with thoughts of the sufferings undergone by all concerned—Mathilde, his family and himself. He tried to get over this feeling by concentrating on his work but the antidote was not to be found there. Neither was it to be found in the gym where he frequently went nor in contacts made through the Cambridge Musical Society that he had joined. He knew what he wanted and it was simple enough "just to talk with a woman. I gained much satisfaction in looking into the faces of some of the women I saw on the street. I had no desire for passion, my desire was for companionship....Alone in Cambridge and no congenial soul. It is not well for man to be alone."

But what of Mathilde during this time? There is a brief reference to her when, during Christmas holidays back home in Toronto, King was reading aloud from Thackeray to his mother and sisters. It was a tale almost too real:

> The whole story reads like an account of my own thoughts & feelings & adventures though there was something more painful in it than one gathers here, painful, I fear for each of us. Still I imagine [Mathilde] knew more than I did of the possible issue, etc., etc. .

. . What I read this morning was very embarrassing, words almost identical to my own being used in part.

It is possible that their meeting in Chicago in the late summer had been so difficult for them both that correspondence stopped for the next few months, but at Christmas he sent her a gift, a pair of initialed cuff-links, presumably to wear with the uniform in which it so pleased him to see her. It is surprising that their relationship did not end with the Chicago fiasco but it didn't: it just changed direction. They wrote twice in March 1899, once when she sent him a Bible and a few days later when he acknowledged this gift which was likely a late Christmas present in exchange for the cuff-links. King's letter gave him a chance to tell her "at some length that I was sorry for all I had done amiss, that I had suffered for it from the time till this present. . . . [I] asked her to forgive me . . . took all the blame to myself." In this letter, too, he asked her to burn all of his letters except two and offered to return hers whenever she wished him to do so.

When a request for a return of Mathilde's letters did come, it was not from her but from her husband. That Mathilde was married did not come as a surprise to King. In early December, 1900, he went to a party in Ottawa where he had been living since July of that year and met a former St. Luke's nurse, Violet Nesbitt. They naturally talked of St. Luke's and of the people there and, as soon as King mentioned Mathilde's name, he was told "But Mr. King, she is not Miss Grossert any longer" and went on to say that she had married her cousin, George Barchet, the previous June.

I said I hoped she was happily married. I did not say I was glad or sorry. I am so glad tho'. If she were not I would never feel free. She has married quickly and, I trust with my soul, is happy. I cannot do other than that with great fondness & compassion of her and wish her life peace & joy....I feel a strange real happiness, my whole soul is aroused, and I seem to feel that God has been wonderfully kind. All I dreaded was having saddened a life, against my will & desire. If she is happy, I can be so too, & the pain endured may make a nobler man of me.

The storm that had raged so fiercely during much of the time since he had met Mathilde in early 1897 was now past. It was followed by a peace that promised new freedom to King whose closing thought for the year 1900 was that 'God has been kind.'

It was in late March 1901, that George Barchet wrote asking for the return of his wife's letters. A few days later, King went to Boston to retrieve these letters which, along with other chattels, had been left behind at Harvard in 1899 when he went off to Europe on a travelling fellowship for a year. On the train trip back to Ottawa he read them over and wrote in his diary that "They are a beautiful set of letters but a strain of sadness runs thro' them & of misunderstanding & unrest, no wonder." His own letters to Mathilde had been sent from Maryland where the Barchets were living and were awaiting him in Ottawa. "I destroyed in the fire on the hearth all of mine. As I look at them I see them to have been the most worthless sort of trash. I am glad they are in ashes." It is not to his credit that earlier that same evening he read parts of Mathilde's letters to his friend, Bert Harper, before doing them up in a bundle to return to her. It was his stated intention to return every one of her letters and it is unthinkable that a man who was so overconscientious about all facets of his life would have done otherwise. Some of her letters had been copied in the back of a journal but, except for a few scraps, these were later destroyed.

When George Barchet wrote asking for the return of his wife's letters, he stated clearly that she had no further wish to correspond with King. If, indeed, it was her wish, she later changed her mind. From 1905 on, they wrote to each other, infrequently, but at length, and this pattern continued until being broken by King's death in 1950. Somehow a myth developed in the Barchet family that King never did return Mathilde's letters as requested and with this legacy in mind, permission to use her letters has been denied to anyone. This is such a pity as her letters are wonderful, showing her intelligence, courage and strength of character.

The Barchets had three children, Stephen, Mary, and baby Nellie, by the time correspondence between Mathilde and King was resumed. Nellie died as an infant and a year later Stephanie was born. Through these children King kept in touch with the activities of a growing family to an extent only shared with his own nieces and nephews. Christmas was one time when he always sent them greetings and gifts and was the recipient of charming little letters, especially from Stephanie. Snippets of these letters reflect the children's warmth for King. In 1919, Stephanie was sent a book as was Mathilde and at the end of her own letter of thanks, Stephanie added a P. S. informing King that "Mother read the book you sent her more faithfully than she reads the Bible." The following year Stephanie's gift was something more exciting than a book: "Thank you very much for sending me that lovely jumping rope. I am having a lovely time with it. I have been jumping with it ever since I received it. It seems you know what little girls like." Just before Christmas that year she wrote him of their Christmas preparations and added "And, Mr. King, I am awfully sorry that you can't spend it with us."

In her letters, Stephanie was always asking King to come back to see them. His busy life left little time for visits but one had been planned for 1908 when he was to be in Washington on business. He telegraphed Mathilde saying that he would be free to spend some time with them on the weekend but at the last minute he had to change his plans. This would have been his introduction to George Barchet and the children as well as seeing Mathilde for the first time since she had married. It was another seven years before this happened. In May 1915, King had been out to Denver to visit his brother, Max, whose health was the cause of much concern, and on the way back he stopped over in Washington. From there he took a train to Annapolis, Maryland, where he was met at the station by the whole Barchet family and they then drove out to Belfield Farm, their home, for a few hours visit. He saw Mathilde next in October 1922; this time she went in to Washington for a short, hurried visit, leaving the family behind. This did not sit well with Stephanie who wrote to remind King that "It has been seven or eight years since I saw you last, and Mary and I regretted very much the lost chance to see you once more, that time in Washington. I hope fate will be more kind in future, and then we will all be happy together."

Meanwhile, the Barchet children were growing up and moving on. When Stephen was in his teens, there was a time when he was a somewhat reluctant student and King wrote to him on several occasions emphasizing the importance of sticking to his studies. By the early 20's Stephen was in the U. S. Naval Academy in Annapolis, at the start of a distinguished career. In 1924, he married and King was invited to the wedding. He was unable to attend, but sent his wishes by telegram to both the bride and groom and to Mathilde. Stephanie was the next to give her heart to someone although she did not yet marry and when Mary married in 1926 the wedding took place in Hollywood. There was no question of King being able to attend this wedding either but in later years he was able to keep in touch with Mary more closely than with either Stephen or Stephanie. She married into the Navy and for some years her husband had assignments on the East Coast of United States, an area where King often found himself on business or pleasure.

Except for the few and scattered visits, King kept in touch with Mathilde by letters. Before the demands on his time became too great he wrote by hand, sometimes from the peace and quiet of his Kingsmere retreat, but after his reentry into politics the letters were mostly dictated. In 1936 he wrote to Mathilde saying, "I should be very glad indeed to have Mary come into possession of any of the letters or small remembrances which you may have received from me, and to which you so kindly attach so great a value." He supplemented his letters by sending her Canadian papers from time to time as well as the *House of Commons Reports* and she had a subscription to the *Ottawa Evening Journal*. By whatever means, King was able to keep Mathilde informed as to what was going on in his life. She could read about him when he entered Parliament in 1908, when he became Minister of Labour in 1909, and could follow his career change when he took up an appointment to the Rockefeller Foundation as their Director of Research in 1914. The news in 1919 was that he was back in politics, having succeeded Sir Wilfrid Laurier as leader of the Liberal Party of Canada. Two years later another pinnacle was reached when he became Prime Minister of Canada. Mathilde's library was added to on receiving copies of King's own books: *The Secret of Heroism*, the story of his friend, Bert Harper, *The Message of the Carillon and other Addresses* which marked the Jubilee celebrations of 1926. And she should not be without a copy of *Industry and Humanity*, the book he wrote out of his experience with management and labour problems. He even sent her several extra copies for her special friends.

From at least 1906, Mathilde sent King pictures of the children when they were small and of herself and received in return a copy of every photograph taken of King over the years. At Christmas, 1940, her gift from King, likely the last one in her collection, was a photograph taken at Kingsmere for some English publications. "Please do not laugh or exclaim . . .", he wrote, "I know full well how many you already have. Having been taken in this previous year, baffled as we are by its many mysteries, the expression is one which, I know, will appeal to you." It was the second photograph she received from him that year. In the spring of 1940, as a souvenir of a visit he made to Belfield Farm recently, he sent along a photo of himself and his little dog, Pat, this picture being special as, he told Mathilde, it has since been used in the recent campaign.

In April 1940, King went to Baltimore for a medical check-up before a flurry of visits in the area. He first went to Warm Springs to consult with President Roosevelt, then to see the Rockefellers in Williamsburg before going to Washington from whence he made his call on the Barchets at their farm. His diary tells of what was to be his last visit there. There was 'that sumptuous repast which you served so largely with your own hands' to him and to other guests and a little talk which he and Mathilde had when they were alone. She had a little gossip for him and brought out some interesting newspaper cuttings which she had saved as well as one of his photographs which had escaped a disastrous fire in their house in 1932 in which many of her most treasured possessions were lost. "We did not discuss the war. Barchet himself is like Henry--strong on Zionism. Gave his account of periods through which we were passing 'as told by the Scriptures', while Mathilde's own sympathies were with the British and against Hitler, referring to him as anti-Christ. We sat and looked at the glorious sunset after which they both came with me to the car. The last glimpse I had was seeing her walk around the house with a white shawl over the white dress which she was wearing, following her husband towards the sunset. I had many thoughts of what she has been through in the years gone by and how little in some particulars she has changed."

Both Mathilde and King were now past their sixty-fifth birthdays and time had been taking its toll on their health. King came away from his visit to Dr. Barker in Baltimore, however, encouraged by the report but Mathilde, who had not been well over the past couple of years had more than her own health to be concerned about. George Barchet had had a series of heart attacks and Mathilde recognized that the outlook for him was not good. At the beginning of 1944 after a long period of illness, he died and was buried on their property at Belfield Farm. After her husband's death, Mathilde's own health deteriorated and, for a time, she was obliged to live in Washington with Mary and her husband, Walter Warlick. It was there that she and King met for the last time:

> *Mary kissed me when I came to the door and her mother embraced me very warmly. She was all in black but seemed to cheer up marvelously when we talked together. Indeed I was delighted to see how well she kept up. Only once did she seem to break down when she spoke of her not being intended to live alone. That she missed her husband very much, not withstanding his long illness through the last few years....Mary had*

some orange juice for health and dates and chocolates. It really was a lovely little break in the morning. It made me quite sad, however, to feel that I could not stay and have a nice long talk with them. I know, however, that my visit cheered them up very much.

The only other contact of a more personal nature than the letters that continued to be exchanged came in the summer of 1949. King was spending some days with John D. Rockefeller, Jr., at Seal Harbor, Maine, not too far from Castine where Mary and her husband (by than an Admiral) lived. An article in the *Bangor Daily News* alerted Mary to the fact that King was nearby and she wrote, at once, asking if it might be possible for him to pay them a visit. A few days later she had a phone call from him saying that he would be able to go over later on in that same day if it were convenient for Mary. This visit was described in minute detail to Mathilde by her daughter who wrote that "This was around three in the afternoon and I began to worry about what to give Mr. King for supper because I remembered you had said he had to be careful about what he ate." It seems she should not have worried about food or anything else:

From the start everything clicked; and after a few minutes it seemed as though Walter and Estelle [Mary's sister-in-law] had been his friends for years, they had so much in common to talk about....Mr. King said he eats everything now....Walter brought out his choicest wine and Mr. King proposed a toast to 'your dear Mother whom we all know is the centre of our thoughts this evening.' And he recalled the days at St. Luke's when he was a patient....Spoke of your bravery and steadfastness under all circumstances, your remarkable sense of duty, your beautiful mind, beautiful eyes. [Did you know that] he still has the cross from the sleeve of your uniform? All through his visit, no matter how far the conversation ranged, he would return to the subject of you....It was past eight-thirty when he took his leave of us. As we stood in the hall, he held his hand up, raising it higher, then lower, to study my face and look for some resemblance to yours.

It seems that, for Mary, as for her mother, the old magic worked. The man whom as a child she had dubbed her 'Knight errant' had been a guest in her home and it was the revival of an old love. "He is utterly and completely charming...his conversation is wonderful, and we felt happy and at ease with him all the while." For King, too, it was a memorable occasion. "I was particularly happy that I had made the trip. The evening was one of the most enjoyable I have had at any time in any place. I know the pleasure it will give Mrs. Barchet that I have seen Mary in her own home in Castine."

In the spring of 1950, King wrote to Mathilde for the last time. He was ill by then, too ill to do much except rest, despite his protestations to the contrary in his letter. Mathilde, as usual, had been advising him on how to take life a bit easier and he was in agreement.

> How wise you were to drop all Christmas activities including the writing of letters, etc. We must all remember that once past the seventies, one cannot live the kind of life one may have enjoyed in earlier years.... I must try to follow your example of doing a little more in the way of reading in the late afternoon. As for letters, they are a nightmare and must be treated as such. Otherwise they are certain to become intolerable burdens.

With a touch of the old acerbity, he added that if friends and relatives did not understand this, 'it is just too bad for them' and went on to congratulate Mathilde "upon your own letter. I mean the strength shown in the writing as well as, if you will allow me to say so, the charm of its composition. But you always have had a very special gift for writing."

Reading between the lines in their correspondence, there are signs that his feelings for her were stronger than he was able to admit although he evidently expressed them personally to her on occasion. His letters of later years, being dictated, were the soul of propriety as was his behaviour during visits made to Belfield where he gained the love of the Barchet children and the respect of their father. Once, after a visit to Belfield, he read through some of their letters and commented that "She has had a hard struggle & has become a mere drudge, where under other circumstances she would have been a woman of brilliant attainments." Was he then thinking of what her life might have been if they had married? Did he ever wonder if this just might have happened had they met in 1900 when both were in Germany, she to visit family and he, on his travelling scholarship from Harvard? He wrote to her on 26 April saying he would like to see her before he moved on from Berlin where he had been spending a month. His next planned stop was to be in Switzerland and Wurtemburg area was directly on his way. His only fear was that Mathilde might have already left. Knowing that she did go home for a visit and that she was married in June of 1900 the probability is that in April she was more concerned with planning her wedding than in meeting up with an old love. In any event, there was no meeting then but, had there been, the bitterness of 1898 was fading and they might have been able to put the past behind them. There, far from the pressures of his parents, he might have acted on his advice to himself in the spring of 1898 when he said 'Here is something that can only be resolved by myself'. He did not have the courage to do so then and, sadly, he was not given another chance.

What was left for Mathilde and King was what can only be called an extraordinary friendship, sustained by letters and the too rare visits. Their memories of the days of their falling in love in Chicago, however, remained and King recalled those far off days in writing to Mathilde to thank her for his visit to Belfield in 1940:

Most vivid of all in my mind will be the calm beauty of the evening hour of sunset, and the lovely scene, with all the wonder of the springtime [and he recalled her appearance], clothed in white, the white shawl over your head. . . .It was a radiant picture [which] brought back many thoughts of the St. Luke's uniform which you wore many years ago and which was so very becoming to you.

As King wrote his Christmas letter to Mathilde in 1946 his thoughts ran to the span of their friendship:

How difficult to believe that it is now almost a full half century since we first met. Those days continue to lend their happy memories to the present. In that interval of time, we have, I think, exchanged greetings at every Christmas season. I hope there may be many more.

Four years later, Mackenzie King's death took from Mathilde her 'liebes Kind'. A short while before his death in July 1950, he dictated his last letter to her. In it, his thoughts went back to Belfield Farm where she was again living. "Pear Point must be quite lovely now. I am able to picture it and the little cottage, quite perfectly, and can imagine what it must be like with Spring flowers beginning to make their presence felt. May the Spring and Summer months bring to you not only the joys of the Easter Season but much in the way of health as well."

Mathilde lived for another ten years, sometimes in ill health, but there can be no doubt but that, when well enough to do so, she relived many of the hours they had spent together, refreshing her memory, if need be, by glancing at the many photographs she had of him and rereading his letters, especially those written in his 'own dear hand'.

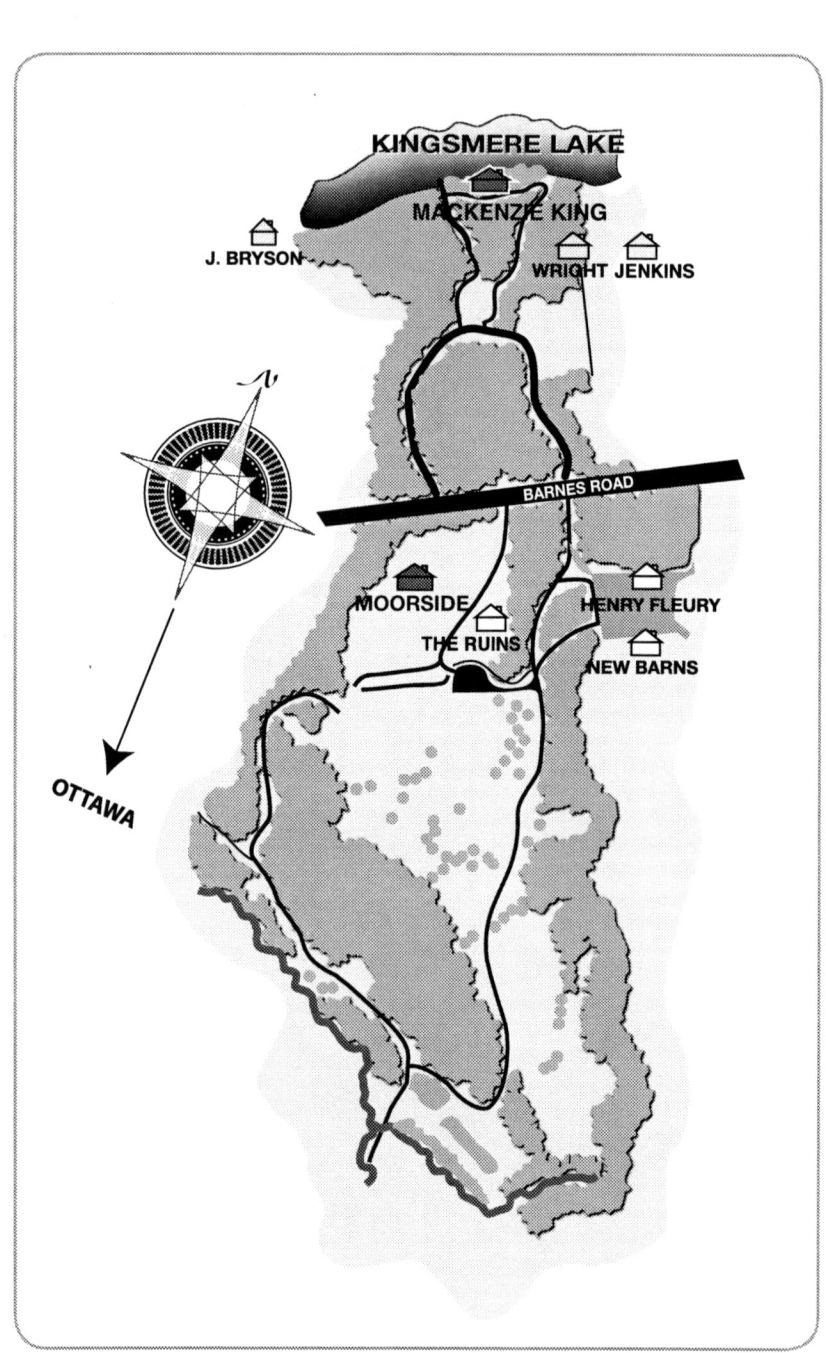

Bert Harper

Winter came early to Ottawa as 1901 was drawing to a close. By mid-November, in his last long letter to King who was in British Columbia on a strike-breaking mission, Bert Harper passed on the news: "This afternoon Harry, Laschinger and I took a long walk in the frosty air—for winter has gripped Ottawa hard, ice covers the ground, ponds are frozen and the sky is stern and gray." A little more than two weeks later King was on his way back to Ottawa and when the train stopped at Barrie, he reportedly had to make a choice between spending his last change on a newspaper or a sandwich. He chose the paper but before opening it he looked across for a moment or two at the Harper house where he had visited Bert many times. Then, as the train picked up speed, he settled back in his seat to read the paper. What immediately caught his startled attention was the previous day's news of the tragic death of Harper, his intimate friend and associate. There had been a skating party on the Ottawa River on 6 December, a party which set out from Government House and which had been led by the Governor-General and Lady Minto. The temptation to use the rink provided by the cold weather and the lack of snow was great but although the ponds, as Harper reported, had frozen quickly, the same could not be said for the river that still had patches of open water. With the Minto's leading the way, others, especially those who were in the social picture, would not be left behind. Bert Harper, Bessie Blair and two other skaters left some time after the Minto party and were still on the ice as dusk fell. At that hour of day the patches of open water could not be easily seen by the skaters and, when Bessie Blair and her partner went too close towards the mouth of the Gatineau River, they were suddenly confronted by a large area of water that they could not possibly avoid. Harper and his friend were a little behind them and went immediately to their aid. While the girl with whom Harper was skating went to shore at Gatineau Point to seek assistance, he lay on the ice as close to the pair as he could safely go and held out his walking stick to see if they could grasp it. The swiftness of the current made any such attempt useless and Bessie and her friend decided they would try to swim ashore. When Harper heard this he tossed off his coat and gloves and jumped in to help Miss Blair despite her assurances that she could make it on her own. Other skaters who came on the scene pleaded with him, cautioning him that it would be useless and could only mean certain death but their arguments were in vain. 'What else can I do!' were his last words as he entered the icy waters. Next morning the bodies of Bessie Blair and Harper were found not far from each other.

The days that followed were as difficult for King as any he had ever known. When his romance with Mathilde was coming to an end three years earlier, he had gone through traumatic days and nights but had accepted the inevitable. Now he was experiencing a new and different kind of loss in the death of his only intimate male friend. The news had reached him so coldly, so publicly, from the pages of a newspaper, bought for a nickel. Had the telegram, which had been sent to inform him of the tragedy, reached him, it would have been, at least, a personal touch. Slight wonder, then, that by the time he reached Toronto where his father was waiting for him at the station, he was in a state of collapse. As soon as he had recovered sufficiently he took a train to Ottawa where, with mutual friends and Harper's relatives, he went through the ritual connected with death and funeral services. There was another service in Barrie and then the interment in Cookstown where Bert had been born twenty-eight years ago to the day. Predictably and unfortunately, what went through King's mind during this period is not known as far as his diary is concerned. Just as was the case when he accepted the futility of the situation with Mathilde and was to be the pattern in future partings of a painful nature, the diary was silent for a time.

It was not until 19 January 1902, with a new volume of his diary in front of him, that he once more began to put his thoughts down. They went directly to Bert.

> *Dear old Bert, my first greeting in the New Year a year ago, next to those at home, was from him, and now he is gone. He has gone quickly, the soul of the man that I loved as I have loved no other man, my father and brother alone excepted. . . . God's purpose was plain in his life—it was wrought out and achieved.*

It was undoubtedly this idea of the fulfillment of God's purpose in Bert's life that prompted King to write what might otherwise be considered a very strange letter to his parents soon after Harper's death.

> *You may wonder at my saying that despite its trials and anxieties the past week has been one of profound peace and real happiness. Whether it is that the sense of loss is more than swallowed up in the knowledge of gain, the triumph of victory so complete over all the obstacles of life and death, or the closer companionship which can come to souls unfettered by the limitations of this mortal existence I know not. . . . Though it may seem strange to other ears, I feel the loss but little so much do I feel the gain.*

Despite what he said in this letter, the pages of the diary paint a different picture. It is one of a man who spends New Year's Day in the room of the friend with whom he shared quarters and where now there were only memories as he began sorting out books, clothing and 'such few one time possessions as may serve to recall a memory or association'.

At the end of that lonely exercise, he could write in a eulogistic fashion of the 'good, true, noble, brave soul', his departed friend, and of 'endless evidences of an untiring energy and ceaseless striving after duty and right.' He had come across a little piece of folded paper such as might have been torn from a school scribbler and on it was written a penitent little note:

> *Private. Dear Pa. You cannot imagine how unhappy I feel and have felt since 5:30 this afternoon. I cannot stand to see Mac [his brother] blamed for a thing he did not do for realy [sic] it was me who took the plums. They were on the table so tempting and nobody being in the kitchen I took them and when you asked me I was going to say yes but a fear of shame came over me but now I come to the conclusion that I would rather take a whipping and have a clear conscience ~~but please do not tell anybody excepting~~ I will try in future to be more honest. Bert. Please forgive me.*

This note which is now tucked in the front of a diary which Bert kept in 1890 is clearly from an earlier date as, in 1890, the entries are those of a boy fast approaching manhood, not those of a youthful plum thief. He writes, in what little scope an eight-line-a-day diary affords of the weather, of church [attending services three times some Sundays], of lectures on

Home Missions, of Bible classes. There are references to school with its Literary Association of which he was always an active member and of the Reform Club. Outside of church and school, seasonal activities such as sailing, tennis, cricket and family picnics filled the summer months. In winter, the annual ice-cutting on the bay seemed to have been a big event in Barrie, the town that Harper later described as 'a quaint old place, which has gone halfway up the hill and sat down'.

Henry Albert Harper (1900)

In September 1891, Harper entered University College in Toronto and there the relationship with King began. Both were in the class of '95 and their paths crossed not only in the lecture halls but also in what King later referred to as the "larger life of the university. [Harper] was always certain to be found as an active participant in those events . . . with which undergraduate life at a large university abounds." The first of these events to be experienced by both Harper, the seventeen-year old student from Barrie Collegiate and King, in from Berlin, were the activities connected with convocation exercises. Harper's little diary didn't give him much room to comment on the high-jinks that went on except to say "[A] wild time. Could not hear much. Students burst their way into the [hall]." King, not yet a diarist, wrote home to his sister, Jennie, giving a more complete story of their antics:

> *We had a great time at the Convocation. I was carried in with the crowd. . . . There were so many they smashed about 50 chairs standing on them and shoving and they made such a racket that you could not hear what was being said. Another big time was at the Grand Opera House on Friday night. All the students went in a body & made such a fearful racket in the Gods that the policemen had to interfere after the opera. They marched up to Bishop Strachan School & serenaded the girls, policemen marching with them all the way to maintain order.*

Another undergraduate event to which Harper referred in his diary was hustling freshmen at a subsequent convocation. King was one of the organizers for this ritual. As he saw it,

> *Today has been a memorable one in the history of college life. This morning I attended the college and did all I could to spread rumours of a hustle for this afternoon. This afternoon we held our college convocation in the Auditorium. I was one of the ushers, the boys filled the top gallery. . . . After convocation the boys lined up on James Street and hustled many of the freshmen.*

For this action some students were brought before the University Council and risked being expelled from residence for their pranks. King was not charged but he did get into trouble later in the month when Hallowe'en gave the students another chance to let off steam. This time he noted, "The chief work of the evening was to tear down an old shed on the Varsity grounds. We sang college songs, tore down fences, etc., as usual. I carried a large flag pole. The police were very rough."

So was the University Council and this time King did not escape being fined for his involvement. Each of those charged was fined $15, a fee that was pretty steep for those days and which they highly resented since they insisted that what they were doing was ridding the grounds of an unsightly building.

King and Harper became friends as well as classmates from their early days at University College. There were visits back and forth to each other's rooms to discuss various Varsity 'politics' or, as King wrote, just simply to have a "rambling talk for an hour or two, but profitable I believe. I really enjoy a good chat with a fellow." By 1893, King was living at home, his parents having moved to Toronto and Bert Harper was a frequent visitor in the house at 104 Beverley Street. It was during the summers though, that their friendship was cemented and geography can be said to have played a role in this. Each year, for part of the holidays, King managed to get himself invited to spend some time with friends who had cottages in the vacation area north of Toronto. He usually stopped off in Barrie en route either to have a chat with Harper at the station or to spend a few days as his guest. In the summer of 1895, King spent part of August on Bohemia Island in Lake Rosseau with a house party. Some of the other guests were also from the class of '95 as well as being members of the same fraternity, Kappa Alpha. With the students in a high-spirited mood now that they had completed their undergraduate studies, it had been a holiday with many fun-filled moments. One of the events was a fancy-dress ball. "Jack Falconbridge and I went as the 'Heavenly Twins' dressed in long baby robes, with little hoods and ribbons. We were blackened with corks. He was 'Angelica' and I was 'Diabolo'."

On his way back to Toronto, King spent a weekend with the Harpers and there, away from the capers of Bohemia Island, there was time to have a quiet talk or two. Possibly it was King's recounting the tale of being a black face 'Diabolo' that reminded Harper of something he had not previously mentioned. "Bert told me what he had thought of me when he 1st knew me—a sort of compound—one that could be a saint or a devil, a 'Dr. Jekyll and Mr. Hyde'. He had since learned to see beyond the external nature which I do not wonder represents the picture to many." They had long talks on the reality of life, talks such as King, at any rate, felt were good for them and which could have a strong influence on their lives. There was time, as well, for a drive into the country where they set a pattern that was to continue in later years—reading aloud to each other. Their choice was Oliver Wendell Holmes' *The Autocrat at the Breakfast Table*. King's bread-and-butter note from Toronto later expressed the hope that Harper had continued reading Holmes.

> *I would like to send you the book with passages marked but you will doubtless feel my kindred soul crawl up alongside of yours and whisper to you just what we were trying to say. . . . You will find 'Iris' a very beautiful creature in many ways. I have added her to my mind's future gallery of beautiful females. I have a number of splendid characters there already . . . Marguerite and Evangeline. . . . But this girl topic is a hard one (I mean to make you talk, etc.) so I will stop there before I forget.*

But they had more on their minds in the autumn of 1895 than 'girl topics' or long philosophical discussions. Both were graduates then but neither had any clear picture of where he was going. Harper's degree was in Political Science but he had never strayed from his interest in writing and had been an active member of the Literary and Scientific Society while at University. In a journal that he began to keep shortly after graduation and which unfortunately is not available now, he wrote that

> *I have not as yet settled upon a course in life. Several weapons lie before me, which might be of use in the conflict with the world, and with all of which I feel I might familiarize myself. Which will enable me to achieve the greatest success? Shall it be law, the ministry, a business career or journalism or what? At one time I lean in one direction and again in another.*

As a stop-gap measure he worked as a Confederation Life Insurance agent out of his father's office in Barrie but he soon found that he was developing a 'cordial dislike' for this work.

> *I shall certainly have to 'make a break' before long, since the state of affairs is preying upon my mind and upon my ambition and my self-esteem. Tonight we have some friends coming in, a minister from the country and his wife. They will probably ask me what I am going to do. I am sick of that question.*

King's career, meanwhile, was also in a holding pattern. He had ambitions and he possessed what one fellow-student termed "a sort of aura of destiny which to me was inexplicable by anything in his personality or performance, and which probably emanated from his own absolute conviction that he had what in religious circles is designated 'a call'." With King, as with his friend Harper, however, it took some time to answer this 'call'. He, too, turned briefly to his father's profession, becoming articled to him in law. This he no doubt saw as a filial duty since he had become increasingly aware that "Father needs my assistance and needs to be looked after. I have resolved to get him out of his money difficulties which are at present wearing out his life." As it turned out, he had no more love for or interest in law than Harper had in the insurance business. It was not long before King wrote that "I am disgusted with law and have made up my mind never to go into it. . . . I am getting most thoroughly sick of the idea of law every day."* By the end of summer he was as restless as Harper and was also getting tired of not having a definite goal. In one respect, however, he was more fortunate than his friend. Through contacts, King became a reporter for the Toronto *News*, later moving to the *Globe* which he felt was a worthier paper, not being so sensational. There he spent the winter of 1895-6 at a weekly salary of $7 (up $2 from his pay at the *News*), covering the action at the police courts. Making the best of a situation that was of more interest to him

---

*On 12 June 1896, King received the degree of LL.B from the hands of his father.

than the study of law but which was still a stop-gap, he rationalized that "I will derive great benefit for my after work. I fully intend to make academic work my profession and am taking Journalism as an extra year of practical experience in the great school of life."

It must have been galling for Harper to see his friend with such ready access to work at a newspaper which was where he himself wished to be. Bert had reflected on the merits of different careers and decided that lacking capital, "my leanings are towards journalism as most likely to give me satisfaction and to aid me in the study of mankind—man." Despite his best efforts, no opportunity presented itself for over a year after graduation. He became discouraged at times, none more so than as 1896 drew to a close: "As the midnight bell rang out the old year and rang in the new, the future was not too encouraging to me. It was with a feeling of bitterness that I took out a note-book and wrote the words, 'January 1, 1897, and still on the market'." But his luck was about to change. In February he was offered a temporary position as a reporter on the London *Advertiser* and, although he know the work could not last beyond a few weeks, he grasped the opportunity. From there he went to the London *News* and, later in the same year, moved to the Toronto *Mail and Empire*, (quite possibly with help from friends of King). Each move brought greater responsibilities, and in 1899 he took a further step up the ladder when he joined the Montreal *Herald* as city editor. He also became that paper's representative in the Ottawa Press Gallery—an opportunity, as he saw it, since "Here at the very centre of the Dominion I see all about me the means of acquiring the knowledge which should make my life a useful one and that, I assure you again, is my chiefest aim." He also made regular contributions to the *Herald's* editorial columns and, in King's opinion, "commenced to help at least to shape and direct public opinion in matters of national concern." It was particularly gratifying to King to read one article on the anti-sweating principle* that noted his own contribution to the cause. "It is beautiful", King wrote, "the way in which things have turned out in regard to each of us working more or less hand in hand on work to which we pledged ourselves in prayer some years ago."

While Harper was at last seeing his career in journalism progress, King

---

*In 1897, while King was working for the *Mail* and *Empire*, he wrote a series of articles on labour conditions relating to the manufacture of uniforms for Post Office employees. This 'sweated labour' problem was brought to the attention of Sir William Mulock, Postmaster-General of Canada, through the offices of King's father, a friend of Mulock.

was still sorting out what he wished to do by way of graduate work. He was certain of one thing: he wanted more out of life than the daily routine of a reporter on the *Globe*. A typical day there consisted of a

> zig-zag route. . . . This morning I was at the police courts recording lists of drunks, vagrants, burglars, orders of prot'n, cases of nonsupport and the like. This kept me busy till nearly noon. I then wrote a little advance notice of a funeral and went to the Cathedral and reported a beautiful sermon by Canon Dumolin [sic] on the prodigal's return. . . . After dinner I attended the funeral of Mr. Vickers and had to go from there to the Toronto Opera House and report a special matinee given by all the Co's in Toronto . . . wrote up account of funeral and then of theatre.

This sort of work was obviously not going to satisfy one with an 'aura of destiny' about him. Before becoming articled to his father, King had applied to various universities for a scholarship in economics. One had been offered by the University of Chicago but King refused it, very likely because of parental pressure to remain in Toronto. In 1896, the university made another offer and this time he did accept it. In the course of his work on the *Globe*, he had met Jane Addams who was lecturing on her work with the settlement house that she had founded in Chicago. King now saw a path opening before him. Impressed by what he heard from Miss Addams, he wrote in his diary:

> I never listened to an address which I more thoroughly enjoyed. . . . The history of the movement, taking it back to the influence and practical work of Arnold Toynbee was more than delightful to me. I love Toynbee and I love Miss Adams [sic]. I love the work in which the one was and the other is and which I soon hope to be engaged in.

It would all fit in so well were he to go to Chicago. He would have his desired studies in economics and, thanks to having met Miss Addams, there would be an opportunity of doing some work of a social nature, something that had interested him throughout his student days. It would also fit in with the philosophy that he and Harper shared, that they should think of their futures in terms of the betterment of mankind. There could not have been two more earnest graduates in the class of '95 than Harper and King. From the days when as undergraduates they had had 'rambling chats' on

Varsity politics, they had moved on to more sober topics. During King's stopovers in Barrie they found themselves in total agreement as to their aims in life. Looking back on this accord a couple of years after graduation, King wrote to Harper, saying:

> *We have both found how few men there really are who take life in earnest. . . . Think carefully, old man, of the work we have to do. There are after all not many of us who are willing to sacrifice everything for the triumph of righteousness but you and I must certainly stand there. . . . Let us face our life problems again together as we did prayerfully before in the past.*

From their writings, either in their letters or diaries, it would be hard to say which of the two was the more dedicated although it was King who sometimes provided the back-stiffening needed to keep Harper on track. When he had found Harper despondent about his future in 1896, there had been a talk and a prayer by the parlor grate in Barrie, a talk which Harper later referred to as "the struggle you made to point out to me what is truly ennobling in life." They come across as being rather pompous and it was in the perception they had of standing 'alone for the triumph of righteousness' that their earnestness also smacks of priggishness.

'Get down to work at once. Let your life and influence tell for Christ'. These were the words written across the top of the page in King's diary as he began to record his year in Chicago. Before leaving home, he told Harper of his great desire to get on with his work: "I have so far, I fear, been playing along the roadside of life." It was with high resolve that he set out. "It will be such a release to get into a higher plane of thought and action in which I hope [to lead] a more spiritual life. I hope the settlement idea will prove to be what I imagine it to be." But the reality did not live up to his expectations: a short period of living in the settlement house proved this to him. In his disillusionment, he turned to Harper with his thoughts about his experience of Chicago's 19th ward. "I will never be able to live a life of idle luxury. I have come to regard wealth almost as a curse, perhaps should say the sad abuse of it on every hand." In a few weeks, the experiment was over and, as he rationalized it, "I had hoped to combine both [university and settlement work] but I find I cannot and the work I accomplish for the neighbourhood here is not worth the sacrifice, at least it does not appear so."

When Harper and King met again in the autumn of 1897 the year in Chicago was but a memory for King, a memory of crushed idealism. His only consolation was that he felt he had come to know a little more of the world. At the same time, Harper, too, had gone through a period of personal development. Like King, he had also recognized that he had to forsake some of his ideas but this, he held, was only proof of his 'honest desire for truth and that I still have much to learn'. He had gone to London with the hope that "I may hereafter be able to subdue whatever weakness there is in my character and there is much." In King's opinion, his friend seemed to be suffering from his old fault of "undue self-depreciation and equally over-appreciation of your friends." After their meeting in late 1897, King wrote to Harper that:

You say you found me a fuller man. You say in your letter that you left London a better man. I found you so. You will understand that this is no underestimation of what you were before. Your manly worth I trust I have always known but there was something, what it was I cannot say which kept telling me all the time 'This is Harper, the same old fellow but he is mightily changed.' There was a greater depth of Life in you than I had ever discovered before.

That autumn as Harper was settling in to his work in Toronto, King was on the move again, this time going to Harvard for a further two years' study. During his first year there, King's work was interrupted by his blossoming love affair with Mathilde. It was only to Harper that he could write fully about this. "I hold you dearer than any of my Canadian friends . . . the scenes are shifting fast and possibly by next Sunday I will have a great secret for you but you must keep it in your heart for no man in Canada will get an inkling of it save yourself." The 'great secret' was displaced a month later by the news that "It is doubtful if there will be an engagement for some little time but I assure you there is a very strong friendship though more than this we have both agreed there shall not be until we have each played a part that was first set out before thoughts of love arose." To Harper this seemed an excellent solution and he was quick to tell King so: "I cannot but feel that what you propose is the best course for all concerned, and, indeed, I must confess some relief as I read your letter. So easy is it for a single circumstance to change the course of a life should that circumstance transpire prematurely." They had set out such lofty goals for each other that the thought of one of them having to make a compromise with these ideals seems to have been unthinkable in Harper's eyes. King's frame of mind in the months following this decision was decidedly low, low to the point where, when he and Harper met in September, "We did not get into one of our old earnest conversations. I am not the man now to talk in the way I used to."

It had long been King's hope that he and Harper might, in the course of their work, spend some time together. In 1899 they were still 'circling in all directions around each other'. Harper was then in the Press Gallery in Ottawa and King was leaving for Europe on a Harvard scholarship. Part-time student, part-time tourist, he was in Rome in 1900 when he received a letter which gave him pause for thought. It was from Sir William Mulock who was the Canadian Postmaster-General and it contained an invitation to accept the "Editorship and management of the new Government *Labour Gazette*, Ottawa. Duties begin in early July. Salary fifteen hundred dollars. . . . May increase. If yes, come." Given King's growing interest in and some knowledge of labour relations he had recently written to Harper "I believe that it is noble cause and I must give my life to it." But the decision as to whether or not to accept Mulock's offer did not come easily. It meant leaving the university world and, as he said, "I have tasted some of the fruits of a life of scholarship and I must confess I am loath to leave them." On the other hand, he could see 'noble opportunities in this other work' and as he wrote to his parents, "It would mean an opportunity to carry on the work that my grandfather began." In the end, he sent a cable of acceptance to Mulock and sailed for home in mid-July.

Ottawa, as he looked about him later that month, did not impress him. Earlier that year, parts of it had been wiped out in a fire that could have been worse had the wind not changed fortuitously but, in any case, and especially in comparison to the European cities which King had recently visited, it would have come out badly. It was 'gloomy' and not interesting but 'tiresome', in his eyes. What made it less depressing was to find that Harper was in town and on the day he arrived they met for lunch in the old Russell House to catch up on the year's separation. Within a few days King had moved to a room ($3 per week) in the Victoria Chambers on Elgin Street. Harper had been in Ottawa for over a year by then and one of the first things he had done was to get himself elected to membership in the Ottawa Rowing Club and, later, to the Amateur Athletic Society and the Ottawa Canoe Club. Within a day of King's arrival, Harper took him to a 'smoking concert' at the Rowing Club and "I had my name put up as a member of the club. It seems a good place to get to know the best fellows of the town & to get some pleasant exercise rowing and swimming on the river."

It was not long before Harper and King decided to find rooms together. It was a step not taken without some qualms on King's part but one that he felt was in Harper's best interests. King himself, was feeling anxious, afraid at times that he had made a mistake in accepting the position in Ottawa. "This work will never please me and I have been a fool to take it in hand. I shall seek to follow it as duty & see if I can gain peace." he wrote in his diary. (He had earlier decided to give up keeping a diary when he returned to Canada, feeling that it made one too introspective and self-conscious. Better, he thought, to just keep a book of jottings but he took it up again 'as one returns to an old friend whom one thinks one can forsake'.)

By mid-October King and Harper had found suitable accommodation—two bedrooms and a shared sitting room at 202 Maria Street (now Laurier Avenue West). Around this time, too, Harper left the Montreal *Herald* and, on King's suggestion, became Associate Editor of the *Labour Gazette*. Such close proximity, both at work and at home, bore out fears on King's part about a loss of privacy. The Harper who now shared quarters with him was, in some respects, greatly changed. For the past three years, his life had been spent in the rough-and-tumble, as well as in the camaraderie of the newspaper world where he led a much more outgoing existence than did King who, until a few months ago, was still a student. In letters to Harper from other friends, there is every indication that he lived life differently when King was not around. The gist of one letter from a friend who had visited him in Ottawa reads:

> *That was a merry pace we set in Ottawa. How did you get home? [I] slept on the train from Smiths Falls to Toronto although I got up a couple of times with an awful thirst. 'Gin and lemon', I think, Bert, is a better combination than Sanderson or Tosh—Try it when you come up here.*

Another letter referred to "the hilarious time you had at the [Press Club] dinner, I presume . . . that you would not be in very good shape to discuss business." With King it was a different story. When he was at Harvard, he wrote in his diary that "I [resigned] my place on the exec. comm. of the Can. Club, . . . partly because of the fact that liquor was brought in at the last meeting." and a more all-encompassing decision was reached a year or two later.

> *Gillespie invited me to a little party in his room. . . . He had invited half a doz. Classical students . . . they drank whiskey & told filthy stories most of the time. I left before the party broke up. . . . How men of university training can in the presence of each other tell & laugh at filth I cannot understand. . . . A drop of whiskey has never passed my lips & never will so long as I possess health & strength & a will of my own. I am glad I find no enjoyment in such gatherings.*

As far as whiskey was concerned, he broke his vow many times but afterwards, he would always be penitent. King was not then nor did he ever become a 'man's man' and it took a lot of tolerance on the part of both Harper and King to live so closely together.

During this period of adjustment they were both lonely. A picture which Harper bought for his room, that of "a lone wolf, standing on a hill of snow, in the moonlight" was, he told King, "a picture of desolation and loneliness in which he is inclined to find a comparison to his life." King's loneliness centred on his single state: "I would give all I have to be married to one I could love and who loved me." While he could close his diary entry for his birthday in 1900 with the words 'God has been kind', there were many times after he and Harper went to live at 202 Maria Street when he would not agree that this was so. He still felt responsible for bettering the lives of both Harper and himself. This weighed heavily on him and he seems to have been constantly watching his friend for signs of weakening. At times he was comforted by the feeling that "Harper has a great soul and it is winning [?] itself Godward." but there were other moments when he was not so sure. "He has gone out tonight. He has been restless all day. Hope he will keep up the fight for noble Christian manhood. I must do all I can to have it so for us both."

There were other problems during their first winter of living and working together. In the office, the business detail of getting out the *Labour Gazette* was hardly bearable for a man of King's nature. The chore of revising correspondents' work he found to be 'a slow, uninteresting and largely worthless task' and dealing with the office routine which, while necessary, took up time that he would have preferred to spend on real and earnest writing for the journal. Harper did not like the routine work either, and there were signs that made King wonder if their working together was a good idea. He fussed about this in his dairy: "[Harper] is inclined to do much of his work, it seems to me, in a slipshod fashion & in scissors & paste rather than research method, and I often feel discouraged with him." It did not help matters when the Ottawa *Journal* ran an article on the Department of Labour which included a two column cut of King and a one column one of Harper. King was upset on a personal level: "I pray I do not look like the cut. It has a nose of a criminal and the eyes of a dissolute, the expression is mostly that of a negro convict. Harper's cut is very good, flattering if anything. . . . I bought 50 copies of the paper, why I do not know." Had he known what Harper wrote in his diary on this occasion there might have been fireworks:

> *Rex and I have been getting some cheap newspaper notoriety. The information is I think pretty much as Rex dictated it. . . . For myself I don't think it proper nor even wise for young men to keep blowing their trumpets too loudly. Vanity is Rex's great weakness however and will I fear remain an alloy in his character to the close.*

It was their shared love of reading that became a bridge between the two men. While Harper's nature was not as pent up as King's, their tastes in reading material were very similar. Almost as soon as they had settled into their new quarters, they continued the pattern of reading aloud, in turn, to each other in front of the fire in their small parlor. Their immediate choice was Thomas Carlyle, a British romantic idealist, whose book, *Hero Worship*, was greatly to their liking, so much so that its inspirational message often led them to talk much of the night away as they rededicated their lives to all that was noble and good. When reading *Past and Present* by the same author, King noted that it was "a good book like all Carlyle's writings full of solid truth, boldly & bluntly expressed." The writer also appealed to Harper for those same qualities: "Grand, bluff, sturdy old Carlyle is becoming a reality to me. . . . I find [him] to be healthy, wholesome and full of moral fibre." They read the poets, too. An evening devoted to Matthew Arnold, a favourite of Harper's, drew from him the comment that "His philosophy, the pursuit of perfection. . . . I find in him more and more the noble minded man as I proceed. . . . The room where we sat before a grate fire seemed filled with the thought of the noble man who penned the poem, and the evening was a most enjoyable one." Tennyson's *The Idylls of the King* provided more 'healthy inspiration' and had its message for them: "The gentle teaching of the poem is that we must be swayed by high resolves and noble motives." They read these writers and others but they did not read for the sake of entertainment. King would

Mackenzie King 1900

have found that type of literature to be frivolous, more 'wasted or worse than wasted time' and, as for Harper, it was true that he was 'less inclined to seek recreation with a book than in other ways.'

Although they professed that it was a heavy cross to bear, both men became part of the social life of Ottawa. They were two young, eligible bachelors, new to the city, and the invitations kept coming. They had mutual friends in the Burbidge family through Henry, 'Burb', a classmate of 95, and were frequent guests in their home. Through this entree into Ottawa society and the contacts they made in the various clubs to which they belonged, they found themselves being asked to teas, euchre parties, skating and theatre parties and At Homes. Far from avoiding these distractions or 'healthy relaxations' (however one looked at it), they actually sought them out at times. One afternoon, after a day in the office, being restless, perhaps, they "Went for a walk. . . . We called at the Robert Allens—they were not receiving, thank Heavens, then at Mrs. D'Arcy Scott's do-do. Then on the Misses Haycocks—a room full of bright and pretty little girls." As always with King, however, doubts immediately set in and he made another effort to end what he called 'this social nonsense'. "I refused a skating party tonight, a euchre party tomorrow at Mrs. Gemmill's & will not go to an At Home at Mrs. Fraser's in the afternoon." Despite their ambivalent attitude towards being entertained, they were aware of the politesse required of their positions and did their own share in returning hospitality. Sometimes they took guests to the theatre or entertained at tea in their parlor but once they arranged something different. Along with 'Burb', Harper and King invited twenty-six of their friends one Saturday evening in March 1901, for a sleighing party. They hired a large 'carry-all' or 'Bandwagon' drawn by four plumed horses and crossed over the Ottawa River to Aylmer for a supper and dancing.

Relief for Harper and King in their love-hate affair with society came only in distancing themselves from it in the summer of 1901. On Thanksgiving Day the previous year, they discovered Kingsmere and from then on the area around this little lake in the Gatineau Hills in Quebec, just outside Ottawa, became an important part of their lives. For King it was an association that lasted until his death in 1950. It was of very short duration for Harper—only that one summer—but it was a welcome retreat for one whose love of nature was great. It was also a place where, seated one Sunday morning high on King Mountain, he could look down on Ottawa in the distance and reflect that "If men could only get to a mountain occasionally and look down upon the world in which they live and move and have their being, there would be less dilettantism, less worship of forms, institutions, baubles and lath and plaster." When they first started looking for somewhere to spend the summer they thought of taking rooms in a boarding-house in Britannia, a popular resort at that time and only a few miles out of Ottawa. They could spend evenings and weekends there by the water and still be close enough to commute on the newly opened Ottawa Electric Railway's streetcars. But Kingsmere, too, was attracting its share of summer visitors and Dr. Herridge, pastor of St. Andrew's Presbyterian Church which Harper and King attended, would have sung its praises to them. Dr. Herridge's wife, Marjorie, was fast becoming a personal friend of both Harper and King and when she, too, extolled the glories of Kingsmere, the die was cast. Getting to and from Kingsmere was, however, not a simple run on a streetcar. Usually they took the train for the twelve or so miles from Ottawa to Chelsea and then they would either go by coach or walk the four miles through the woods to Caroline McMinn's boarding house where they were staying. They each had their 'wheels', too, Harper's Model 51 having been considered 'the nicest one on the market' when he had bought it the previous year. King's bicycle was also almost new and he had been very proud of the fact that, having been taught to ride by a friend, he was able to ride up and down alone within a half-hour. Nevertheless, he was not committed to this means of transportation, complaining that it did not provide the right sort of all round exercise. Harper was the one who was a keen cyclist to the point that he sometimes made the entire trip this way even if it was 'eight miles a day on the wheel, four of them uphill'. During the month of July, King was on holidays in the United States and, having enquired of Harper how the travelling back and forth was going, was told that "I have several times ridden in from the hill and once last week made a record run by coming in from the house there in 55 minutes."

By early August, King was back and rejoicing in that "It is most delightful to be back again and I enjoy more than all the days in the States those evenings in the woods and on the moor, alone and free." Harper was there for a short overlap before leaving on his holidays, and Mrs. King came up from Toronto for a visit. Marjorie Herridge and the children were also there along with her sister, Emily Duncan. Thus King was hardly 'alone' but he and Harper were 'free', not in slavery to the At Home and tea party hostesses in Ottawa. It was a time for relaxation as they indulged in long talks on the verandah of the boarding house and in such simple (not to say boyish) pastimes as tossing knives and pitching coppers on the lawn. Sometimes the party took long walks, often to the top of King Mountain, and one afternoon Harper and King slipped away for a walk to Pink Lake and a bit of skinny-dipping. Inspirational readings were less necessary away from the pull of society and the regime of 'Early to bed, early to rise' along with night and morning plunges in the little lake made for a very satisfying change.

Harper's holidays that year took him to the Maritime Provinces on the annual excursion for members of the Canadian Press Association. On reading Harper's diaries after his death, King noted that there were many references to the beauties of nature as seen along the way but, on his return, it seemed to King that "a considerable part of the time was devoted to speaking of the girls he met. I fear Bert has a weakness for the fair sex." There seems to have been no serious romance in Harper's life. There had been early references to Ida L and various other girls, 'summer girls', as he called them and a letter from one of his friends once referred to him as 'a young man that is in love'. There was also the possibility according to Mathilde that there might have been an attraction between her nurse friend, Violet Nesbitt, and Harper, who saw each other from time to time socially in Ottawa. Nothing came of this and when Miss Nesbitt next appears it is as a nurse in South Africa during the Boer War. Harper had asked one of his friends who was going to South Africa by the same ship to be of any assistance he could during the voyage. When he had a letter back and found out that this friend seemed to be more than willing to be of any possible help, he wrote a cautionary note saying:

> *I am glad you found Nurse Nesbitt interesting. I think she is a first-rate sort of girl, but take care, old chap, prenez garde de votre coeur! It is a dangerous thing for an energetic young man to devote too much of his thought to a girl, when there are not a lot of other girls around. Prenez garde, Monsieur.*

Whether Harper's cautious stand could have been because of King's influence is hard to say. He had witnessed the turmoil of the affair between King and Mathilde in its early days and again in 1901. At Easter that year King made a quick trip to Boston to collect his papers and other effects including Mathilde's letters. On his return, he did the unpardonable and

> read aloud to Harper parts of [Mathilde's] letters, then did them up in a bundle to return to her. Burb came in about 10, at which time I destroyed in the fire in the hearth all of mine. As I look at them I see them to have been the most worthless sort of trash. I am glad they are in ashes.

As for Mathilde's letters: "They are a beautiful set of letters but a strain of sadness runs thro' them & of misunderstanding and unrest. No wonder." Ever since King and Mathilde had decided to go their separate ways, he had been cautious to the point where Harper observed that there was "a proneness to talk to girls with an earnestness to which they are unaccustomed." Whether or not King was conscious of this approach, it served as protection and it seems to have had an influence on Harper except when he was out from under King's watchful eye.

When King was away from Ottawa, Harper became the Acting Deputy Minister and editor of the *Gazette*. Both the Department and the journal survived these absences as King was never really out of touch. There were frequent letters back and forth and while King was not always satisfied that Harper exercised proper control, there was no open friction. This came later in 1901 as King prepared to go to British Columbia on another labour dispute. The problem involved how to take into account the mixture of races and cultures in that province with Harper urging a cautious, reflective course if trouble did come. It seems that King was at odds with this thinking and evidently made no bones about it around Ottawa. So clear was the difference between the two men that Ottawa began to gossip about the Deputy Minister and his assistant. Distance cooled tempers when King went away in early November. During this time, they corresponded often and the letters seem to have put to rest any dissention between them.

In his first breathing spell after King's departure, Harper wrote to him, extending good wishes for the success of the mission and, in what sounds like a fence-mending mood, went on to say:

> *My dear Rex, I assure you it is not the prejudice of a friendship . . . that tells me it is not the strong arm of a commission, nor yet the power of public opinion, that is your strongest weapon in this important crisis; but the commanding influence of a high-minded manhood moved by noble impulses and unalloyed by selfish motives.*

He was surely saying the right thing to bridge any gaps and he went on:

> *I miss you very much in the office, but still more out of it. Indeed when you are away I realize how much we are together.... Your life has grown into mine to such an extent that your hopes and aspirations are mine as well.*

In the last long letter that he wrote to King, the feeling was still the same. "I miss you, Rex, very much. The meaning of an individual is sometimes emphasized when the individual is absent from the associations which are eloquent of his individuality." At the close of this wordy letter, after saying that he must settle down and do some work, he added: "The house is singularly quiet, without any movement in the adjoining room." And quiet it was to remain. King had wished for a year in which they might share their lives. They had that and a bit more but this association was suddenly broken by what can only be called a tragic and senseless accident when Harper drowned in the Ottawa River before King's return from the west.

But Harper was not to be forgotten. Within days of his death, a meeting was held at Ottawa City Hall to discuss erecting a memorial to mark his heroism. King was, undoubtedly, the guiding force behind this movement and as the one who had known Harper more intimately than anyone else, he was in a position to guide the project in the different stages. It had been decided that a monument should be erected and that it should be of bronze and stone with a figure on it which would symbolize Harper's character and his heroism. To King, the choice of a figure was an easy decision. On the wall in Harper's study and where he could see it each time he went to his desk was a reproduction of George Frederick

Watt's painting of Sir Galahad. He had often remarked to King and others that this was his ideal knight and thus this became the choice of the committee in charge of the work. A public subscription was opened and the commission to do the statue was awarded to a young American sculptor whom King later learned was born on the same day and in the same year as Harper. Had he then been interested in coincidences to the same degree as he was in later life, he would have instantly known that the committee had made the right choice of sculptor. It was in early November 1905, that King finally saw the statue as it was being prepared for mounting. "After all my endeavours to secure the head of Metcalfe Street as a site ... I was fearful lest it might not be all that we could wish and desire. My mind was relieved beyond measure when I saw the figure—a wonderful piece of work, splendidly executed—a 'Sir Galahad' every inch of it." Two weeks later the Governor-General, Lord Grey, unveiled this allegorical representation of Harper's ideal knight. In his remarks to the three thousand or so persons gathered on that cold November afternoon, he said that "I shall seldom pass this monument without being reminded of the example which [Harper] has bequeathed as a precious legacy." The statue still stands today, the bronze 'Sir Galahad' set on a granite base in which are carved the words from one of Harper's and King's best loved idylls, 'If I lose myself, I save myself'. Had Lord Grey's expressed hope on this occasion that "this statue may be only the first of a set of noble companions, which, in the course of time, will make this street the Via Sacra of the capital" been carried out, the memorial to Harper might not be as ignored as it is today and its story so lost to history.

Two months later, a further memorial to Harper appeared when King's book, *The Secret of Heroism*, was published. Shortly after Harper's death, when King was packing up Harper's books and papers, he came upon his friend's diary and the idea of publishing parts of it came to his mind. "The more I read of it, the more beautiful I discover his soul and real purpose to have been." He decided to go ahead with this project and to augment the diary excerpts by quoting from letters which Harper had written to members of his family and to King himself, his avowed purpose being "to weave from them the story of his inner life, in the belief that its beauty will bring courage and inspiration to many." King's emotions, when he received the first copies of this book in January 1906, were ones of relief in that 'the bookmaking is all that can be desired' and "mingled sadness and joy as I walked to the [Rideau] Club for lunch with it in my hand

and saw Harper's monument with the sun shining on it." The book's public reception at that time was probably similar to opinions expressed by writers at a later date. When it came time to write biographies of King, the book was mentioned and lauded or put down depending on the author's feelings for King. It was said that "It displayed King's literary talent at its best: great simplicity, careful and even fastidious expression" and it was also described as being 'a tortured little book' written in a 'turgid and self-conscious style'. The charge was later made, not without some justification, that it was not simply a memorial to Harper but that there were actually two prominent characters in the book, Harper and the author, King, who was accused of having used this book as "the first overt sign of ambition for a public career." A partial confession of the duality of characters in the book is found in a letter which King wrote in 1919 to B.K. Sandwell, an old Toronto classmate, in which he admitted that "[*The Secret of Heroism*] is perhaps as much an expression of my own convictions on some of the fundamental things of life as it is of Harper's character and aims."

This book, like the person about whom it was ostensibly written, is now largely forgotten; but, as long as there is an interest in Mackenzie King with specific reference to his friendships, there will be questions as to the quality of the relationship between those two men. Violet Markham, an English friend who was so close to King in their thoughts on many subjects, was not able to understand their association and see it as it was. It was her feeling that Harper was good for King, that he was drawing him out, and that, "Had he lived, his influence would probably have served to break down the barriers which Mackenzie King increasingly built between himself and his fellow men." Right on so many other issues, she was wrong in this, an understandable error when her only idea of what Harper was like and what he stood for in King's life came from King himself. From the start, back in their student days, King was the dominant one. After graduation when their paths divided, it was King who took the high road. Leaving Harper behind learning the ropes of journalism, he continued with his studies, meeting and hobnobbing with the rich, the famous and the learned in Chicago, Boston and later in Europe. During this time their friendship continued, cemented as it was by their common idealism as well as by their need of each other. To whom else could King confide the depth of his wish to work for the betterment of mankind? Not to his parents who took a dim view of his straying into settlement work in Chicago; neither might it have been understood by the summer crowd on Bohemia Island or by his wealthy friends in Newport society. Nor was there anyone else, seemingly, to whom Harper could turn when he was overtaken by feelings of self-depreciation and self-distrust. It was only King who could reprimand him for this attitude and encourage him by saying that: "The seed has been planted and taken root—the seasons must do the rest." This was the pattern of their lives to the end of their days together. It was changed so abruptly in the dusk of that December day in 1901 and King was left to carry on alone. Whatever may be said about the quality of their friendship, after Harper's death there was no other man who took his place in King's life, ever. He could only do as he had done before in times of personal upheaval and turn back to his friend, his diary: "I am taking up this diary again as a means of keeping me true to my true purpose." He could also turn to Marjorie Herridge who had been a friend to both himself and Harper although, as it turned out, this was not a wise move.

Marjorie Herridge

There was a strange Minister & when he prayed for the Minister's wife, she grabbed me by the knee & began to laugh." Oddly enough, this is a direct quote from Mackenzie King's diary. The date was 10 March 1901, and the place, St. Andrew's Presbyterian Church in Ottawa. 'She' was Marjorie Herridge, wife of the incumbent of that church, Rev. Dr. William Herridge, who was out of town that day while his wife shared the family pew with King and his friend, 'Burb'.

It is true that, as a boy, King's own actions in church were less than reverent at times but by 1901 his youthful high spirits had given way to the dignified behaviour expected of a Deputy Minister. Embarrassing for him, then, to be grabbed by the knee in the midst of the morning service and to be further discomfited by the laughter that accompanied this sudden gesture. In a disapproving tone, he indicated that 'She was inclined to laugh too much if opportunity given at all.' King was likely not in the mood to pay too much attention to the sermon that morning. As a young man he had become what one biographer called a 'sermon taster'. In the company of other students while at university, he attended services at churches other than the Presbyterian one in which he had been brought up; what he found was seldom to his liking. At St. Michael's Cathedral in Toronto, his reaction was that "The whole service was to me worse than a mockery as far as teaching religion was concerned. The ceremonies, etc., were explained." While still in Toronto he went

> to Milligan's church but was greatly disappointed in the man I heard. . . . It is a poor plan for a Minister to try and handle metaphores [sic]when he don't [sic] know how, or to draw absurd comparisons and run too much into his own personal affairs.

In the summer of 1899, while he was in Newport, Rhode Island, tutoring Bob Gerry, a friend from Harvard, he heard a sermon that was, in his opinion, truly reprehensible.

> [The Episcopalian Minister] was preaching to a very fashionable congregation, outside were footmen standing on the street, inside he was telling them that the poor should have the gospel preached to them, and hinting at an equality in man before God. . . . What contradictions!

During the year he spent in Europe, visiting many of the grand and famous cathedrals and churches had broadened his religious experience. The effect on him was not positive: "The more churches I see, the more do I become out of patience with 'formal' religion. Catholic churches are like centres of idolatry & in many Protestant ones, the bible is a sort of fetish." When he came to live in Ottawa, he found that he had some complaints, too, regarding St. Andrew's. Dr. Herridge, in his sermons, sometimes disappointed, sometimes pleased King whose reactions ranged from finding him 'a teacher of Ethics [sic], not a preacher of religion' to outright praise when he "preached on the text, the things of earth & Heaven. It was one of the finest sermons I have ever listened to. The way in which he spoke of the reality of the invisible & eternal."

Away from the pulpit, though, King was highly critical of Dr. Herridge, finding him to be vain and conceited. And, as for Mrs. Herridge, it did not take him very long to note that she did not behave like a typical Minister's wife either inside or outside the church. At a public lecture in March 1901,

> Malaria and Mosquitoes . . . a most interesting lecture, delivered exceptionally well, without notes, in a popular & yet cultured manner. . . . I sat beside Mrs. Herridge who was inclined to laugh as usual & behave badly.

Yet, he still thought, at that time, that she had 'ability & sense'; she was also fun to be with even if she sometimes was an embarrassment to the very proper King. It was in the same month as the lecture on Malaria and Mosquitoes (an odd choice of topic for Ottawa at that time of year) and the episode in church, that King, Harper and 'Burb' hosted their sleighing party to Aylmer. When they decided to have a chaperone along, it was to Marjorie they turned and, according to reports, she was full of life and kept the party in good spirits.

In the summer of 1901, King and Marjorie were thrown into each other's company a great deal while at Kingsmere. She was there with her four children, Gordon, Bill, Irene and Gwen as well as her sister, Emily Duncan. Dr. Herridge was in England that summer but Harper was there at the beginning of the season and King joined the group after a brief holiday in the United States. Isabel King was also present for part of August. By all accounts, she was her usual vivacious self and King was able to report that even the rain during the stagecoach ride in from Chelsea did not dampen her spirits. She and Marjorie had already met during the previous summer in Muskoka and on that first evening together at the McMinn boarding house, where they were all staying, their shared reminiscences of their past meeting elicited much laughter from them. This was duly brought under control by King's reading aloud to them from "Emerson's *Essay on Nature*, the part on Idealism & Spirit with the truth of which I agree heartily and feel the strength & beauty as of soul inspiration." That set the pattern for the next few weeks, moments of lightheartedness and of sober thought. There were walks in the surrounding woods, including one to the top of King Mountain, a fairly steep climb in parts, and, to King's astonishment, his mother "got all the way to the top with only a rest or two at the most. . . . The view from the mountaintop beside the cross was grand. . . . All that is associated with altitude & loftiness was with us in part."

Soon after Mrs. King's arrival, Harper left on holidays but King was able to get out to the country most evenings after work. Occasionally there was a problem with this arrangement. When his Minister, Sir William Mulock, returned from a trip to Australia, he insisted that King remain in town that night. Not to leave the two ladies by themselves, King phoned and asked them to come in for midday dinner with him.

> *They drove in from the country this morning with a white horse which looked like a bag of bones & a rickety old carriage—the whole makeup Harper calls a 'dromedary'. I laughed and laughed to see them try to make the brute go with a wooden whip.*

The following weekend, King's time with his mother and Marjorie was threatened by further demands from Sir William but he put his foot down. This was in the days when civil servants worked on Saturday mornings and King had no quarrel with that but to work overtime past one o'clock—no!

I will do my work faithfully, and give it my best energy, thought & abilities, but I will not serve any man, nor will I allow my own personal private life to be crushed or crowded. . . . Office hours end at one so I simply declined to remain over & left at one.

(Many civil servants who had their weekends and evenings disrupted by King in later years surely wished that he had learned something from his own experience.)

At Kingsmere, on weekends and in the evenings, the walks continued. As a rule, it was usually just King and Marjorie. She would meet him at the Chelsea station when he arrived after a day's work in town and they would walk back together to Mrs. McMinn's, being joined at times by Mrs. King and Emily Duncan for the last part of the way. There were walks and there were talks, talks in the moonlight with 'Mrs. H.' as he still referred to her in his diary. There were talks that went on so late on occasion that he overslept the following morning and had to go to the station by stage instead of walking or cycling there. One night they all went to the Maingy's [sic] to play cards. "We passed the evening with euchre. The moonlight was beautiful on the fields and about here and I had a pleasant walk & talk with Mrs. H. in it." Another evening,

After dinner, Mrs. Herridge, Miss Duncan, Mother & I went to the lake. Miss Duncan & Mother took the punt & we went in a canoe. It was a beautiful moonlight night. I never laughed more than to see Mother & Miss D. with only one oar trying to make progress & going round in circles. We played a mean sort of trick by leaving them to themselves in this way.

On a quiet morning or afternoon, the verandah provided a pleasant setting for reading aloud, sometimes with Mrs. King, sometimes with Marjorie. It was on a Saturday evening, though, in early September when they, King and Marjorie, began reading Matthew Arnold to each other. Dr. Herridge was back from England but he had gone in to Ottawa to prepare for the Sunday services; Mrs. King had returned to Toronto and Bert Harper was nowhere in sight. Had he been there, the evening would have had a different emphasis. Bert had long been an admirer of Arnold and had rediscovered his poetry during the winter of 1900-01. 'The Buried Life' was one of his favourite poems, appealing to what Arnold himself called 'high seriousness', a condition from which both Harper and King suffered. It was the practice of Harper and whoever was with him to put aside the volume of poetry that was being read and 'to allow a deeper searching of the heart [to] follow'. Without Harper's presence, it seems that Marjorie and King did not follow this custom but read on and on

> till nearly half past one. The night was a revelation to me of a new soul, a supremely refined intellectual and spiritual beauty characterized its thought and expression. My whole nature roused as I read [the poems] and Mrs. H. and I gave her [our?] whole thought and mind to their beauty.

'Tristan and Isolde' was one of their choices that evening and, whether or not King already knew the poem, it clearly took on a new meaning for him. The tragic love story retold in the company of one who was on the verge of becoming more than just a friend to him made a deep impression. On Sunday, they continued reading Arnold. "I shall never forget these two nights. . . . They have added so much to my life".

Gossip about Marjorie, Harper and King was heard in Ottawa in the autumn of 1901. It appeared unseemly to some that the Minister's wife should be seen so much in the company of the two men but King was quick in coming to her defense: "Tho more impulsive in her goodness of heart, Mrs. H. has twice the head and heart of these people and not their meanness." If there seemed cause for tongues to wag at that time, the gossips could have had a field day some months later. After Harper's death, King turned more to Marjorie (and for a time to all at the Manse), and had anyone been looking in there as the year 1902 came in, they would have observed a strange domestic scene.

> Mrs. Herridge and I stood before an open grate with bowed heads. . . . The children had returned from a party and we kissed them anew, Gwennie was asleep, Dr. Herridge in bed beside two lighted candles, I kissed him & Miss Duncan and Willy later.

After reading part of Emerson's *Essay on Friendship* beside the fire with Marjorie, King went back home only to return later that day for the family dinner "which I enjoyed greatly. Gordon played a while of [on?] the violin, the Dr. on the piano, Gwennie with her arm around my neck and Irene beside me as we looked over some pictures together."

Taken at its face value, this was just a family entertaining a close friend but there were undercurrents that would make this an occasion rarely to be repeated. During the next few months, relations between the Herridges and King changed dramatically. His diary entry for that day—his first since Harper's death—expressed his desire 'to seek to be true to what I record in its pages' but truth eluded him at times. It was blurred by his naïveté in trying to deal with something more complex than anything he had previously experienced. His one love affair had been with Mathilde and he did not handle that with great success. Nor did he learn anything from it. One of his concerns about Mathilde had been his suspicion that she was older than he was but, here he was, in 1902, becoming involved with someone who was sixteen years older than he, who was married and had four young children. The reality of the situation seems to have been beyond his comprehension.

Marjorie Herridge (1914)

As he and Marjorie greeted the New Year with bowed heads, his thoughts were first of his family in Toronto and then 'of her beside me, and of he who is gone'. There was no doubt that Harper's death was much on their minds and it was having an effect on their feelings for each other but there was another element, too. Dr. Herridge's odd behaviour on New Year's Eve was symptomatic of a recurrence of the melancholia from which he suffered and, early in January, he went away for a few weeks. At this time Marjorie relied more and more on King who, without quite knowing why, seemed to feel that he was able to be of some comfort to her. 'Poor soul, she has more to bear than a woman's heart deserves' and during this period, scarcely a day went by when he did not spend at least part of it with her. On the day that Dr. Herridge left, King spent the evening at the manse at which time Marjorie seemed to be "most anxious to unburden her heart, tho' holding back from so doing. . . . She has had a most terrible strain. . . . How the innocent suffer!" The next day he tried to ease her distress in a rather questionable manner by reading 'an extract from pages of pain in an old diary'. (Could he have been reading his account of his unsuccessful wooing of Mathilde?)

In late January, Isabel King came to Ottawa for a visit. Earlier in the month, Max, her younger son, had left with the Medical Corps for South Africa where the Boer War was still raging. A change of scene under those circumstances would be welcome and she always enjoyed her visits with 'Willy'. For his part, he was always proud to show off his 'beautiful mother' to all 'of the right political and social stripe'. During the time she was in Ottawa, the capital was busy, socially. There was a State Banquet while she was there; she attended private dinners, receptions and teas. She went 'calling', too, this in the company of both King and Marjorie whom she considered a friend by then. These calls were 'extremely short & formal & to my mind, the most utter farce' in King's eyes although he could note, doubtless with some satisfaction, that "Lady Laurier was very pleasant and sd. she hoped I wd. come often to see them."

Later, after Mrs. King had returned to Toronto and had written her Thank-you notes, there was also one for King which was 'from her heart, the most loving note from a torn and loving heart'. Her time in Ottawa, while diverting in its own way, could not have been easy for her. She was nobody's fool and it would not have taken her long to see that even if King himself was largely unaware of it, his constant association with Marjorie was unwise. Dr. Herridge came home in early February but he was still in a disturbed state of mind. Certainly relations between himself and Marjorie reached a new low in this period which led King to remark that "I cannot admire the way he treats his wife, who is a most loving, affectionate, warm-hearted soul, as good & pure as God ever created woman." To give King his due, he had begun to feel somewhat uncomfortable each time he and Marjorie were together after the Doctor's return. He even went so far as to wonder if "I have been too constantly to the manse, and I seem to feel that perhaps there is an injustice to the Dr. in my doing so." Having come this far in his analysis of the situation, King found himself up against a brick wall. Could he change his attitude? Should he, perhaps, not go to the manse so often? After a short talk with Marjorie, it was all resolved: '[I]t resulted in the candid confession to each other that our friendship was too real to suffer any break'. On 25 February, the blow fell. Marjorie had spent the evening at the Kings' and had stayed on rather late, so late that when she had not returned by midnight, Dr. Herridge called for her. By then, she and King had left and had taken a walk around the block before going to the manse. When they arrived, the Dr. was home and they found

> *the front door was locked. Mrs. H. rang twice and then the Dr. came himself, unlocked the door & stepped back. When I said good night to him, he did not reply, but in the most direct manner possible slammed the inside door shut on both of us. It was in so many words 'You may both go your way, I scorn you both.'*

There was no way now to avoid the issue and, during the last two days of Mrs. King's visit, there was a flurry of discussions taking place. The morning after the incident at the manse, Marjorie visited Mrs. King who may or may not have been her confidante at this time. She would want to talk to someone and there could not have been many others to whom the wife of the Presbyterian Minister could turn at such a time. At noon that day, it was King's turn for a talk with Marjorie and, in the course of a long walk, they openly discussed their friendship and the propriety of it. What had remained unspoken until then all came out as Marjorie told of

> *Dr. Herridge's indifference to her, the want of any true love between them—for years past, his going his way & she her's, his justifying her action by his friendship with other women, his leaving her alone for months each summer, & the rest.*

On the day following the closed-door episode. King called on Dr. Herridge for a few minutes and heard his side of the story.

> *He sd. he had been annoyed with his wife . . . the only reason was what the neighbours might say. If there were but the three of us, I was welcome to go where & when and be where & when I liked with Mrs. H. but we had to consider the outside world. . . . He was quite worried I cld. see & had nothing to say for his own act.*

As might have been expected, this behaviour of Dr. Herridge's which Marjorie considered 'entirely unpardonable' and 'the action of an insane man' had the effect of increasing her bitterness towards her husband. It also turned her even more to King. A few days later he found out how deep her feelings were:

> *The truth is she loves me, and my problem is here. I am determined to do nothing that will cause any estrangement of feeling between her and the doctor. She does not love him. Her love for me is no robbery, but perhaps it may enable me to cause her to think more of him. This must be my purpose and is. The love I have for her, and it is a real love, is not to win her to myself. That is impossible—is not desired, but knowing her to help her, knowing the doctor to help him, knowing them both to be a blessing to their home.*

Then King set about implementing this high-minded thinking. He first turned to Dr. Herridge on the following Sunday, walking to church with him 'taking his arm, asking him to let me be a help to him in his life and work.' That evening, he was back in the fold, having been invited to supper at the manse. This gave him a chance to speak to Marjorie and to advise her to

> *do what she cld. for the Dr. to love him well. When she seemed to resent my being drawn closer to him, my soul rose against her. It will do this. When I think he is responsible for the lack of love, I sympathize, when I think she is the cause, or fosters it, it turns my heart against her. . . . I wd to God she loved him more.*

Had King kept up his diary a little more regularly in the spring and summer of 1902, some of the mystery of his true relationship with Marjorie would have been revealed. As it was, there were weeks at a time when he wrote nothing at all. What few entries there were showed what seemed like a real determination on the part of both Marjorie and King to see less of each other and to live their lives to the 'highest and best'. Alas, for high resolutions! These had even less chance of working for King and Marjorie than they had had with King and Harper. Despite King's avowed wish 'To know duty, to love it and do it' there was constant backsliding on the part of both of them. Early in July, King took holidays and went to Toronto to work on his long-delayed Harvard thesis. There was some hope of being able to finish it in the atmosphere of the family home; there was no hope at all of concentrating on it in Ottawa with Marjorie nearby. For the rest of the summer, King commuted between Ottawa and Chelsea, boarding again at Mrs. McMinn's. Marjorie and the children were there as usual but Dr. Herridge was off by himself in the Maritimes.

What went on between King and Marjorie that summer has been a matter of no little conjecture. His diary was silent until 21 September when he was back in Ottawa and from it one learns that

> *The story of my life for the present is the story of its relation to the Child [a recent name for Marjorie]. Our summer has been lived together, lived to ourselves and now the fall and winter has [sic] come and we are to live apart and the duties of life rather than its pleasures are to receive their emphasis. What is to be the outcome of this love, the love which binds her to me and me to her, that is the problem now.*

The solution to this dilemma—for such it appeared to King, at least—was "not in seeking to turn away, or in ceasing to be, it must be worked out in the full presence of each other by a fuller presence of God. I see no other path, either certain or right." A further entry for that day came after a talk with Marjorie

> *whose love is such that she is unhappy one minute alone. We talked earnestly & I sought to tell her of the need of allowing my action to be free, with no misunderstanding. This she feign would do, but cannot, nor can nor do I blame her with what her life's experience has been. God has never drawn us so together unless for a purpose of His own. This alone I can feel.*

There is also a comment that has intrigued readers over the years. When he wrote that 'I have reason to love her as I never had reason to before', what, exactly, was he saying? It would be easy to jump to the conclusion that they had become lovers during the summer but that is out of character for King. A sense of propriety had governed his behaviour with Mathilde at all times but, lacking any evidence, it is not possible to say what happened between him and Marjorie in the summer of 1902. It is plain that she was in love with him while he seems to have become swept up in the headiness of the situation. In the long view, it is more than likely that their relationship was platonic, in deed if not in thought.

It seems clear that King had been at least thinking of making an effort to break away when he wrote of 'allowing my actions to be free' but, if so, he did not completely succeed. Marjorie was still dependent on him to a great extent and he seemed incapable of doing anything about it. Life for both followed pretty much the same pattern as in past years. King often attended services at St. Andrew's with Marjorie since his presence in the family pew was something the Dr. thought to be above reproach. He was as usual a frequent caller at the manse and there were evenings in late 1902 and into the following year when Marjorie went over to his rooms for an hour or two. If the view is accepted that their relationship was more than likely platonic, this idea is reinforced in reading King's diaries. There is no evidence of guilt in what he wrote. It seems that they read and they talked. More often than not, Marjorie used King as a shoulder to cry on as she told of "the injustices to which her life is at times subjected. . . . Poor soul, how little the world knows how great a sorrow is hers."

King was absent from Ottawa for a period in the spring of 1903 when he traveled to British Columbia where trouble was brewing between the CPR Company and officials of a union. The train trip provided King with time to read and reflect and to observe, with horror, how some members of the clergy, other than Dr. Herridge, behaved. 'It was the most deliberate performance I have ever witnessed', wrote King of this episode. It evidently attracted the attention of all the passengers in the railway car and, as he observed, it did break the monotony of the view outside as the train made its way from Moose Jaw to Calgary.

A priest . . . was on the train with a young woman. . . . They seemed to be having a jolly time together and he bought sauterne and benedictine for her at meals & drank a good deal himself. . . . After the other passengers had gone to bed I saw the priest get out of his berth & get into bed with the girl.

Possibly it was King who alerted the porter (since he seemed to be taking a great interest in what was going on) but soon the priest was sent back to his own berth, promising not to stray across the aisle again. 'I have both their names', King noted. What use he planned to make of this information is difficult to say. Next morning his first thought was of "how little profession or calling or vows or anything external can mean as compared with innate goodness."

As for Dr. Herridge, the member of the cloth whom King knew at first hand, relations between himself and King actually reached a point where they were able to work together in late 1903. A Men's Club was to be formed at St. Andrew's and, instead of Marjorie spending the evenings with King, it was the turn of her husband who had enlisted King's help in forming this club. After only two weeks of talks, the club was officially launched, with King as its 1st Vice-President and seeing in it great possibilities for good. His intention at the time was to make his 'influence felt for good through it'. Although he went on to edit the first edition of The *Message*, a monthly publication of the club, this was just about the last time he and Dr. Herridge saw eye-to-eye on anything.

Lapses in King's diary keeping were nothing new. Often it was the torment of his personal life that contributed to the long silences but, during the spring and summer of 1904, nothing was written for a completely different reason. Kingswood, his first cottage at Kingsmere, was being built. It was a modest structure but it was ample for his bachelor needs. There were four rooms—a small bedroom, a kitchen and, facing the lake, a living room and a dining room. As well, there was a verandah overlooking the lake and King was immensely proud of the whole thing. "The bare floor, the timbered walls & ceilings, the brick hearth & fireplace are more beautiful to my eyes than the best interiors of the city." The fireplace that he referred to provided King with his first opportunity in building to express his love of the romantic. In design, it was modeled on one which he had seen in Shakespeare's home in Stratford-on-Avon and which was a more suitable style for an old English kitchen with its heavy iron hooks for holding kettles and cooking pots than it was for a Canadian cottage. When the cottage was officially opened to a few friends, this fireplace was the focal point of the evening. Marjorie read aloud from Matthew Arnold and not from Shakespeare which was undoubtedly a mistake. The fireplace was dedicated to the memory of Bert Harper and the fire lit but the solemnity of the evening was broken when it became obvious that the chimney would not draw and the guests had to flee the smoke-filled room.

> *This is an ideal spot for a house and the house itself is as quaint as it can be. I don't think it at all tiny and [it] is certainly awfully pretty. [Billy] has shown remarkably good taste in his curtains etc., & I only wish you could see it too. All his doors, windows, etc., are painted white and it makes the place so fresh. I sleep in the big room and we use the other bedroom for a dining room. It is all lovely and Billy is so happy.*

So wrote King's sister, Jennie, to their other sister, Bella, who was at home in Toronto. Mr. and Mrs. King also spent the summer with King and after the family left, he took two weeks holidays to catch up on work around the cottage, work he had largely put aside while he was playing host. In the spring he had been busy painting his new home, even 'working on the Sabbath', much to his mother's disgust and he had tried to ignore the huge piles of brush that still remained from the tree-trimming which had been done in preparation for building. This could no longer be ignored so

> *Got Buckley to help me part of the time and we had a huge bonfire, managed to clear away the whole pile, chopping and sawing up the pieces suitable for burning in the grate or stove and burning the underbrush. Then went in for a swim and had lunch.*

Although it was late in the season, being well into September, King was not the only cottager around. By 1904, boarding-house days were a thing of the past for the Herridges as well as for King. The decision had been made at the end of the summer of 1901 that both parties should build their own summer places. King arranged to buy a piece of land on the shore of Kingsmere Lake for $200 and that same weekend, he helped draw up plans for Edgmoor, the Herridge cottage, which was to be built on a part of the moor beloved of King and Marjorie for moonlight walks and talks. When King was busily cleaning up around Kingswood, Marjorie and the younger children were still out at their own cottage and this worried King. "I felt anxious about the Child & the children being alone at the house & made up my mind not to leave them alone at night again. She is an heroic woman to stay alone in that large solitary house, with two little children & neither servant nor even dog about." So concerned was he that he did spend a couple of nights at Edgmoor but this came to a stop when one of his staff came out from Ottawa and stayed overnight with King who could not very well risk any seeming impropriety.

From the time King's guests left until he returned to work in Ottawa, part of each day was spent in writing his memoir of Bert Harper. The rest of the time, when he was not clearing away brush, he and Marjorie began to read the first volume of a life of William Ewart Gladstone, the British statesman and long-time Prime Minister. It did not take long for King to find a similarity between his connection with Bert and that of Gladstone to his friend, Hallam. Like Harper, Hallam had died young and King found "a similar parallel between [their natures], an earnest cheerfulness, and a plaintive seriousness or even sadness which made them much akin." He did not go so far as to draw comparisons between himself and Gladstone but there was evident approval of the latter's character: "[His] generous nature . . . is splendidly portrayed as is his conception of duty & obedience to the Divine Will." When the *Gladstone Diaries* were published in 1974, it was apparent that the two men had much more in common than could have been learned from the book King and Marjorie were reading in 1904. Then, it could be seen that the problem of expressing ones sexuality was common to both:

> *Priggish and hypocritical he may have seemed to enemies, foolhardy to friends but his struggles with his body and his conscience, when seen in the diary in the context of his religious, political and family life, cannot but seem noble.*

By 1904, King was becoming restive, finding his career as a civil servant unfulfilling. Entering politics had never been far from his mind although he had put the idea on hold for a time. Lack of funds ruled out any consideration of entering the election of 1904 but by the following year he was ready to set the wheels in motion. He had saved a little money by then and, coincidentally, Sir William Mulock offered his resignation as Postmaster-General. To King, who had been Sir William's protégé, this seemed to be a good time to consider changing careers. The country was still three years away from a General Election and during this period King continued to press his case with vigour and audacity. The machinations of how to get his political career launched took up so much time that he had very little left to spend with Marjorie. This did not please her and when his calls at the manse became less frequent, she expressed her disappointment strongly. When they were together, however, he was in such a tense state that he admittedly spoke to her in an impatient manner at times. It seemed, according to King's diaries, that their relationship (although it continued sporadically), had none of its earlier intensity. When there is any mention of her it is in the context of what had brought them together in the first place, their shared relationship with Harper. In 1904 the unveiling of the Sir Galahad monument to their friend's memory was a time for recalling those earlier days and what they had all meant to each other. They still had their shared love of books but there was even one Sunday afternoon when King, fatigued and discouraged about his future, fell asleep while Marjorie was reading to him.

During this time when he was so preoccupied with thoughts of politics, Marjorie was busy doing all those good deeds in which the wife of a pastor is expected to be interested. Her work in 1906 centred on raising money for the work of the Grenfell Mission in Labrador, a popular charity with many at that time. But her heart was not in such deeds any more. With the approach of spring, she had reached a point of nervous and physical exhaustion where she decided on a prolonged visit to her brother, George Duncan, a Presbyterian Minister in Glencairn, Scotland.

> *Sometimes, [she wrote in a note to King], I wonder if you understand at all why I am going away—or if I understand it myself—The incessant pain at my heart, the desire to get back all that is best in ones life, drives me to something desperate, not for my own sake, dear Boy, but for yours and all those who are dear to me through love and duty.*

While she was away letters crossed the Atlantic with great regularity and paint a picture that is at odds with what can be read in King's diary. When Mathilde wrote to King, her greeting, sometimes, was 'My dearly beloved Mackenzie King' but Marjorie usually addressed him as 'Boy, darling' or 'Dear Boy'. She was nervous about those letters especially since she wrote exactly what she was feeling and wanted King to do the same, the stipulation being that both sets of letters should later be burned. When it came time to commit his letters to the fireplace, she found that she simply could not do so and mailed them back to him through her sister, Emily. These letters somehow escaped destruction but, again, as was the case with his letters to Mathilde, there is only one side of the correspondence available. However, there is plenty for a profitable reading between the lines.

During Marjorie's self-imposed exile in Scotland, she wondered from time to time if she had hindered King in his career (and suspected that the answer was 'Yes'), still she was not prepared to give him up. All she could think of was being back in Kingsmere, in their old familiar haunts. It came as an unpleasant shock to her to learn that their time together there would be short. By mid-September, King was off to England on government business, leaving Marjorie in a reflective and unsettled mood. Before coming home, she wondered if any lasting good would have come from her trip but she took comfort in the fact that she had 'honestly and faithfully' done what she could to recover in mind and body. It seems not to have been enough. As she said good-bye to King once more, her promise to him was that "I will try and get some rest if I can—for I know I cannot keep up much longer for everything about me is literally dead. . . . When you can, think kindly of me, Boy, do so—I need it."

Before a year was out, Marjorie had to bear a new personal cross. Her elder son, Bill, then in his early 20's, became ill while out at Kingsmere.

Wherever the peripatetic Reverend was that summer, it was King who came to the rescue by having two doctors brought out from Ottawa in record-breaking time. Their verdict was not good.

> *I will never forget the sadness on Mrs. Herridge's face when she came down to my house about 6. I was getting ready to go up to see what the Dr. had said when I met her. She burst out crying & wept bitterly telling me that it was tuberculosis of the spine that Bill had.*

For the next few months, Marjorie's only concern was the care of her son. She spent weeks with him in a sanatorium north of Ottawa towards North Bay where both the isolation and the strain of Bill's illness were very difficult to bear.

Bill's recovery was slow but eventually he was able to take up his university studies once more and Marjorie's interest shifted back to King. Despite his aggressive start in 1904, he still had not made his way into politics but, early in 1907, he took up the battle again. Marjorie's interest in his endeavours was a source of joy to him. "[She] is a woman who has great discernment in some things & none in others.... She feels that public life with all its risks would be better for me than the civil service." Public life for King was a matter to which she had given a great deal of thought during the days when she saw that he was suffering from what she termed 'satiety' as a civil servant.

> *Boy, I don't believe that the best that is in you is being brought out now....Don't be hurt at that, dear heart, for I have such a great idea of that best. I know what you are capable of and I believe that there are things in your life now that use up much of its energy without giving an equivalent compensation. . . . [You] must be a great power in the world.*

That was in accordance with King's own belief that he had a 'call' but in order to accomplish this it was time to give Destiny a nudge. With the election of October 1908 coming up fast, King still did not have the Prime Minister's blessing in the choice of a seat. This had to be changed and "So I went in to Sir Wilfrid's office at noon. . . . I said that I wished to show him letters from N. Waterloo. He glanced at the clock when I pulled out the long one but I sat still." The outcome of this meeting was that King agreed to run in North Waterloo, having Sir Wilfrid's word on it that a separate

Department of Labour would be set up with King at its head in due course. Tenacity won the day and five weeks of hard struggle won him the seat.

Over the years King had been away from Ottawa on different occasions on labour related matters; often his travels were within Canada but he also went to England and to the United States. Before the newly-elected M. P. for North Waterloo was even able to take his seat in the House of Commons, he was off on a series of meetings which took him as far as the Orient. This time he was away for almost five months, and Marjorie found this long absence to be very difficult. It is evident in the letters she wrote to him that her health was in a precarious state. The mental problems that would beset her a few years later were beginning to have an effect on her daily life in 1909.

> *Several times, [she wrote], I have not been well, but I did not let go. I feel sometimes just what Peter must have felt when he was walking on the water—that because his faith was failing he was sinking.... What strange mysteries the soul & mind are & how little we know of their true relation to the body.... I know how glad you will be when I tell you I have not gone to Montreal [to a hospital?].*

Letters that she received from King during those months were some comfort to her but

> *I miss you, Boy. The winter has been long & cold & very changeable but I am thankful I have not minded it very much. My long fur coat & hat have been a comfort and I am told look well (so much for appearance).*

And she was looking forward to his return with a heart full of hope: "You will come back with the first of spring, Boy, & will bring spring to many hearts." By early May, he was home having served what she termed his "forty days preparation for what is to follow.... It is wonderful how your guiding star has gone before you & led you into paths that were made for you."

But a short three years later, King was out of office, defeated at the polls, and left to wonder whither his 'guiding star' was to lead next. Marjorie's advice, freely given, was that 'There is a tremendous work to be done in the world outside of politics'. She, the daughter of a clergyman as well as the wife and sister of one, had this to say on King's future:

> *I have thought much last night and this morning about your going into politics once again or Varsity or the church. Now, my mind is made up. It may not influence you in the least but this is what I think.*

Clearly, her thoughts were leading towards the church and

> *Something tells me strongly that . . . you would be greater and happier in this work. A man may be Premier of Canada, and not have the profound love & loyalty that comes to those who have given joy and spiritual light to those who want it—You have so much of this quality, Boy dear. . . . God help you to decide aright.*

It was neither Varsity nor the Church that King chose in the interregnum between 1911 and 1919. The pros and cons of both were considered but in 1914, he accepted an appointment as head of the Department of Industrial Relations with the Rockefeller Foundation in New York.

During the days following his electoral defeat, when his future plans were vague, he was sure of one thing only and that was that he should seek to marry. 1912 was the year when he carried out this deliberate search and he discussed it with both Mathilde and Marjorie. Mathilde enthusiastically took up this idea but it was much more difficult for Marjorie to wish him well in his quest. In what must have been an emotional and uncomfortable evening, they talked about this situation with King evidently not mincing words. Its effect on Marjorie was devastating.

> *Last night after you had gone away & through the long hours of the night I lay thinking of you, your life, the crisis it is at now & all you said to me. Your longing for a home of your own. . . . I feel humiliated dear Boy to think that my selfishness & want of faith in God has hindered you so far—for I dreaded to face a life without you. . . . I must strive however rough the path to prove my faith in the same God & my great love for you. . . . Make then that home, Boy, & may God send you the love you need. . . . One thing I ask, dear, don't talk to me now about this—let me work it out.*

As is well known, King's search failed and so, eventually, did the bond between him and Marjorie. By 1914, he realized that "There is no longer a welcome for me [at the Herridge's] because I have drawn away, & now see it was selfishness that lay at the root of friendship, tho' perhaps I am wrong in this." While still willing to give her the benefit of the doubt, he could not fail to see that she had changed. In 1906, when writing to him from Scotland and commenting on the foibles of women, it was her opinion then that

> *I think women with us [i.e. around her in Ottawa] are narrowed by the jealousy of display, the love of finery & superficiality. If one could only help a few to look for the treasures in nature & art & literature instead of the jewel box & the lace shop. . . . It is such folly to think that clothes cover up a poor spirit, a weak will or a mean heart.*

If he thought back to that earlier view of hers, it would have been difficult to reconcile it with what he currently observed of her and her family. 'The more wealth, the more selfishness with most people' was his conclusion. What really annoyed him occurred during a visit by his mother in the spring of 1914; the Herridges, it seemed, were not suitably attentive.

> *I have been considerably hurt at the indifference and selfishness [of the Herridge family]. Not one of them have put themselves out to see anything of or do anything for Mother. . . . This has decided me in the matter of further concern for any of them.*

When Marjorie even forgot his birthday that year, it was the last straw. 'How strange & sad!' he mused, 'What changes the years bring.'

Although he had vowed to have nothing further to do with them, his contacts with the Herridges were, by this time, a part of the very pattern of his life. A couple of weeks after his forgotten birthday [his fortieth], he unbent in order to make an attempt to be of help if possible in a most difficult situation that had developed around Dr. Herridge. In 1914 he had been named Moderator of the General Assembly of the Presbyterian Church in Canada but, detracting from this honour, there were problems in his pastorate which led to calls for his resignation. A phone call to Marjorie at this time only confirmed his worst fears about them.

> *I feel sorry, but what terrible selfishness & vanity & pride & conceit is bundled together with a sort of arrogance in both the Dr. & his wife. . . . For neither . . . can brook the least opposition, if it is not worship & admiration of them, it is nothing or worse than nothing. . . . I should*

like to help to lessen the pain that I know Mrs. H. is suffering, but it is useless to attempt, only flattery could do it.

They saw very little of each other from that time on. Soon after the night in 1912 when King had spoken to her so plainly about her perceived selfishness, Marjorie took the stand that things could not go on between them as in the past. "I must forget, and you must forget 'not because we will, but because we must'. . . . Say to yourself 'Old past let go and drop in the sea'." Events conspired to make this possible for them. King's work with the Rockefeller Foundation meant that he was often out of the country for weeks at a time and then Marjorie, too, went away. Both her sons, Bill and Gordon, were with the Canadian Army in France during World War 1 and, in 1916, she decided to cross over to England to be near them. She lived in Folkestone on the south coast and soon after her arrival there, she saw an opportunity for service. 'I can say it is a work which is one of the most needed', she wrote to King of her new responsibilities as head of a committee which helped look after casualties passing through Folkestone from hospitals in England and France. Once in a long while, they met in later years in Ottawa. It was in the late summer of 1918, after she had returned from England, and they were both in Kingsmere that "Mrs. Herridge sent a note inviting me to tea tonight. I think she did not like the summer to pass without doing this. I went and spent a pleasant evening with her and Irene and Emily. Irene's beautiful little children were quite attractive."

In late 1919, Marjorie suffered a mental breakdown and was sent to the psychiatric hospital in Guelph for treatment. It was her son, Bill, who concerned himself about her condition and worried as to whether or not she was in the right place. "She feels she is losing ground but she is trying so hard to pull through. It would break your heart to see her fighting against the cursed thing." And, remembering times past, he turned to King for help.

> *Will you go to see her. Just drop in, without letting either her or the hospital people know in advance. She was speaking of you and I know your visit will bring her happiness. Besides, I must have advice and I believe yours will be best.*

Unfortunately, there is no record of any follow-up by King on receiving this letter but he did see her in the summer of 1921 when she was able to spend some time at Kingsmere. She was, he said, greatly aged and in a distressed state over 'evil thoughts'. Poor Marjorie was to suffer yet another blow when, in 1922, her younger son, Gordon, died as the result of a shooting accident. Dr. Herridge was the family spokesman at that time and wrote to thank King 'for the kindness you have shown in these sad days—for your wise insight'. Showing a less than sensitive nature himself, he added that "It is too early to say what the effect of the shock may be upon my poor wife though I have hopes that the morbid subjectivity which is part of her affliction may be broken, in some measure, by her thought for others."

After Gordon's death, Marjorie could no longer bear the thought of spending any more summers at Kingsmere. There were too many memories and with the other children having moved away, they decided to sell the cottage. This came at a time when King was interested in adding to his own property there and had, in fact, already bought some parcels of land adjacent to his first purchase. What more natural than that he should look up the hill towards Edgmoor and think of adding it to his 'estate'. In one of those ironies of fate, he was in the act of trying to reach Dr. Herridge by phone about purchasing it on 22 March 1924, when the news of Marjorie's death was brought to him. His immediate reaction was one of 'release, a great release' for her.

> *[She has] often said there were many worse things than death, often too has she lately expressed the desire to die. Her life has been a great tragedy. The greatest I have known in human life. The past ten years our friendship has meant little, my first ten years in Ottawa it was in some respects apart from home ties and affiliations the most real experience of my life, full of happiness and pain. Selfishness marred it in the end, selfishness and self-indulgence. I could not have believed I could have felt so little the word of her death.*

During the following days King felt calm, secure, powerful. "I can account for it in no other way than that Mrs. Herridge's spirit, freed from all the pains and sorrows & limitations of her terrible infirmity, is now in the presence of God and is making its influence known to me."

In a matter of days after Marjorie's death King arranged for the purchase of Edgmoor, intending it for the use of his new friends, Godfroy and Joan

Patteson during the summers. In 1928, however, he decided to move into the former Herridge cottage himself. Extensive renovations were carried out and by late summer he was installed in the house on the moor, now, appropriately renamed Moorside. It was his summer home for twelve years, a home where, at times, the ghosts of the past came to keep him company. During one of the many trying periods of Marjorie's life, she had written to King, saying,

> *My mind goes back to the old days when everything seemed good. . . . I would like tonight to see the sunset at Kingsmere—to smell the fresh earth and hear the whip-poor-will and [see] the stars come out. It might, for a night at least, make me feel rested again.*

One night in the summer of 1934 during the period when King was deeply engrossed in spiritualism and communicating with those whose lives had special meaning for him, he felt that Marjorie's spirit was, indeed, 'making its influence known' to him. Even the whip-poor-will was in attendance,

> *thrashing out his notes only a few yards away, very loud & clear & strong. I walked around to the front of the house & walked on the lawn in the moonlight and suddenly there came over me, as if bursting upon me, the meaning of it all. I said we are back again to the Matthew Arnold days—the Child and I. This means that all that there has been of saddness and [?] has been forgiven, forgotten, and we begin anew where we were in those days . . . and our souls are revealed as God meant them to be in highest service and gladness. . . . I thought the dawn—that is the picture the Child gave me—the Corot I put in the place in my bedroom . . . near the room she had. Then I looked at the willow tree she had planted. It filled such a space—so magnificent in the moonlight, so expressive and symbolic. . . . I was convinced I was again with the Child as we had been, that God had answered our prayers.*
>
> *I came into the house. It was 'home' at last—the end of the journey from the past to the future—the old to the new. When I went upstairs before going to my own room, I went to the room which the Child used to have and I knelt beside the bed and thanked God for His grace & mercy and asked Him to bless her as never before.*

He did not go to bed until dawn and when he went it was with words from the oft-repeated poems of Matthew Arnold and Wilfred Campbell, (another favourite of his and Marjorie's) echoing in his mind. "Dear Campbell & Marjorie H —those were beautiful days & times. They have not gone, they are here again, they live on forever. I knelt by my own bedside & I prayed God's blessing on all that He knew was in my heart, and thanked Him for His loving kindness."

Violet Markham

It chanced that the hazard of a journey across Canada brought me to Ottawa on Trafalgar Day, 1905. I was staying with the Governor-General and Lady Grey at Rideau Hall, and after dinner Lord Grey came across the room followed by a young man, whom he introduced with the words: 'You must meet Mackenzie King, he will be Prime Minister of Canada some day.'

Such was Violet Markham's recollection of her first meeting with King who, she said, smiled and shook his head on hearing this prediction. It was a large dinner party that evening, arranged to include various itinerant English people who had taken part in the ceremonies of that October day. Violet Markham, herself, was one such itinerant. She was an Englishwoman of wealth but with a social conscience which made it intolerable for her to live the life that was expected of her, that of a young society lady. Her energies had earlier been devoted to opening a Settlement House in Chesterfield, Derbyshire. There, she was involved particularly with educational matters but, by 1905, the work "had served to deepen in me a sense of the squalor and misery which had resulted in England due to her neglect of social conditions at the time of the Industrial Revolution." It was her curiosity that brought her to Canada to see whether a young country was able to avoid any of the errors for which the Old World was paying so dearly.

By the time she reached Ottawa, Violet had traveled Canada from coast to coast, and was grateful for an invitation to be the Greys' guest for a few days in order to rest up after the rough-and-tumble of her trip. On the evening in question she said "it was indeed a change to find myself in the atmosphere of a delightful English country house. I recollect coming into a drawing-room full of flowers" and with guests mingling after dinner. This atmosphere was one to which King was no stranger either: he had often been a guest at Rideau Hall ever since his arrival in the capital five years earlier. In fact, he sometimes felt that he was becoming 'a little too conspicuous with the Government House people' but that did not mean he turned down all invitations. Violet's impressions of him that evening were that he was "a pleasant-looking man of medium build, with a round face and abundant fair hair" but that he seemed to be very young for his position as Deputy Minister of Labour. At the end of the evening she summed him up in her diary as being "a most charming and able young man, full of the right ideals."

During the course of the evening, they discovered just how many interests they did have in common. King could empathize with Violet as she told him of her aims and her frustrations at the Chesterfield Settlement. When she related what she had seen in her cross-Canada visits to factories and what she had learned in talks with officials and inspectors along the way, King was, undoubtedly, the one person in that room (and quite likely in all of Canada at that time) who could best appreciate her feelings. As a student, he had first-hand knowledge of conditions at settlement houses in Chicago and Boston and, later, at Passmore Edwards House in London during his travels in 1900. In fact, the Governor-General could not have made a more suitable introduction that night. But what neither of the three suspected was that Violet and King were laying the foundations of a friendship which lasted for nearly half a century, never wavering. "We were both young and enthusiastic, so friendship between us was natural." Violet wrote many years later in her autobiography, *Return Passage*.

As friendship it began, and so it remained without any of the stresses of King's relationship with Mathilde or Marjorie. It was a friendship without strings—just what King needed (but not always what he got). Violet herself put her finger on it when she wrote later to him about

> *All the ties & intimacies of a friendship which as you remind me has lasted now for nearly 20 years. . . . Few friends have been to each other what you & I have been. My dear—I sometimes think that the fact of our not having been 'in love' as the phrase goes with each other & that we never met on any plane of disturbing emotion has made our love & affection for one another the great & abiding thing it has been in life to both of us. No one has ever been so near to me in spirit as you have done & it has been given to each of us in critical moments in the other's life to lay a helping hand on bowed shoulders & make the drinking of the cup more tolerable. We have adventured very greatly together in the things of the soul—Please God we shall so adventure together to the end of our pilgrimage.*

Her prayer was answered and, as had been the case in Mathilde's story, it was an association broken only by King's death.

Before Violet left Ottawa in 1905, she and King met again on more than one occasion. During talks in his office he was able to further enlighten her about labour conditions in Canada and they visited the governmental experimental farm as well as what she called a "pulp and match factory"— surely E.B. Eddy's. Never one to mince words with King, even from the very start of their friendship, she fired a salvo in a farewell note: "Those poor children in the match factory rather haunt me! In a young country like this with a high standard of adult wages such things should not be." On a more conciliatory note she added

> You gave me not only much to think of, but renewed hope and courage to take back to the old country with its many difficult problems. . . . It has been the greatest pleasure to meet you & our talk yesterday was indeed a delight. . . . I need not say how much I hope we shall meet again.

When she was an elderly lady, Violet wrote a book called *Friendship's Harvest*, a collection of personality sketches of some of her closest friends, and it is here, in the chapter on King, that she shares her impressions of him across the years. A reviewer of this book, while welcoming a fresh view-point on King, 'our Spectacular Sphinx', was of the opinion that it was likely written by a woman who 'viewed him as it were through a telescope', and offered the thought that she never saw him for very long in her whole life. Not so. They met again within the year, this time in England, and in the following autumn in Canada. From then on they saw each other whenever King paid one of his frequent visits to England at which times Violet's home was a regular port of call. Two World Wars intruded and the demands of King's political life as well as those of Violet's own career and her family responsibilities made for gaps in the visits. Then they had to resort to letter-writing to keep in touch. And what letter-writing! As was always the case when King wrote to intimate friends there would be pages and pages filled with his tiny, cramped script. In Violet he met his match. Her writing was the exact opposite of his in style—large, round and free-flowing in form, and it also filled numerous pages. While there was no shortage of things to write about there was a definite unease as far as the choice of salutation went. 'My dear Mackenzie-King', Violet wrote in the beginning of their correspondence (and she even hyphenated it in good English fashion). In time she changed this to 'My dear friend. (This seems a good compromise, does it not?)', and, eventually, he became 'My dear Rex'. To King she was 'Dear Miss Markham' for a few years even though he had progressed from signing his letters, 'Your sincere friend, W. L. Mackenzie King' to 'Always affectionately yours, Rex'. Gradually he summoned up the courage to write 'Dear Violet' but, taking into account the propriety of it all in those post-Victorian times, he felt forced to explain that it was not until he had paid a visit to Chesterfield and met her mother that this became possible for him.

> *It may interest you to know that it was her speaking of you to me always as 'Violet' that makes it seem to me very natural to call you by that name now she is gone, though before I always felt as you know some diffidence about it.*

While it was their common interests in social and industrial matters that brought them together, it was family problems on both sides of the Atlantic that cemented their friendship. The 'laying of a helpful hand on bowed shoulders', as mentioned by Violet, was one of the characteristics of their association from the start. When she was in Ottawa in 1905, Violet was already carrying a burden of worry about her mother's health and on her return to England, the depressing report to King was that 'Life has gone very heavily with me since we met'. Her mother had become a complete invalid and Violet was forced to give up most of her own work to care for her. During visits to England and in letters over the following years, King was able to express his sympathy and understanding and, while he had failed miserably in his resolution to be of help to the Herridges, he had some success in trying to guide Violet through this distressing period in her life. As she wrote him in 1908, "You made clear to me . . . the spiritual continuity of existence and that the spiritual ideal must be followed at all costs whatever sacrifices it may involve. I see now that if my whole life of work & action has to be given up—even so."

Violet, who considered herself to be 'a weak and twisted vessel', found it difficult to lead this life of self-sacrifice but she assured King that she was 'fighting, not well and with many a failure against the misery and despair of tragic private circumstances.' In December of that year there was a further opportunity for King to be supportive of Violet when he was in London for discussions on the eve of his trip to the Orient. By that time, Violet had brought her mother to a hospital in London and she, herself, was living in

Violet Markham (1912)

her little house on Gower Street in Bloomsbury. Her welcome to King was warm: "Could you possibly come in after dinner? I spend the evening with Mother and return about 9.30. Then I work half the night! . . . I shall indeed be glad to see you." They met again on Christmas Day when they worshipped at St. Margaret's, Westminster, but it was then becoming clear to King that little he could say would be of lasting help to her. Seeing her mother suffer both bodily and mentally without any seeming hope was making her life what she termed 'a confused nightmare'. King's travel to the East took him by way of the Red Sea and it was from a P&O liner that he wrote to Violet expressing his "regret that in the great mysteries the shadows of which fall across your path at the moment I seemed so helpless in unfolding a meaning."

Words alone were not the answer: this he had seen for himself. As his ship traveled through the entrance to the Red Sea, bringing him close to the Holy Land 'where all that is most sacred in association has its home', the idea of sending Violet the gift of a cross occurred to him. This would be a symbol to her of those 'great mysteries' which so beset her; as well, it would be something tangible which she could hold—something of a talisman—which might help her to remember some of their talks. It was undoubtedly not the right time or place to shop for such a gift but, at each stop, he looked and had no more success than when he wrote from India that he had found little demand for 'ecclesiastical jewellery'. It was not until he returned to Canada in May that he found what he wanted. On receiving it, Violet wrote:

How much I value your cross! I never possessed one before & I am more than glad that this symbol of supreme endeavour in the light of which alone work can have worth or value should come to me from you. I shall always wear it & have it fastened on the chain which carries my pencil—a chain I wear year in year out. The pencil &

the cross—the practical & the ideal will always be together & even in this brief week I have drawn patience from the symbol at my belt; when sorely tried (& I am often sorely tried) my hand goes to it for strength & silence.

For more than two years this cross was to Violet a constant companion and help in her struggle. Then she lost it and, after a particularly difficult period in her mother's illness, realized just how much she needed it. "I feel it's very barefaced to ask you for another cross" was her apologetic plea to King just before Christmas, 1912, " but I can't do otherwise." A replacement was shortly on its way as well as a long letter from King reflecting on Violet's plight:

I have sometimes thought I was wrong when I advised you not to forsake the cross that has been placed upon you. You will never forsake it, but I am almost inclined to say you must not live with its shadow too wholly upon you. . . . I know how one suffers who feels as deeply as you do, and I am human enough to be the fonder of you because from what you tell me, you now and then can stand the injustice of it all no longer; but take the little cross which is, at last, on its way to you, and let it speak to you of a love that forgave the world all its abuse and wrongs and be quick to forgive, no matter how hard that may be. . . . When the moment is very hard go away and be alone, and when you are alone know that I am beside you telling you that you are not alone.

'Perhaps the losing of the little cross only signifies that the great trial is going to pass away' was King's initial reaction to its loss, and for a time Mrs. Markham's health did improve, but at Easter 1912, a cable from Violet said 'Mother died peacefully yesterday'. Letters alone did not seem to offer enough consolation and when King suggested that he would like to go over to see her, Violet was quick to respond. Despite having many friends near her at this time, her reply was:

It is the one thing I want and which would comfort and strengthen me beyond any other. No words can express what I feel about the friendship which is ready to undertake such journey for my sake. . . . I have no friend with whom I can share every memory of my Mother's death as I feel I can share them with you. You must help me to be brave, Rex, help me to get back my hand on to the helm of life.

As she envisioned his visit it was to think of "What walks & talks we will have! In the morning I must work & you shall read & rest & evolve. The rest of the day we will do things together." It was August before King could make the trip and he spent two weeks with Violet at Chesterfield. On his departure she wrote to him that

> *There seems such a great light over those wonderful days we spent together that I am still a little dazzled. I have missed you more than I can well express. . . . You always bring me that great sense of the eternities:—it has been so from the first in the most mysterious otherworldly way. The tie between us I always feel is one which transcends time and space. Somehow I think we were fellow spirits when the morning stars were made.*

While King was able to be supportive of Violet during this difficult period, his own life was in turmoil. He had been out of office for over a year and not only was he seeking some casual employment but he was making a determined search for a wife. When he took up his duties as Minister of Labour in 1909, Violet wrote to congratulate him, saying

> *I have visions of very goodly things for you. And of course I want personal happiness for you too, for the right sort of home means everything to a man with such work before him as yours. You must marry some day & I want her to be very nice when you make your choice! You are too busy at present to think of that side of life but you mustn't miss what is after all the most wonderful experience life holds.*

King's response was heartfelt:

> *You spoke of my having a home. I never lay my head upon a pillow that I do not pray for it. But it is all such a mystery. I believe in love as I believe in Life but I know little of the one while I have seen much of the other. Perhaps some day this gift will come to me.*

Two years later, Violet was still of the opinion that he should marry one day but was somewhat alarmed by the timing of his present crusade. In words that are reminiscent of what Jennie wrote in 1897 when it seemed that King and Mathilde were about to become engaged, Violet now said: "I am desperately anxious you shouldn't miss [married life] but I don't quite see how marriage is going to be possible for you unless you have a modest competence assured. It isn't a question of wealth but it is a question of a certain financial security."

Shortly, however, it did become a question of wealth—too much of it. In January 1912, he went to New York on business, intending to be there for only for a weekend but, as he wrote Violet,

> *I found myself quite unexpectedly the guest of two brothers [the Gerrys] each of whom I used to tutor at Harvard, and each of whom have had a lasting regard for me. They are very wealthy men and have married very wealthy women. They were amazingly frank in their statement to me that it was their wish to repay a lifelong friendship by helping me to gain one in life who could share its opportunities from the circle of their intimate personal friends. They asked me to stay with them until this was accomplished, and are insistent that I shall return in the spring, and go with them and a house party to Virginia to spend a month in the open.*

He stayed a fortnight 'out of politeness' and 'much against my desire' but he did not accept the invitation to Virginia nor did he succumb to the matchmaking efforts of his hosts. As he wrote Violet,

> *I need not tell you that the thought of marrying a woman for her money is abhorrent to me.... I have vowed to myself that on this the one great step in life I will effect no compromise with my soul, and that even if it means the forsaking of my career, or no career at all. With God's help, my work alone will determine that issue for me.*

Wealth, albeit on a more modest scale than what he had seen as a guest of his old Harvard friends, got in the way of matrimony once more on this trip. Although at this time, he was still writing to Violet as 'Dear Miss Markham', his thoughts poured out freely even if, at times, he felt he was writing too frankly. Violet had earlier written of his marrying when the timing was right and it was her hope "that when that moment comes you will feel able to tell me about it knowing you can count most surely on my affection & sympathy when that great troubling of the waters comes." King took her at her word in telling her of the unsuccessful efforts of his friends, the Gerrys, and then of Martha McCook whom he saw briefly while he was still in New York. "If I were independent I should not hesitate to ask her to share my life....I have known her for some years and have felt that way about her from the day I first saw her". But there was a snag. "She has been brought up in comfort, and according to standards here, almost luxury [but] I doubt if she has an income of her own, and I have therefore recognized from the outset the life I could offer her would have too many hazards."

For this he received a sound reprimand from Violet.

I feel very strongly no man has a right to deny a woman the happiness she may crave from his love merely on the score of poverty. It is her business to say whether or not she will share that poverty. I can only speak for myself—if I loved I would share a crust & glory in it. Also in one respect you must have a good conceit of yourself. You have a great deal to offer any woman, a fine position & a fine standing in the eyes of the world. Other things being even your lack of means wouldn't matter. But of course these are only generalities (though I am sure you should bear them in mind) & I am bound to say I more than appreciate all the practical difficulties & obstacles which stand between you & the girl of whom we talked. I have no clear 'shewing' in the matter & so I dare not say to you at this moment, 'rush in and try to win her' though possibly that moment may come.

It did not, of course, and money was only part of the reason why not much more is heard about Miss McCook. This was never an affair of the heart as had been the case with Mathilde but merely another possibility in his vain search.

Meanwhile, he kept alive, in his own heart, the need and the desirability of having a home of his own and the hope of finding the right person with whom to share it. The search went on from time to time and it has been tactfully recorded by one early biographer who wrote of serious possibilities one of whom he referred to only as 'Miss C' (who can now, with the passage of time, be identified as Martha McCook) and others, all the way through to 'Miss I'. There was no 'Miss A' in this list but, obviously, this was Mathilde. 'Miss B' was Frances Howard, a granddaughter of Lord Strathcona. On his way to New York in 1912 he stopped over to see her in Montreal but said he did not 'feel at ease' with her. In each case there was some impediment to marriage, real or imagined, but Violet was quite concerned that King, despite his protestations, might yet marry for wealth. There was one way she knew of which might point out the dangers of such a union and that was by putting it in a personal context. The story she wrote about to him was that of a young man who had married someone whom he liked and respected but with the object of improving his finances. Later, he met and fell in love with another woman who returned his love, the result of which was that "She lives out her life as best may be, but his fatal error has wrecked life for her as well as for him." In complete frankness, she went on: "Dear Rex, in what may have been an hour of temptation to you I draw back the veil from the sanctuary of my own life for I am that woman and now you know a little of the supreme anguish life has brought me." Violet's confession to King was likely prompted by a letter she had had from him a short time earlier in which he admitted that

> *with the weariness of fatigue, and the knowledge of how all but impossible it is to accomplish anything in the field of politics without some measure of independence, I have wondered at times if I have not been too hasty, in turning away from even considering suggestions that had been made.*

Violet later philosophized that

> *There are other things [than marriage]. It is difficult to put some things into words but I think to those of us who have been denied the sweet personal happiness of life there comes at times moments of exaltation and revelation so great that nothing in existence comes like it—moments when one seems lifted through and above all human relationship into the great Divine Heart itself where one rests in a sense of completed and perfect love. At least so it has been with me. Pray God it may be so with you. My dear, I have written you a sermon!*

A month or so after delivering this 'sermon' (on which King, by the way, left no recorded comment), Violet set out on a trip to South Africa. This was in the period following her mother's death, and while she felt she needed a change, she confessed to a pull at the heartstrings with no one to care whether she went or stayed home. She took along a recent letter from King, which she said would be to her 'as the touch of a friend's hand'. In the spring of 1913 she was back home and

> *splendidly well . . . Africa healed me in the end. It took time for I own during the first three months of my travels I was supremely miserable. . . . But after my return to Cape Town [from Rhodesia] in January the sunshine & the flowers & the grand scenery of the Peninsula made me*

feel happier & little by little life came back. . . . [I am] fully determined to do no work of any kind until next winter. I am like a bird outside the cage & I am not going inside again just yet. I am immensely impressed with the value of stepping aside from all work & rush, of possessing ones soul in peace & of having leisure for the personal concerns of life.

This was what she had earlier tried to impress on King—to lie fallow for awhile—and although he was not an apt pupil, taking her own advice worked well for Violet. King had anticipated her return with some cautionary words:

Do not, please, please, do not begin too much. The spirit is restored not by too constant strain, but by the ministering angels of silence, budding leaves, the voices of birds, and the twinkling of stars. The calm of the night, the sweep of the marshes, the love of a few friends, these are what our poor human natures need the most.

He need not have feared, for Violet meant just what she said:

I am being pursued by the imprecations of scores of people who fondly hoped I was returning to work their jobs. But I laugh & for the time being I am a Trappist. I am buying some pretty new clothes & mean to see my friends this season."

This was a side of Violet's nature of which King had seen but little. To date there seemed to have been so many serious, intense moments in their friendship with the result that King had decided that Violet was a 'noble, true woman'. This was an image which she had tried to dispel, telling him that 'Friendship to be real must see with open eyes all the weaknesses as well as the strengths', and she had even gone so far as to write that "I wish you would see me as I am—faulty, passionate, hot-tempered, failing a hundred times. . . . I am terribly undisciplined even after the terrific discipline life has given me." He may not have wanted to see her faults but one thing he had been aware of and that was her unabashed love of beautiful things, clothes included. This had been the inspiration for a gift that he sent her while on his trip to the Orient and her enthusiasm for it ran high:

And now I must thank you . . . for that quite lovely kimono . . . it will make me a most lovely & unique coat. Fancy having a cloak from the Palace at Pekin! I shall burst with pride when I wear it

> *at an evening party. . . . I shall revel in my beautiful Chinese coat and feel real superior in it.*

That she should now decide to buy some pretty clothes and see her friends during the season was to King an indication that she was rested and ready to take on life, albeit in a less dedicated manner than previously. It came, then, as a bit of a shock to learn in October that she was travelling again. This time she was off to Moscow, en route to China to 'look into the East and its novel problems in its most unsettled state!'

It was not until the following year that he learned that it was not only the East that was in 'an unsettled state' but that such had been the case with Violet herself. She now wrote to tell King of her own situation and its outcome, something which was totally unexpected.

> *I am engaged to be married. Yes, under the very shadow of war I am engaged to a soldier! It's already an old story. We met in S. Africa when I was there two years ago. . . . We learnt to care for each other in S. Africa but I wasn't sure of myself then—it all seemed so incredible. And he felt I was in no state wreck as I was then to make so great a decision. So he would ask nothing from me but sent me back as free as I came to try my old life. Well, I went back to it all & it didn't satisfy me; I went off to China only to find how surely my heart was in Africa.*

Violet did not find it easy to explain her soldier-fiancé, Captain James Carruthers, on paper but she wanted King to have some idea of what sort of person he was and how he was received by her family and friends. Her brothers totally approved but "Some of my friends expressed surprise that I of all people should marry a soldier. To one impertinent woman, who asked what had induced me to take such a step, I replied 'Because he sings in his bath. No Markham has ever sung in his bath'." As to his character, "He is not intellectual, he is not literary, he knows nothing about politics [but] he has capacity and wisdom and an unfailing sense of humour. . . . I want you to be very glad for me, dear Rex."

King did "rejoice to know that happiness, so strong, so beautiful has come to your life", but, on the other hand, "how lonely withal I am in the rejoicing. The years that I have shared what was most personal in my life with you, make me feel now as if something that was a part of it was being taken from me." Violet had told King in a letter that "[Jim] is not jealous or tiresome or possessive. He will give me ample elbowroom & seek to close no doors. Those who I love need fear no jealous interference from him though he will probably poke fun at us if we grow too serious!!" And sensing that King needed further reassurance, Violet continued:

> *All that you have been to me in the past I pray you will be to my life's end . . . & I pray I shall fill no smaller place in your life than I have done heretofore. You can't think how utterly painful nay intolerable it would be to me to think that any new ties could weaken much less break those of the past. . . . Had you been the first to marry honestly it would never have occurred to me that I should be less in your life than I am today. . . . When you told me of your deep feelings for Martha McCook & pondered whether you should see her in New York I didn't think for a moment that a happy marriage coming to you . . . could unknit one tie between us. So far as I am concerned dear Rex, I shall want you just as much in the future as in the past.*

On 11 February 1915, Violet became Mrs. James Carruthers in a small, intimate ceremony at St Margaret's, Westminster, and while congratulations went immediately from King he had to admit that he found it strange to be writing to her as a 'Mrs. Somebody'. He had problems, too, over what to call her husband. "I have imagined that Jim—I cannot call him your husband—and I suppose I should call him James—or more properly 'Mr.'—has crossed over from the front and may be returning." It was not until after the war that the two men met. When King went to see the battlefields of Europe in the late spring of 1919, Violet asked him to try to see her husband who was then at Cologne as Chief Demobilization Officer of the Army of the Rhine. She was a bit apprehensive about the possibility of the soldier finding the politician 'a trifle on the serious side'. She need not have worried. A letter from Jim put her fears to rest:

> *You have your friend Rex to thank for my not getting a letter off to you yesterday. He turned up just after lunch. He is a bloodthirsty fellow. Came up here expecting to see guns pointed into Germany, loaded and just waiting for the order to fire. I, being a man of peace, told him we never did anything rough like that and took him to see Faust at the Opera instead. That was almost too much for him. . . . It was a particularly good show, Marguerite being perfect, figure as well as voice. He dined with me and so to bed! I found him a most interesting person and liked him awfully. You paid*

neither him nor me a compliment when you thought I might be bored with him. He is a splendid fellow.

Before crossing over to France, King had spent a few days in London which gave him a chance to see Violet again. It had been seven years since they last met but, in the interim, the distance had been partially bridged by the exchange of letters although this was not always easy. For Violet "This awful war seems to paralyze one in many directions. I have found letter writing so difficult. I suppose intimate letter writing means looking into ones heart and feelings and neither of them bear examination these days." But their letters during this period bore little change from the earlier ones. Violet's marriage, as she had told King, left her relationship with him the same as it had always been; her letters reflect this while his, if handwritten, were a frank expression of his thoughts and feelings. The typed ones, as had been the case with those he sent to Mathilde, were necessarily more reserved in character.

Personal sorrow still stalked their lives during those years and by 1917, they were both writing on black-edged paper. At Easter 1915, Bella, King's elder sister, died after years of indifferent health. In the following year, Violet's brother, Arthur, who had been very close to her, died suddenly and a few months later, King was awakened one morning in his little cottage at Kingsmere by a farmer's boy calling out news of a phone message saying that his father was dying in Toronto. Death came before King could get there and, although in life John King was not always above reproach in the eyes of his son, it was now quite a different story.

> *Dear Violet, what you have written me of Arthur is what I meant to write you of father. Never, never in my life have I seen anything more majestic. . . . Such a look, such perfect peace, such dignity. . . . Nothing in art or imagination has ever equalled it. My own father! I could not realize he was gone. The first thought that came to me was what a gentleman! Such refinement of features, such intellectual and spiritual grace, such majestic calm. He looked as a man would look in the presence of God.*

The last, the ultimate loss that King suffered in this period came in December 1917, when his mother died. It is a story often told of his having taken his mother to live with him in Ottawa some time after his father's death, of her illness and suffering and of King's attempts during this time to run a campaign in North York prior to the election of 1917. He was not home when she died, nor was Violet present at the time of Arthur's death. Thus, in turn through those years, Violet and King comforted each other and their belief, jointly shared, was that

> *Life is too great, too wonderful to be extinguished by the incident of death. All that is precious and beautiful and lovely in the human heart can never die; all that makes of personality and light here must flame into fresh force and beauty in the Beyond.*

Where their lives touched outside of personal sorrows, Violet and King constantly exchanged ideas and sometimes criticisms on different issues. On some Canadian political matters, Violet's opinion was quite different to King's. Arguments flew back and forth across the Atlantic as they discussed Borden's Naval Aid Bill of 1912 with King making a case for an independent Canadian navy as opposed to contributions to the British navy. Violet, although a Liberal, sided with Borden and warned King of what would happen

> *If you young people with your own fleets & your own policies go poking around & getting into rows with other powers which we have neither made or controlled! Australia & Canada might conceivably involve the whole Empire in war on such terms & again the brunt would fall on us.*

She took him to task, as well, on a more personal note:

> *I would—very lovingly—ask you to guard against two tendencies which might if they develop destroy something of your wholeness as a man. Don't become too hot a partizan [sic] seeing your fellow men exclusively in terms of Liberalism & Conservatism. . . . [This] has a tendency to narrow the man or woman who looks at life that way. Still more would I urge you to guard against the assumption that spiritual truth is with your own beliefs & your own beliefs alone. . . . To assume that our beliefs are better than those of other people is to launch oneself on the first wave of an unprofitable sea of self righteousness.*

Only Violet could get away with writing to King in this manner and receive in return only his comment that "I have come to be amused at your fears in regard to my partisanship. . . . I think events ere long will prove conclusively that what you have feared was partisanship was in reality conviction based on foresight." Years later, in a book of reminiscences, she noted that time had, indeed, vindicated his thinking.

During the war, Violet became disillusioned with the British Liberal Party for its conduct and advised King that she would probably 'look for a home among the Labour people'. In January 1919, she ran as a candidate for them in the general election and was defeated, a defeat which King likened to his own in 1917.

> *I pride myself in the thought that your political integrity and mine are akin, and I am particularly confident, therefore, that in defeat you feel exactly as I did, a thousand times stronger than any of those can who won their way to Parliament at the sacrifice of principles which are as dear as life itself.*

In 1914, when Violet wrote to King about her engagement and how there would still and always be a place in her heart and in her life for him, she took a leap forward in saying "There is this great work to do at the end of the war, you in the New World, I in the Old & we will do it together. I don't expect Jim to help me; he's a soldier & it's a soldier's job to fight."

On his way back to Canada from visiting the European battlefields in 1919, King spent a few days with Violet in Chesterfield. Shortly after his return to Ottawa he would be making a bid for the leadership of the Federal Liberal Party and he spent part of his time with Violet discussing a program for presentation at the Convention.

> *We were in the midst of this work when we heard a whistle blow, about four in the afternoon. As it continued we both said, almost simultaneously, 'Peace has been signed' [The Peace of Versailles]. It was a very solemn moment. 'How deeply those people have drunk at the cup of humility', was the expression which came from Violet Markham's lips. She went at once to open the windows to let in the new light and air. . . . The sun came out beautifully from behind the clouds as we gazed from the windows, and the swallows began to fly in circles as if inspired by a new life and joy. The cattle were resting peacefully on the side of the hill and the sheep grazing nearby. It was a picture of perfect peace, a wonderful symbol of the world at rest after a great storm.*

They then went for a long walk across the fields, continuing as they went to discuss the best policies for King to advocate and by the end of the evening, he had the outline of his proposed Liberal program. "May God be with you in all that lies ahead. . . . This time of testing & trial has left you ten fold more fit for the great task of leadership if that onerous duty is to be yours." were Violet's thoughts at this time. Then, drawing a parallel she often used during the years when he had been out of office, she continued: "Like Moses you have had to keep the flock of Jethro in the back side of the desert. And now I think the hour of the Burning Bush and the leadership is at hand."

Violet was at Cologne with Jim when news of King's victory reached them.

What a strange place to hear of this great event in your life! But how glad we both were! We were just going out for a picnic up the Ruhr Valley & we first drank your health under a clump of trees outside a German village & success to the Liberal cause in Canada & again tonight when we came home. . . . I gather from the Times that it was no easy victory. . . . My very dear friend—how I have longed & hoped for this recognition of your worth & services.

Two years later, as Violet walked down Oxford Street in London, her eye was caught by a newspaper headline that said 'Liberals Sweep Canada'. "I could have knelt down on the pavement then and there and thanked God. . . . I am proud, happy and full of thanksgiving." She had followed the Canadian election campaign closely and, although it had taken time, Lord Grey's prophecy had, indeed, come true: King was Prime Minister of Canada. She kept a watchful eye on him as he took up his new role and it wasn't long before she was writing to take him to task for something that is now legendary—his aptitude for taking on too much work and being engulfed by it.

It's clear that somebody ought to descend with a very strong hand on the Prime Minister & organize his work for him!! I was really aghast when I read the account of all the various burthens & offices under which you are struggling. The Labours of Hercules are as nothing by comparison. Prime Minister, President of the Privy Council, Secretary of State for External Affairs, Acting Minister of Finance and a variety of other offices! . . . Delegation is the secret of all successful work. . . . You must keep your time & strength for organization & direction & policy & free yourself from all this executive & departmental work.

She was no stranger to administrative work through her Settlement responsibilities as well as from various positions she held during the war, and with her closeness to King she sincerely hoped that she could make him change his ways. As soon as she knew he would be in London for the 1923 Imperial Conference she wrote and asked if it might be possible "to carry you off in a swift motor to Moon Green [her country home in Kent] for Sunday the 23rd? Just our three selves. No one else—unless, of course, you want to bring a secretary. But I am all for leaving the secretary behind!" That she failed, despite all attempts to effect a change in King's work habits, goes without saying but the visit to Moon Green was not without its positive side.

Some months previously, King had put forward Violet's name as an acting member of the Governing Body of the International Labour Conference in Geneva. It had become the practice before King was in power to select someone, not necessarily a Canadian, to stand in for the Minister of Labour at the trimonthly meetings but Violet's appointment caused some controversy. When it was raised in the House of Commons in Ottawa, Meighen, the Leader of the Opposition, referred to her as 'an English woman politician who forsooth had written a book'. She could not dispute the facts but she did take exception to reading in Hansard that she belonged "to a capitalist coal owning family & therefore must necessarily be biased against Labour!" This condemnation on the one hand and, on the other, a brother who thought she was a Bolshevist, stirring up the working classes. "I wonder which of the two extremes is the more absurd! I must confess Mr. Meighen's displeasure does not keep me awake at night." Her appointment, while having a ring of patronage about it, still meant that Canada was ably represented by Violet in Geneva. As she told King, she was willing to 'put any small social knowledge' she possessed at his disposal but she had some reservations about the practical value to Canada of her being a part of this international gathering. It was to discuss this and other related issues that she wished to have talks with King at Moon Green. As a result of this, she later said that she urged the Canadian Government to get things in order and to appoint one of their own people as a permanent delegate.

'Just our three selves' was how Violet put it as she looked forward to

King's visit to Moon Green. It was, in fact, the first time the three of them—she, King and Jim—had all been together. Nine years of marriage had gone by happily for the Carruthers, marred only by concern for Jim's health. Even some time spent in the balmier climate of South Africa did little to improve his condition but, despite all, he did not lose his sense of humour. Violet later recalled many more visits by King, either at Moon Green or in Chesterfield or in the little house on Gower Street when he so much enjoyed Jim's company, laughing heartily at his stories and jokes. "I always wished Rex could have had a touch of the joie de vivre which was so marked a feature of Jim's nature." On 27 June 1936, Jim died suddenly and it was Violet's turn to experience deep sorrow. In vain, King tried to convince her to "Hold to the belief, dear Violet, that Jim is at your side which in the very truth he is. You will become conscious of his presence the moment you give him a chance to tell you of it." In spite of this assurance her reply was: "I wish I could feel that Jim was just the other side of the hedge. I am afraid I am only conscious of silence and separation that increase as the days go by. I wish I had your faith and conviction."

At the conclusion of this letter, Violet had a request to make of King. It was "If ever, in your [psychic] experience, you touch Jim, you will tell me, will you not?" She was one of the very few friends who knew of his interest in spiritualism. In the mid-1930's, it would be rather difficult for so close a friend not to be aware of his increasing thirst for the revelations of the 'little table'. Having shared all else over the years, during a visit to Moon Green a few months after Jim's death, he told Violet about his experiences in this field and they tried the 'little table' together both then and on the following day. Looking back on this later she wrote that "This was a line of thought in which I was unable to follow him, but friendship would be a dull affair if friends in all matters thought alike. So I listened to his views with interest if without conviction."

Although Meighen described her as having been a politician, Violet's active participation in politics ended soon after her defeat in the 1919 election. She did some work in local organizations and took on some public speaking on behalf of others but there was a sense that the great days of British Liberalism were gone and her energies turned more towards local government. In 1925 she won a seat on the Town Council of Chesterfield and two years later became its Mayor. When King heard of this appointment his response was: "As you know, I have never been very keen about women participating too actively in public affairs. I confess that you have caused me to feel entirely differently." Violet's reaction to this was that "I am very glad if you have come to think differently about women in public life. I am all for leaving the door of opportunity open for any person who is capable of passing through it." But she was talking from a privileged position and she acknowledged this.

> *I am convinced women will be a negligible factor in political and public life and that it can never be a career for any save exceptional individuals by which I mean individuals exceptionally placed. Women with children and ordinary home ties can't give the necessary time. The servant question grows more and more difficult and is handicapping women more and more. Obviously if you have to choose between giving a lecture on Ruskin and cooking the dinner, the dinner wins hands down every time. Women can be good citizens because they can think at home. But whole time positions can only be undertaken by the very few. Nature's Salic Law holds and the men needn't worry about our competition.*

As they say, 'How times have changed' and one wonders what Violet would make of today's situation. Back in 1928, her thoughts echoed King's earlier reflections on women in the public place: "It is part of the changed spirit of the age—a restlessness good neither for men or women—I am sure whatever good women may do a cause in public life, public life does them harm."

Violet's term as Mayor of Chesterfield was cut short by a severe bout of influenza and for some time she was out of action but not any longer than she could help. There were always more books to write and during the 30s she held a position on the Unemployment Assistance Board, becoming Deputy Chairman in 1937. As well, she turned her hand to speechwriting for King. He constantly thought himself ill-served in this respect and, just before the Coronation and the Imperial Conference which followed it in 1937, he asked Violet for 'a suggestion or two as to appropriate themes e.g. The Foundation of Empire, the Secret of Imperial Unity, The Dominion and Britain, etc., etc., with supporting ideas.' What he got in response was a warning.

> *Remember we shall all be surfeited with oratory about the Empire and the appalling poppycock to which it will give rise. . . . [Be] brief . . . tell us about your country . . . Drummond's poems*

and Wilfred Campbell's poems. . . . Campbell: We are the dream which they did dream.

She did prepare a draft speech for either the Guildhall or Mansion House and another on The Secret of Imperial Unity as he had asked, but again urged him to try to see his way clear to giving some cultural addresses because 'Everyone gets so sick of speeches about the Empire!!'

During the 30s, Violet's wealth, so often a burden to her, began to decline. "Like the rest of the world I am very hard up. Coal is in a deplorable state and of course the reactions on my income have been serious." But, being 'very hard up' was a relative term. She no longer had a home in Chesterfield, this having been sold after the death of her brother, Arthur, but she still had her house at 8 Gower Street and she had her 'hidy-hole' at Moon Green in Kent. Although she, Derbyshire born and bred, felt that she was 'somewhat of a Ruth standing amid alien corn in Kent', yet she assured King that 'Here at Moon Green with my garden and dogs I am perfectly happy.' In 1937, after the Coronation and its attendant ceremonies were over, King had time one day to drive down to visit Violet, to enjoy her lovely gardens and to become reacquainted with Bush, Jane and Fafnir, her Labradors which were as much a part of her life as the little Irish terrier, Pat 1st was of his. Had there been Carruthers children and King children doubtless they would have written little notes to each other. There being none, "We even indulged in the whimsy of a canine correspondence—Jane writing to Pat to give him the latest news of the Moon Green kennel.", Violet confessed in her memoirs of King.

It was not until the summer of 1939 that Violet made another visit to Canada, her first since 1906, and was King's guest at Kingsmere. It was far from being a relaxed visit. "The shadow of war was deepening perceptibly over the world during those anxious July days. I found a very weary man when I met my old friend, a man weighted down by the all too sure foreboding of the catastrophe that lay ahead." Time to be host had to be sandwiched between Council meetings and Violet was largely left in the care of Joan Patteson, King's neighbour. When he did have time to spend with her, he was frustrated in his attempts to show off Kingsmere.

While it cleared up during the morning it remained very sultry and damp and the mosquitoes were bad. The result was that a walk we took from the Farm to the Ruins and then on through the woods to the falls and back by the creek and around by the nursery of trees, while helpful and pleasant from the point of exercise, was not too enjoyable.

What time they had for talks on this short visit centred on Violet's concern for King's future and her insistence that he make some plans. Giving up the leadership of the Liberal Party was high on the list, as was the need for him to decide the disposition of his various properties. King told Violet of his "intention of leaving Kingsmere to the nation, if I did not make of it some memorial to my sister Bella for the establishment of some small clinic, should I later come to have one of my nephews [Lyon King, a surgeon] come to live in Ottawa." Further discussions would have to wait for another less hurried time. Violet returned to England on the Aquitaine, arriving home, as King wrote her, 'in the nick of time'.

Letters were almost non-existent during the war years but, as Violet remarked when it was over, "What could we have said to one another but platitudes. So we have kept in touch at the feasts of the Church by cable." They did, however, meet on two occasions during the war. One was in September 1941, when King flew over to England in a converted Liberator bomber to have talks with Churchill. He had earlier heard from Violet that she had been in London "throughout the blitz and am very proud to be one of the garrison of the old town. There has been heavy bombing all round Gower Street but so far we have escaped serious injury except the blowing out of all the windows at the back of the house." By the time King saw her, however, she had made a small concession to the bombings and told him that "When the blitz comes she runs into Vernon Bartlett's house. He lives next door. They go out to the kitchen and play a game of cards—some racing game. It is a sort of patience. They do this until the blitz is over." When they met in 1941, she expressed her delight at seeing that King was no longer the weary man whom she had visited in 1939 but that his appearance bore out what John Buchan, [then Governor-General of Canada] had written her. "I hear you seem and look 20 years younger, that you are full of life and vigour and were never more on top of your job! As you truly say it was the uncertainty that was getting you down." In 1944, the other time when they met in London during the war, King dined with Violet at her home and had further insight into the character of his remarkable friend, now well into her 70s. He was told that despite wartime conditions one thing she never gave up was contact with her friends. "She says once a month she has a dinner party of about thirty or forty people in the house. She saves up her ration coupons for the occasion. Makes sausage rolls. They all lend a hand when arranging the party."

After the war it became clear to her that it had been will-power, not a resurgence of vigour, that had carried King through the struggle and, in late 1948, when they met in London, it was to the bedside of a sick man that she came. He had been in Paris for meetings and was then in London for the first postwar Imperial Conference. As it turned out his contact with it was limited to discussions with his Commonwealth colleagues in his suite at the Dorchester Hotel. When Violet visited him it was not to talk about affairs of state but about King's retirement. When they had met in 1944, Violet had urged upon him the wisdom of not continuing in public office after the war but to become an elder statesman. She warned him that "If one were to remain in public life, all that one had done during the war would be forgotten, and one would be saddled with endless abuse. Her reading of history showed that it was invariably so." King had told her at that time that he had no desire to stay on and would willingly step aside at any time. It was not, however, until August 1948 that he did give up the leadership of the party.

That step having been taken, there was another matter that was of concern to Violet. For all she knew he was entering the last few years of his life as an impoverished man, a view which she could attribute directly to King's own words on the matter. As he faced up to retirement he told her that

> *As I give up my salary as Prime Minister, my indemnity as a member of Parliament, the government allowance for a car, free transportation on the railways of the country, the use of a frank, etc., I shall be giving up a great deal, indeed, all that has left me without concern for the wherewith-all of existence from year to year, and day to day, over many years past, and I shall be without pension or remuneration of any kind.*

This news confirmed what she said were her worst fears,

> *that after this prolonged service to your country you should find yourself at the end without pension or an income adequate to a position of honourable retirement even on a modest scale. . . . Is Canada bereft of people without one grain of imagination? Or do they think you have been carrying on transactions in the Chicago*

wheat market or some kindred enterprise and have been piling up a snug fortune in dollars against your old age? . . . I who can claim to be one of your oldest and closest friends want to see an adequate cushion for the inevitable bump!

It was to suggest such a cushion that she came to see King at his hotel. Her finances had recovered from their low in the 1930s and she was now in the position where it would be to her advantage with regard to taxation to dispose of some of her wealth. What she had to tell King was that she had left him a sum in her will but that she would prefer to give him the amount at this time since it might be helpful in tiding him over a difficult situation. In the end this did not prove possible as such a gift would violate laws which prohibited money from leaving England and she was thwarted in her immediate wish. "However it has struck me since we parted" she later wrote him, "that if you want to come over on a visit to England then the money will be available in this country for your expenses. I quite understand that you don't want any special exception to be made for you in the regulations."*

King was never able to visit England again and so could not make use of what Violet called his 'legacy', but they met in Ottawa in October 1949. She had been on a trip to California and the plan was for them to meet on the Eastern seaboard, possibly in New York, before she went back home. More and more it became apparent from the tone of his letters that he was not well enough to travel so Violet changed her plans and went to spend a few days with him at Laurier House, his official residence in Ottawa. There she found 'a very sick man, sleepless and showing signs of nervous tension'. She had hoped that being free from the cares of office, his health might have improved but, for him, freedom came too late. In an effort to relieve some of his worries, she suggested plans for changes in Laurier House which she found not to her liking. "It was not the kind of house any woman would wish to live in. There was too much furniture to be dusted; too many knick-knacks etc." As well as trying to help him regarding Laurier House, they discussed the writing of his memoirs. Some months earlier, Violet had offered to return the letters he had written her over the years. She felt that these might help him as he turned his

---

*In 1910 she sent money for election expenses and again from 1911 to 1914 she helped King financially.

hand to the reconstruction of his life, containing as they did much information about his doings and also his thoughts. Arrangements were made through the office of the High Commissioner in London and early in 1949, King received a packet that weighed some seven pounds. As Violet remarked when preparing these letters for return, 'We certainly corresponded at length in our youth'.

It became clear to Violet that the memoirs could not be written given the state of King's health and also because of the sheer size of the task.

> *As he showed me the material piled up in the Archives, I was conscious of the nervous tension with which even the sight of the papers filled him. They stood for a task to which he was committed, but a task that he knew at heart was beyond his powers. I suggested that, for the time being, he should forget all about politics and dictate a few reminiscences about his home and childhood. To make some sort of a start might have helped his sense of frustration. But even that small effort proved impossible.*

As she sailed back to England, Violet wrote expressing the thought that "This weary time of physical weakness is a sore trial dear Rex. It will pass & there lie before you I hope serene days of renewed health and leisure." In her own case, the many years of her dedication to country and causes came to an end finally in the summer of 1950. "I have now been retired on age from all my government work and on June 1st was placed on the Supplemental List of Magistrates. I may sign certificates but not sit in court! It's like the whole framework of life falling in & I can't pretend I have not felt a little sad."

Less than a month later there was the sorrowful but not unexpected news from Joan Patteson that "Our friend's condition has taken serious turn. Will keep you informed'. The next day's cable confirmed Violet's worst fears: "Rex's life drawing rapidly to close. Unconscious since Thursday. Your letter last he read. Love Joan."

After King's death, Violet corresponded with Fred McGregor, who had earlier been King's Private Secretary and who had returned to try to assist in King's work on his papers. She spoke of King in these terms:

> *He was always a constant and unchanged background of unswerving affection and friendship in my own life. Through all its trials and vicissitudes he was always so to speak there. Now he has gone I feel the*

rent is great indeed. The penalty of a long life [and I am 77] is that inevitably one outlives many friends. But no loss could be more painful to me than that of Rex.

On 9 February 1959, Violet's death down at her beloved Moon Green, brought to a close the story of a special friendship which had lasted fully half a century, spanning two World Wars and a multiplicity of contacts both familial, political and social when they had each been able to 'lay a helping hand on bowed shoulders'.

The Governors-General

"Going to lunch [?] with His Excellency's [Lord Minto's] daughters & seeing them home was a fine stroke. Nothing like it. The social recreation, too, was all right. You need that, even a little small talk also." It was the same gratuitous advice which John King had given his son when the latter went off to study in Chicago: 'Get in with the right set'.

This fatherly wisdom was not well received then nor was it appreciated in 1901 when King was trying to adjust to life in Ottawa. He was determined not to be drawn too deeply into its social scene, so it annoyed him to be told that "No man can get through the world properly without being able to command at will a certain amount of small talk." King's reaction was blunt:

> [I cannot regard] the mastery of small talk as a good thing, or other than wasted effort, and, along the same line, the going to church and home with the Minto children—saving the fact that they were bright and natural—rather a series of flunkeyism than a thing to be admired. . . . The aims and ideals [of the society world] are false, petty, vain and belittling to one of intelligence and strength. It is the hot-bed of dilletantism [sic] . . . and a thing to [be] shunned rather than courted or envied.

Rideau Hall, the residence of the British Crown's representative in Canada, was at the very heart and centre of social life in Ottawa. It had been so since Ottawa became the capital and anybody who was anybody was either on the invitation list or wished to be. While still a student at the University of Toronto, King had already met one Governor-General when Lord Aberdeen had been invited to address the students there. After the speeches, Their Excellencies were exposed to a little fun. As King's diary records,

> *[We] took the horses out of the Governor's sleigh & the boys got a couple of hundred feet of rope which we fastened to it. I acted as Footman & when Lord & Lady Aberdeen came down showed them into their carriage, then I ran alongside it & talked to the Governor-General and Lady Aberdeen all the way to Victoria College. I enjoyed the conversation with them very much.*

There could not have been much time for any sort of conversation but, had there been, King would have found a soul mate in Lady Aberdeen. One of her stops on the visit to Toronto was to look at conditions of women working for clothing manufacturers and what she saw she found appalling; it was this same problem that King was to investigate four years later. Lady Aberdeen, it seems, was one step ahead of him all along the way. While he later became an ardent admirer of Gladstone, she was already on that bandwagon. Her father and Gladstone had been close friends and, given Lady Aberdeen's strong character, it is not surprising to learn that her husband also embraced Gladstonian philosophies as warmly as she did. King and the Aberdeens had much in common as they were to discover in subsequent and more relaxed meetings. Lady Aberdeen's work on behalf of Canadian women brought her back to Canada from time to time following the end of her husband's term in 1898 and, when King was in London in 1908, among the many social calls that he managed to fit in alongside a heavy work schedule, one was on Lady Aberdeen. They were both reminded of their first meeting when the Toronto students involved in 'playing horsey' each received a bunch of forget-me-nots as a 'Thank you'.

In 1909, after the Aberdeens' son, Archie, died as the result of a car accident, his parents relied on spiritualism for consolation. This had been a latent interest of theirs for a time, and they turned to it more and more as the years went by. Lord Aberdeen died in March 1934, but King kept in touch with Lady Aberdeen and, just as one might pass on the name of ones doctor or lawyer to a good friend, she advised King in choosing a medium while he was in London that autumn. She went one better and made an appointment for him with Mrs. Hester Dowden who was well known for her work in transmitting messages from those in the beyond by means of automatic writing. A year later, when King was sorting out some papers on psychic matters, he spent hours writing a long memo to Lady Aberdeen with emphasis on "the conversation with Lord Aberdeen on April 22, 1 year ago—exactly a year to the day of the memorial to Lord A., unveiled in Ireland [?]

The Countess of Aberdeen (1898)

by Lady A. [Also] the talk with Lord Aberdeen through automatic writing of Mrs. Bowden [sic] in London in Nov., & a talk with mother of Lord Aberdeen, myself writing."

While King was in Geneva for League of Nations meetings in September 1936, he again met Lady Aberdeen who was there in her capacity as president of the National Council of Women. She phoned and asked King to give her a 'good deal of time' on the following day. He was in a testy mood, having on his mind speeches to prepare and, as ever, no one to really help, as he saw it. His annoyance showed as he wrote of her request: "I limited it to tea. . . . People are merciless . . . seek one for social ends. I am determined to see that no one, on this trip, gets the best of me." But he mellowed when he called on the elderly lady at her hotel. "We talked from five until nearly a quarter to eight. She looked remarkably like Queen Victoria in the side face, seemed to be quite keen intellectually and was exceedingly friendly." This was Lady Aberdeen's chance to bring King up to date on the state of psychic matters in England. What interested him was that "a society had recently been formed embracing clergymen and persons interested in psychical research who were holding regular meetings for the purpose of further researches. She spoke of Davidson, the Dean of Canterbury, being one of this number and of other clergymen including McLean of Edinburgh with whom she had had many talks." With Lady Aberdeen's death in April 1939, King lost this source of psychic information and although his 'little table' talks continued, there is no evidence that he was ever in touch by this or any other means with either of the Aberdeens in later years.

'The Queen is dead. Long live the King'. These words were heard within a few hours of King's writing in his diary:

> We feel a sense of personal loss at the thought of [Queen Victoria] parting from us. Her life has been before us from the days we came

> *out of consciousness upon the things of this world. . . . Often during the day has my voice thickened when I spoke of her and my eyes dimmed when reading the references to her. [Harper] & I were speaking of her reign tonight and of how future generations will see a golden & glorious age in it.*

Such were the sentiments of King and Harper, arch Victorians both, but over at Rideau Hall the same was not true. The Mintos who took up residence there in 1898 were representative of that new class, the Edwardians, who were just waiting to burst upon the scene. "They were a distinct new species of proconsul: a glossy and worldly couple entirely at home within the chic, fast, raffish, Marlborough House set that surrounded the Prince of Wales. . . . They brought to Ottawa, Edwardian style at its most seductive and evocative." It was quite a change for Ottawans but where the Governor-General led, there were always those who were ready and willing to follow. As for King himself, one knows that he would have preferred to be an habitué of Rideau Hall while the Aberdeens were there. Before he had even crossed the threshold all remaining pictures of Gladstone, 'dear Mr. G.', had been relegated to the attic or the trash heap and, like any new tenants, the Mintos put their own stamp on the residence. Invitation lists were purged after Minto observed that guests had often been embarrassed by meeting their own tradesmen at social functions during the previous regime. That had to stop. Some names were dropped and some added, among the latter being King's to the obvious delight of his father back in Toronto.

One of the passions of the Mintos was skating, even to the extent that some grumbled that 'the skating people' were the ones the vice-regal couple singled out. One could not call King a lover of the sport but on occasion he did his turns around the rink at Rideau Hall. In January 1904, he

> *went down to Govt. House to the Skating Party. The sight was a most beautiful one. The Chinese lanterns across the rink & on the sides of the toboggan slides, the huge bonfires, the ice palace & coloured lights. . . . I skated with Lady Violet [a daughter of the Minto's] in the grand march, torch light, following immediately after Their Excellencies. I did not want to but Lady Violet took that place. I made one bull in turning the wrong way once, otherwise got through all right. . . . I did not feel well tonight but the skating did me good. Lady Ruby seems almost too much to hope for in any way.*

And in this last sentence there hangs a tale. Lady Ruby Elliot was the second youngest daughter of the Mintos and she had captivated King. Marjorie Herridge and what she meant to him was put aside temporarily as he sang Lady Ruby's praises. "I think very much of her as a fine, noble girl, with high ideals, generous, kind and true nature, sweet & lovely." When he realized that he had first met her almost three years previously, he had to ask himself why he had been wasting so much time. That this period coincided with his most intense association with Marjorie Herridge should seem to have been cause enough. Smitten as he was by Lady Ruby, King did not delude himself into thinking that he could aspire to someone of her position. She was out of Canada for most of 1904, returning shortly before Lord Minto's tour of duty was up in November. King had his chance to say 'good-bye' to her at a Sunday afternoon tea party during which he asked if he might write to her when she was back in England. Her answer, 'now and then' seems to have been what was needed to put their relationship into focus. Although stung by this blow, King rationalized that "She knows I admire her greatly . . . [but] we really do not know each other. . . . She played 'The Evening Star' very beautifully and said it was because I had asked her to." And so Lady Ruby passed out of King's life. She was never really a part of it and thus was not eligible to be among those listed as 'Miss A to Miss I'.

The Earl of Minto (1904)

King's own future began to take form during the tenure of the next Governor-General, Lord Grey, who arrived in Ottawa on 13 December 1904. At noon the next day, King called on His Excellency, the reason for this somewhat premature act being to invite Grey to address the Canadian Club of which King was President. The invitation was refused for the present time, Lord Grey saying that he wished to learn more about Canada first. Despite this early setback, a closeness developed between the two men. While King did not fit in with the Minto

Earl & Countess Grey (1904)

set, he found in Lord Gray himself echoes of his own attitude to public duty. He learned, as well, that he was being envied his youth and the opportunity of coming to terms with humanitarian issues. Their common sympathies were reflected in their bookshelves, Arnold Toynbee having been an inspiration to both. During the course of an afternoon walk a few days before Christmas 1905, Grey shared with King his pleasure in the works of the Italian patriot, Mazzini, and presented him with a complete set of these books for Christmas. A few weeks later King began reading this author aloud to Marjorie Herridge, thrilling in the author's "having regard for the eternal things, believing in them & recognizing that properly presented they would find a response in the hearts of the people."

It was not only Lord Grey who drew King back very often to Rideau Hall but also his friendship with Lady Evelyn, one of the Governor-General's daughters. This had none of the complications of that with Lady Ruby for they met on a different level. Lady Evelyn, who was active in working with the May Court Club (a young ladies' service club formed by Lady Aberdeen in 1898), had asked King for some guidance. One of her projects was to have Professor Stephen Leacock of McGill come and speak to some of the working girls in Ottawa, particularly the 'typewriters, clerks and others in the [Civil] Service'. Don't put the lectures forward as being on Political Science as Lady Evelyn and the Club members had suggested, was King's advice. Be more specific and don't charge a $3 fee for the course. A dollar was enough to ask and the more democratic the whole exercise was the better since 'the Maycourt [sic] had a tendency towards exclusiveness'.

King's constant to-ing and fro-ing to Rideau Hall could not escape drawing some criticism and when he received the C. M. G. (making him a Commander of the Order of St. Michael and St. George) from His Majesty King Edward VII in 1906, the word was out that 'Dinners at Rideau Hall . . .

had paid off. According to an early biographer, "It was an open secret that the honour had been obtained on the personal initiative of Earl Grey and not of the Canadian Government, which might well have looked askance at singling out a junior deputy minister for preferred treatment." The more senior Civil servants in Ottawa were incensed and so was Marjorie Herridge who came to King's defense. When asked "Have you seen William Lyon Mackenzie King in his uniform? Boy, I could have struck her. When I said I had, she asked what I thought of that."

King had much for which to thank Lord Grey, both on the personal and the political side of his life. It was at a dinner party at Rideau Hall that he had been introduced to Violet Markham and thus began their long and satisfying friendship. It was Lord Grey who unveiled the statue in memory of Bert Harper and, as thanks, was given copies of *The Secret of Heroism* which he offered "to send with letters of favourable reviews to London *Times, Spectator, Outlook* and one to Carnegie asking him to get out an edition for his libraries." It was Grey who first called King 'the Peace Maker', having in mind King's success in settling labour strikes, and who was convinced that King would one day be Prime Minister of Canada. It was the Governor-General who urged Laurier to send King on the trip to the Orient and who lost no opportunity that might benefit the budding politician. What a boost to King's ego to be told "that no one would be a better representative than myself. That I had come to be indispensable." It was not every son who could write home to his mother as King did in 1910 that "Of all the honours and events in my life, I think I prize most the friendship of Sir Wilfrid and Earl Grey." In Toronto, John and Isabel King could relax: their son had, indeed, got in with 'the right set'.

During much of the terms of the next two Governors-General, the Duke of Connaught (1911-16) and the Duke of Devonshire (1916-21), King was not at Government House as often as previously. The necessity

H.R.H. The Duke of Connaught

of earning a living was borne in on him after he was defeated at the polls in 1911 and before he became a Rockefeller Foundation employee in 1914. It was his own decision to avoid social engagements whenever possible but not to the point of becoming a hermit. Government House was not completely shut out of his life, however, and shortly after Christmas 1911, he was invited to a large dinner party. He had gone expecting it to be 'a formal evening with reserve and caution and what not' but it turned out quite differently. His host, the Duke of Connaught, was a son of Queen Victoria and King evidently did not know what to expect now that the Vice-Regal representative was also a 'Royal'. At table he was seated beside the Duchess whom he found "comparatively easy to talk with, more so than Lady Grey. I noticed that the [she?] took a good deal to drink, both champagne, liquors, etc." After the ladies left the table, according to the custom of the time, and the gentlemen were left to their port and cigars, the Duke invited King to sit beside him. It is hard to visualize this but "H.R.H. passed me a cigarette from his own case & gave me his own lighted cigarette to light it with." Cigarettes alight, the conversation between the two men ranged widely and, at one point, when the Duke said that, of course, he was an imperialist, this gave King an opening to say that "I had often wished for an opportunity to say to a member of the Royal family that [the Rebellion of 37] was not directed against the Queen of England or the Br. Monarchy but against the prostitution of British Institutions in Canada." Having thus put the rebellion led by his grandfather into perspective, King relaxed and by the time he wrote up his diary the next day, he concluded that

> *I found [the Duke] ... an exceedingly affable & agreeable gentleman to talk with. I was really most agreeably surprised at the strong personal liking I took to both him & to a lesser degree to the Duchess. There was a genuine kindliness & friendliness in his attitude and the air of the entertaining was like the hospitality of an English home. . . . I spent one of the happiest evenings I have ever enjoyed.*

King also met Princess Patricia, the daughter of the Connaughts, that evening and, again, contrary to what he had expected, he found her to be 'a truly lovely girl' but it was not until two years had passed that he got beyond superficial polite conversation with her. Then, one evening when he sat beside her at dinner, she told him of her interest in psychic forces.

She introduced the subject herself. . . . She thought the psychic sense might be developed by concentration . . . that it ought to be possible to control [it], . . . that it was annoying not to be able to do so. . . . She thought the invisible reality greater than the things seen, was sure there was a psychic wave at the present time influencing thought.

While being sympathetic to Princess Patricia's beliefs relating to psychic forces, it was a field that was not yet of consuming interest to King.

Although his work for the Rockefeller Foundation took him away for weeks or even months at a time during these years, Ottawa was still his home but when there he was almost an outsider as far as political affairs were concerned. He was still invited to the occasional dinner party at Rideau Hall, however, or to skating parties but even that latter had its drawbacks and, this time, not because he had 'made a bull in turning the wrong way'. The problem now was much more serious in his eyes. It was early in January 1917, and Rideau Hall once more had new tenants. The Duke of Connaught had been replaced by the Duke of Devonshire in the previous November and, war or no war, the traditions of Government House were upheld by passing the winter months in all the usual outdoor sports, including skating. Full of high resolve, instigated by some criticism that had come his way, King refused the first invitation of the year to attend a skating party, "not really caring to be seen skating at a social function with other men away fighting. I know there is really no reason why I should feel this way, but I am sensitive to comment, and am too conscious of it at times."

The end of 1917 saw King's work with the Foundation over except for the formalities of making it a fact. For the next two years he busied himself with industrial consulting in the United States before returning to Canada permanently. Back in Ottawa he was about to become a regular guest at Rideau Hall again. That summer, the Prince of Wales, the future King Edward VIII, came to Canada on his

The Duke of Devonshire

first tour of the country. By the time he reached Ottawa, King was not just another guest, a 'filler of tables' at Rideau Hall, but a person of some stature in the country. Laurier died in February 1919 and King had been chosen by the Liberals as his successor. As such, he was thrown into closer contact with the Prince than would have otherwise been the case. Seated beside each other one day at a luncheon at the Chateau Laurier in H.R.H.'s honour, King learned how the Prince felt about speech-making. He wished it could come first and the lunch after, King wrote, and

> *I spoke of all speakers having much the same feeling. . . . The cold grape juice caused me to remark on the prohibition throughout the country. H. R. H. sd you can't make a speech on that stuff. He told me he liked a glass of port better than anything else before speaking. . . . As it came the time for speaking he got more and more anxious . . . straining every bit of his body. . . . When he got up he really did splendidly.*

At luncheon the Prince had made some critical remarks about Canadian women who he said did not know how to dance. "I told him," King noted, "he should see some of the younger group of Ottawa girls who are often at the Golf & Country Clubs, that they were splendid dancers." This seemed to interest His Highness and "He said I wonder if they dance in the afternoon at the Golf Club. He then told me he was not going to Blue Sea Lake but wd go out to the Club instead, was hoping to get out that afternoon for a game." It is likely that the Prince, who had been complaining of a bruised hand from the constant hand-shaking, went out to the Club to find a dance partner rather than to play a round of golf. That evening there was a State dinner and dance at Government House which King (and one hopes the Prince of Wales, as well) enjoyed. "[I] was on the floor soon after the first of two or three [dances], never missed a dance till we left at 1. Had [as one of my partners] Lady Dorothy Cavendish,* daughter of His Ex.—she looked very smart but her sister Lady Rachel was perfectly beautiful." When the Prince of Wales was back in Ottawa at the end of a tour of western Canada, the May Court Club held a Charity Ball in his honour and it is hard to say who enjoyed the evening more, the guest of honour or King. Tucking his C.M.G. into his coat pocket on arrival at the Chateau Laurier (because 'I hate wearing an order around my neck'), King made no apologies for his pleasure at being on the dance floor. 'Once I start dancing I enjoy every number'. The only fly in the ointment was that he found it difficult 'not to

---

*Lady Dorothy later became the wife of Sir Harold Macmillan.

pick favourites rather than do duty dances'.

While King always found that he and the daughters of the various Governors-General were compatible (except for Lady Ruby and his unrequited love of her), the same easy social relationship did not always exist with their mothers. He and Lady Minto had little in common either when the Mintos were in Ottawa or later. After seeing her again in 1921, King's terse remark was that she was 'as usual frigid enough'. For some reason he found Lady Grey difficult to talk to but, to his surprise, he had no such problem with Princess Louise, Duchess of Connaught. As for the Duchess of Devonshire, his feelings about her (and her husband) came out only after their departure and on the arrival of the new Governor-General, Lord Byng, and his wife in 1921. "The note of youth & vigour & absence of side was noticeable in Lord Byng and of naturalness and pleasantness in Lady Byng. A refreshing contrast to the heaviness of the Duke of Devonshire and the formal exclusiveness of the Duchess. I feel sure that both Lord & Lady Byng are going to be most popular and acceptable." If only things had worked out so happily for their relationship, but that was not to be.

During their first autumn in Ottawa, the Byngs and King saw little of each other. An election had been called and King spent a good deal of time campaigning across the country. When they met on 7 December, the day after the election, King had changed hats and was no longer the Opposition Leader but Prime Minister of Canada. Two years earlier he had been assured that this was in his future, having been told so by none other than the formally exclusive Duchess of Devonshire.

> *At a dinner last night, [she] told me that some time ago when she & her daughter & Angus McIntosh & one or two others were amusing themselves with a 'weege' board, she called it, someone asked who is to be the next Premier & the reply, to use the Duchess' own words, 'the thing rammed out Mackenzie King'. She laughed quite heartily about it.*

King's new responsibilities left him with little time for socializing. A skating party at Government House became only a few minutes on the ice, long enough to make an appearance and to have a 'duty' skate or two. On one occasion, a dance given by Their Excellencies which began at 10 p.m. suited him well at the end of a busy day. When he wrote this up in his diary, however, it is evident that he foresaw an uneasy relationship with Lady Byng: "Took Her Excellency into supper. Find it a little difficult to talk with her, mostly because of lack of subjects & interests in common." While acknowledging that she "has not had the training or background of the wives of previous G.G.'s", he added that she was 'unconventional'.

On the day the Byngs arrived in Ottawa, King had not been introduced to Lady Evelyn Byng but his impression of her then, as an onlooker, was that "She seemed to me to have an intellectual face, not a beauty at all but a sensible woman." According to a biographer of Lord Byng, Lady Evelyn had

> *about her none of the aloofness which characterized some of the other chatelaines of Rideau Hall, [but] she was not a 'comfortable' mistress of the household. She had a spectacular temper and, in the privacy of her home, was apt to give it rein, startling everyone nearby with the range of her profanity.*

It was lucky for King that there was not a reason for her to draw her sword on him sooner than she did. She claimed that she never liked him, never trusted him and had warned her husband about him, but this may or may not have been that convenient thing—hindsight.

In any event, for most of the first four years, politeness prevailed between the new Governor-General and the newly-elected Prime Minister. While King had his doubts about Lady Byng from the start, he found Lord Byng to be "very retiring, a little standoffish & shy, a feeling I can well appreciate as I feel it in myself." King's nerves were in a sorry state as he tried to cope with his new responsibilities as well as with the move into Laurier House, his official residence. It seemed to him that he had

Lord & Lady Byng

to do everything himself: "It is no job for a man alone running a house & a country at the same [time] & laid up with grippe to boot." By the spring of 1923, and before the pictures were even hung in his new home, the Byngs were invited to tea and given a tour of the house in which they 'seemed genuinely interested'. It was a relaxed visit with 'Her Ex. Presiding' at the tea table while the two men discussed phrenology, a special study of Lord Byng's.

Opportunities for such visits were rare. The Byngs and King more often met on formal occasions such as dinners and 'Drawing Rooms' at Government House. These latter were King's bane, not because he didn't enjoy them but rather the contrary, the one exception being in the matter of dress. Of one reception in the spring of 1924, he recorded that "I wore the full dress Windsor uniform, white breeches, etc for the first time. To tell the truth I was far from happy in them." And he would not have worn them except that Lord Byng emphasized 'keeping up the ceremonies, etc. if in the position'. On other matters, King and the Governor-General were often of one mind whether the issues were international or domestic. One Canadian question that would not be settled for decades, that of a flag, also saw them in accord.

> *He [Byng] agreed we shld have a Canadian flag with Union Jack & our own distinctive emblem on the field. I suggested each Dominion adopting the same design, putting their distinctive designs in field keeping Union Jack in upper left hand corner, when flag out to right on pole. He agreed absolutely.*

So much in tune were the two men that it seemed to King that "Lord Byng is truly anxious to be of real help & is most kindly and generously disposed towards myself."

Alas, this congenial state was not to continue much longer. A General Election was called for 29 October 1925 and when the votes were counted, King and his Liberals held only 101 seats; the Conservatives under Arthur Meighen had 116 while the Progressives with 24 seats held the balance of power. The first shot in the King-Byng controversy had been fired. This constitutional wrangle has been covered in depth by experts on the subject as well as by those with political biases or informed opinions. A brief background look is all that is required here to cover the development of deteriorating relations between Byng and King. Shortly after their arrival in Ottawa, Lady Byng took King aside one evening to tell him that he "would find Lord Byng very good at keeping everything secret, that having been in military life, they were not in politics." She went further when writing in *Up the Stream of Time*, her autobiography, that both she and her husband 'always shunned and detested politics'. As one early King biographer noted, this was, "if we are to believe [her], an extraordinary frame of mind for [Byng] who had chosen to live in that milieu for four or five years." During his first long talk with King soon after he arrived in Ottawa, the new Governor-General expressed some concern about his lack of knowledge of constitutional matters but told King that "I have only one object, that is to be of what service I can. I have no axe to grind, only to do what I can where opportunity offers."

When he met with King on the day after the 1925 election, he soon discovered what a difficult task he was facing. As Byng saw it, there were three ways of dealing with the situation: "The first is dissolution, that I hope you will not ask for, that I do not wish to grant at this stage, the people do not want another election immediately, the next is that Mr. Meighen having the largest solid group should be called on, and the third is that you should continue." In strongly urging King to accept the second alternative, Byng stressed that 'as a friend of yours' he felt that 'it would be the more dignified thing not to try to carry on under such circumstance'. There was some logic there, King concluded, but said "I wd. wish to talk matters over with my colleagues first, that they would probably oppose the idea." His assumption was correct; no one except Vincent Massey would hear of it. When Byng was informed of this, "He said to me almost immediately . . . I shall be obliged to say that while I accept your advice, I differ from you in opinion. . . . I pointed out how serious it wd be were a difference of view between himself & me to take place." In a flurry of activity the following day, King read a statement to the waiting reporters that he was going to continue in office. There was no comment and no questions were asked. As King thought about the hours of discussions with his colleagues and with Byng, it seemed to him that "Lord Byng has certainly tried to be fair & just & has been fair & just. The natural Tory could not helping [sic] in the feeling that the Govt. shld resign & let the Tories come in, but this I truly believe, was meant as much, if not more in my own interest, than from any love of or desire to help Meighen—I do not think he likes Meighen."

'It is given to me to carry on' was how it appeared to King then and until June 1926, Canada continued to have a Liberal government, but it was a gruelling time for King. The Governor-General tried to control any resentment he may have felt towards him for remaining in office but Lady Byng did nothing to hide her feelings. Insults seemed to pile one on top of the other. One such snub occurred in November when King accepted an invitation from Lady Byng to extend his patronage to a hockey match. Hockey had become a passion of hers when she and Lord Byng decided that the ice at Rideau Hall held little interest for them. She never learned to skate without the help of a chair and Lord Byng soon found that his skill on the ice was limited but they were often to be found rink-side in the Vice-Regal box. It was a slap in the face to King when he was, at no time that evening, invited to the box.

> *After all I am the Prime Minister of the country and His Ex. is a visiting governor. The fact that at the moment there is a difficult situation only makes me the more indignant that they had not the courtesy to recognize the situatio n as meriting a little graciousness. . . . I confess to a certain feeling of genuine indignation at the action of Their Excellencies tonight.*

But this, trying as it was, was as nothing compared with what was to follow. In early December he learned that the dates of the State Dinner and the Drawing Room, the two big social events connected with the Opening of a new Parliament, were being shuffled around. After a dinner at Government House on 12 December, King and his host retired to the library where the subject was brought up. King's concern about the changes elicited the explanation from Byng as to the real reason for the delay.

> *"[It] could not be given that week at Govt. House. He went on to say that Her Excellency's birthday party had been arranged for 3 months ago, that with the house full of people—people coming out, it cld not be done. . . . [He] spoke of the inconvenience of the State Dinner, upsetting the house more than anything else did. I agreed & said I regarded it as an imposition but it was a sort of State function."*

King might raise his arguments but nothing was to be changed. All in all it had been a difficult evening. At dinner, he was "seated next to Miss Sanford [sic] who I do not care for and to the left of Her Ex. who looked very tired and worn. There was no pleasant or conving [sic] conversation,—chit chat of a critical character—There is too much of that at Govt House, making light of others, dwelling on limitations etc." The lady on King's left was Eva Sandford who had come out from England as lady-in-waiting to Lady Byng in the summer of 1924. While she was undoubtedly highly satisfactory as far as Lady Byng was concerned, King did not like her but at dinner that evening he made what polite conversation was expected—had she found time to get out on her own, time to make any new friends in her first year in Ottawa and so on. We have Eva's own words for what happened next.

> *Suddenly I was horrified to feel a pinch on my thigh. A short time later it was followed by another. Instinctively I raised my foot and kicked downwards with my high heel against his [King's] leg. There was a moan as I turned my back on him. For the rest of the evening I ignored him and talked only to the man on my left.*

Were it not that the story came from Eva, herself, one might be inclined to treat it as a malicious rumour but there is little doubt that it did, in fact, happen. The question is why. It seems highly uncharacteristic behaviour for King but the answer may lie in the stress that he had been undergoing for some time. Early that year, he took himself to task:

> *Have been making a great mistake sitting up so late, eating & drinking the amount I have and not exercising and disciplining myself as I should. I seem to get in a mood, thro' the pressure of work, which makes me more or less reckless in behaviour and I let my impulses control as I should not do. It is a curious sort of conflict of the two natures which I know is all wrong and yet seem unwilling to change.*

Just a few days previous to the incident he was, once again, berating himself for taking too many stimulants, too much wine and liquor, this despite a resolve to cut out drinking altogether. Possibly the dinner that night was so full of 'chit chat', was so boring, that his hand went automatically to his glass with a result that was most unexpected.

When both Lord and Lady Byng soundly scolded Eva for her seeming rudeness towards the Prime Minister, she blurted out the truth. "If I had thought about it I wouldn't have said a word for who would believe such a thing about the Prime Minister?" Fortunately for her, Lady Byng believed the story and "I've never seen her in such a rage!", Eva went on. "She went straight to Lord Byng and said she'd never have that man under her roof again. Of course that was impossible but Lady Byng did her best to avoid Mackenzie King in future. Whenever he came to see the Governor-General, she'd say to me 'Here he comes-let's go to ground."

Appearances had to be kept up, however, and King was back at Rideau Hall early in January 1926, for the contentious birthday party for Her Excellency. It took the form of a fancy dress ball and King had to admit that "[It] was an attractive affair. I took her Ex. in to supper. . . . Stayed until end of Ball at 3 a.m., which was a mistake. I should have left at midnight. I never seem able to control my own will." He may not have known it but the story of the 'pinch' had made the rounds in Ottawa by then and there was great giggling when one of Eva's dance partners, a rotund figure in a clown's costume, asked her to dance and immediately gave her another pinch. This time the culprit was not King. Despite thinking it all 'a piece of nonsense' he had entered into the spirit of the occasion and went dressed as a courtier from the time of King George III.

As Byng's time in Canada was drawing to a close, the final phase of the King-Byng affair was played out. The Liberal government which had been in office with the support of the Progressives was faced with a vote of censure in the House over a scandal in the Customs Department. King asked for dissolution and the Governor-General refused. There was nothing for King to do but resign at which time Meighen was asked to form a government. He was Prime Minister for only three days before being defeated in the House by one vote. It was then his turn to ask that the House be dissolved and this was granted almost immediately. This did not go unchallenged by King who made full use of his interpretation of the matter during the election campaign, which followed during the summer and early autumn of 1926. When the votes were in, he was back as Prime Minister and remained so until 1930.

It had been a rough campaign and Byng fully expected that during his last few weeks he would see King take 'a very vitriolic line' against him. But, with the exception of what was said during the campaign, King's manner "took the inverted form of a conscious rectitude and a determined cordiality." Shortly before the election, King did the proper thing and had the Byngs to Laurier House for a farewell dinner. It was not the most pleasant occasion. King wrote that at this dinner-party, Lady Byng "looked as if it was the trial of her life to shake me by the hand; the expression on her face was a terrifying one." Four days later, they left Ottawa but not before one last official act, the laying of a corner-stone for the altar in the Memorial Chamber of the Peace

Tower. At the railway station, the formal farewells were said and, again, "Her Excellency was as unpleasant as she could be. She looked at me like someone from the Chamber of Horrors; all that she said was 'Mr. King' and shook hands. I know the words were used instead of 'Prime Minister'. . . . No one proposed a cheer for Her Excellency."

Reconciliation—if such it can be called—between the Byngs and King came late. There was one regrettable incident in 1932 when the Byngs visited Ottawa and, in a private tête-à-tête with the former Governor-General, King, overcome by the emotion of the long-ago events, burst into tears over what he said had been a misunderstanding on the part of both. This did nothing to clear the air and only gave Lady Byng a chance to say, in effect, to her husband 'Now, you see what kind of man this is'. In early June 1935, Byng died. His passing was marked in Ottawa by a memorial service that was held at the Capital Theatre. As King sat alone in the left front box, his thoughts were on the differences of opinion that had characterized the last months of Byng's time in Ottawa. "Throughout the service I felt as if it were the ending of a chapter which had been a very important one. . . . My conscience was perfectly clear. . . . I felt a complete serenity in viewing the past." He felt even better later that day when he sat at the 'little table' with his friends, the Pattesons, and had the following 'talk' with Byng:

> *Byng:* I have not forgotten the time you advised me to grant a dissolution. You were right and I was wrong.
> *King:* How was that?
> *Byng:* I was wrong in not believing what you told me.
> *King:* Yes!
> *Byng:* Try to forgive me. . . . I am sorry for any wrong I have done you.
> *King:* So long as you can see into my heart and know the truth, that is all I want."

A sort of truce was later realized between King and Evelyn Byng. In 1940 she came to Ottawa for a visit of somewhat long duration* and, one evening at dinner at Government House, she discovered to her great consternation that King was one of the other guests. While the men remained at the table,

---

*Willis O'Connor said that Lady Byng stayed with them in their private residence, Byng House, for six months. Due to money restrictions during the war years, she had to depend on help from her Canadian friends and he used to refer to her jokingly as the 'kept woman'.

Viscount & Lady Willingdon

the ladies went back to the drawing room. There, Lady Byng had taken up her knitting and just as King came back into the room, her ball of wool rolled off under the grand piano. King made the instinctive gesture of helping her retrieve it and the sight presented to the other guests of the two posteriors in this odd situation was too much for them. It brought down the house and even King and Evelyn Byng had a smile for each other as they rose to their feet. But the peace did not last and, to the end, Lady Byng had nothing good to say of King whom she had once called 'our dear little roly poly friend'.

After the Byngs left, Rideau Hall moved into its purple period. Lady Willingdon, wife of the new Governor-General, loved the colour and some of its softer tints such as mauve. She wrote on mauve stationery and touches of the colour showed up in every decorative touch possible as she turned Rideau Hall inside out soon after their arrival in late October 1926. This redecorating was long overdue and it gave her ample outlet for her abundant energies while Lord Willingdon took up his new responsibilities. They had visited Ottawa earlier in the year at which time the talk turned to whether or not Lord Willingdon might succeed Byng. In private conversation with King, Byng did not favour such an appointment. "[He] did not think a military man wd suit, most of them thought in terms of their training, they might do for India or a Crown Colony but not for Canada." This view, perhaps not surprising in light of Byng's own experiences in Canada, did not carry the day. Both the Willingdons were keen on the idea of coming with Lady Willingdon having only one reservation, which was whether or not the allowances were adequate as they had little personal wealth. It was not until December when King returned after attending the Imperial Conference in London that he saw the changes which had taken place in the Vice-Regal residence. He had scarcely time to greet his little dog, before going over to have lunch with Their Excellencies. "It was a delightful home party, only the A.D.C.'s at lunch in addition to

Lord & Lady W. . . . They shewed me over the house—the new room for receiving—the whole place looks much prettier than before."

After lunch, King briefed Lord Willingdon on the Conference and, in particular, on one aspect of it, which brought about a change in the role of the Governor-General. Henceforth, whoever held that office was to be the representative of the ruling sovereign and all business between Canada and the Mother Country would, in future, be channelled through High Commissioners. King's advice to Willingdon was that, under the changed circumstances, "He was the King's representative & should model his acts on the King's." A word of caution about not making too many speeches seems to have fallen on deaf ears and before too many months had passed, King was remarking that it was difficult to keep the Governor-General from public speaking but that 'He speaks well and likes it'.

On 1 July 1927, Canada celebrated the Diamond Jubilee of Confederation and, in Ottawa, the occasion was marked by much pomp and circumstance. For King, the day got off to a confused start when the water overflowed in his bathroom and the new butler got his foot stuck in the lift door where he was imprisoned for an hour or so. While others were trying to free the poor butler, King went over his speeches for the last time before meeting Their Excellencies in front of the Confederation Building. For King, the most exciting item on a busy day's program was the dedication of the Carillon in the Peace Tower. The bells had arrived in May, huge bells which made King fear for the strength of the tower. Thanks to the Governor-General's decision to review the Guard for a second time that morning, the ceremonies in front of the Peace Tower got off to a slow start and as a consequence, King was rushed with his speech and decided to cut out part of it thus finishing it a full five minutes before the clock in the Tower struck 12 noon.

Working relations between Lord Willingdon and King were, on the whole, very cordial, a welcome change from affairs during the latter part of Byng's tenure. The only bone of contention—and it was a small one—appears to have been on a matter of precedence during a visit later that summer by the Prince of Wales and Prince George (later King George VI) as well as Stanley Baldwin, the British Prime Minister. King greeted them at Quebec City and escorted them back to Ottawa where a full program had been arranged. Two of the events, the dedication of the altar in the Memorial Chamber in the Peace Tower and the unveiling of the statue of Sir Wilfrid Laurier called for the correct protocol and this created a difference of opinion between King and His Excellency. King was never at his best in such a situation. He fussed and fretted especially where Royalty was involved but the Governor-General took a conciliatory stand:

> *I can't alter my view that my suggested arrangement is the best one and that your anxieties as to what the public will feel at the party driving up unescorted by their host are really, if I may say so, exaggerated. . . . .Anyhow, H. R. H. and Baldwin are the guests of the Government with you as its Prime Minister and you have a perfect right to organize the matter as you wish.* Pray, [the Governor-General continued] *don't look on this as a serious disagreement between us two. These wretched details of arrangements as to ceremonial matters are not of grave constitutional importance!*

King took this advice but he was just a bit annoyed when Their Excellencies arrived on the scene about ten minutes early. All went well in the Memorial Chamber but when it came time for the unveiling of the Laurier statue, the gremlins seem to have been at work against King's big moment to honour his old political hero.

> *To my great chagrin, just as we arrived the flags fell off & the officials of the Public Works had to mount ladders & rearrange them. The seating was in the open without a canopy overhead, or 'loud speakers' provided. . . . This made our distinguished guests very restive & restless.*

They obviously found King's speech too long and boring but he persevered because "I was thinking not of them but of Laurier & the country". While this was going on, the Prince of Wales, now on his 'third imperial tour' of Canada, "was in anything but a pleasant mood . . . talking . . . laughing . . . behaving really badly in the presence of the large throng." So upsetting were the circumstances that when his speech was over at last, King forgot to ask H.R.H. to unveil the monument and had to go back again to invite him to do so!

It was with a sense of relief, quite likely on both sides, that the Royal party moved on to western Canada a few days later. Official Ottawa could relax but at Rideau Hall, the bills were just coming in and, as a result, King was asked by the Governor-General for a grant of $5000 to cover expenses. This exasperated him: "I am beginning to be 'fed up' with this English invasion & all the Diamond Jubilee celebrations and ceremonies."

But this was not the last time the King Government had to dig deep to cover costs during the Willingdons' stay in Canada. In Quebec City, the Citadel, the summer residence of the Governors-General, was in a sorry state of repair. Lord Dufferin and his family had first used it when he was Governor-General in the 1870s but by the 1930s it was hardly livable. Lighting, heating and plumbing were brought up to date and then Lady Willingdon stepped in to oversee the decorations. Her colour scheme was as expected: "Those who are familiar with Lady Willingdon's color preferences would expect the lilacs, amethysts and soft greens that are in her private room. Her bedroom walls are tinted Primrose . . . the rug is lilac." During a visit to the Citadel in December 1928, Lord Willingdon wrote to King about "this wonderful home you have given us and to thank you and your colleagues for having the courage to organize this ancient spot."

In September 1927 when the Prince of Wales and his party were still in the West, the Willingdons took a short holiday.

> *My only trouble, [the Governor-General wrote back to King] is that I can't keep off the golf links and am in a state of complete exhaustion every evening. . . . I hope you are really taking a holiday. The life of the Prime Minister of Canada is and must be one of increasing stress and strain and you must, please, take every possible step to ensure yr. complete health and wellbeing before the session comes on. You will be saying this Governor-General is a perfect nuisance with his constant lecturing about yr. health.*

Their Excellencies were both concerned every time King was a bit under the weather. A message might come from Willingdon saying 'My dear Prime Minister, I'm sorry to hear you have a cold. . . . Can I come down tomorrow evening and have a cup of tea with you and we'll have a talk.' Another time it might be a note from Lady Willingdon, telling him of a tonic that she was sending over to him. 'P.S. Swear to me to take the tonic, won't you?' It was only when King found that his Sundays were being intruded on that he began to consider the Governor-General to be a 'perfect nuisance'. "Sunday is my right", he insisted, on being asked to "come down to Govt House any time today, to lunch or dinner, or any other time, except tea time. . . . I felt I must make my stand for Sunday rest, recreation & chance to be quiet & reflect & work & right to go to church." And it was not until after the church service that he went to Rideau Hall where he made his point clear. "I spoke out about my desire [to keep] Sunday free of engagements. His Ex. accepted all in fine spirit. . . . I had to take the stand. It was a bold piece of business on my part to turn up in morning clothes, not dress clothes, etc., and to make quite clear that I was not going to yield on Sunday entertainment!"

There were other things which annoyed King about the Willingdons, some important, some less so but to a person of King's sensitivity they loomed large. His diary gives one instance of what was, to him a slight to the office of the Prime Minister of Canada. He had been staying at the Citadel with the Willingdons in June 1929, and one day they drove out to a luncheon party in the country. King had been given the little 'jump seat' and had to sit sideways as they drove along. He was not happy about this seeming indignity: "I know nothing was meant, but it shows what a wrong sense of proportion people come to have & especially those from the old country in relation to people here. The truth is this whole business of Govr. Genl. (from the old land) is getting completely out of date. It will disappear ere long. I have favoured keeping an old country gentleman in the position but it will take very little to cause our people to end it all." Another little thing that irked King was the Willingdons' propensity for 'rushing to and fro'. This was a trait of Lady Willingdon in particular and the Governor-General sometimes referred, jokingly, to this in letters to King but nowhere, in their correspondence, is there any hint that the Willingdons had other than the most congenial of feelings towards him. If they sensed his testiness at times, they ignored it. Absences of either party from Ottawa were marked by letters that speak for themselves. "We miss you horribly and Ottawa does not seem half so nice and interesting without you here to talk about everything." and "We look upon you as a real friend", were typical messages to King. In January 1931, Lord Willingdon's tour of duty came to an end with his posting to India as Viceroy and, writing on shipboard en route to England, Lady Willingdon expressed their feelings:

> *I cannot tell you how I felt about saying goodbye to you, dear friend. You have always been so wonderful to us ever since we landed in Canada till the moment we left. God bless you and keep you until we meet again and may that not be very far distant. Anyhow, anyway, anywhere, I shall never forget you and love you always. Your ever grateful, Marie Willingdon.*

By the time the Willingdons left Canada, R. B. Bennett had replaced King as Prime Minister as the result of the election, which had been held

Earl of Bessborough

on 29 July 1930. Over at Rideau Hall, the 14th Governor-General, Lord Bessborough and Roberte, Lady Bessborough, took up residence in the spring of 1931. In a letter from India, Lord Willingdon asked King about them: "I do hope the Bessboroughs are doing well. You say nothing about them in yr letter, but I hope you have met them & formed a good impression of them." Actually, King saw less of the Bessboroughs than of any Governor-General and his wife since he had first come to Ottawa in 1900. Even during the years when his work took him out of the country, he still had enough time at home to participate in the social life of the capital. He was still young then, an 'eligible young bachelor'; in 1931, he was fifty-seven years old and with the exception of Lord Willingdon who still urged him to give up the celibate state, no one seriously thought of him any longer as a 'good catch'. But for a period in the late twenties and early thirties, he appeared on the social scene as little as possible and that, grudgingly. "Another dinner . . . luncheon . . . tea. These social problems are hell, when it comes to work & efficiency therefor & yet it seems impossible to stop them." In his determination to cut out what he felt were non-essential invitations, he was helped and guided by messages received through visions, dreams and from mediums who contacted those in the Beyond. It was a comfort to him that their advice coincided exactly with what he was thinking himself: eat less, exercise more and get more sleep.

All of these contacts, especially the ones with 'dear Mother' helped him through the years when he was leader of the Opposition and feeling left out of things. He did not adjust well to seeing Bennett as advisor to the Governor-General, a role which he, himself, had played during most of the twenties. One diary entry during this time shows his pique at being overlooked. In August 1931, he attended a dinner party at Government House in honour of Their Majesties, the King and Queen of Siam, and was not presented to the Queen until late in the evening. It was galling, too, "to find an A.D.C., General Panet, who is a flunkey on the tour, introduced before me. . . . After being Prime Minister of Canada, for nearly 9 years and a member of both the Canadian and Imperial Privy Council, this was hardly befitting."

King reserved his criticism then and on subsequent occasions not for Lord Bessborough himself but for the office which he held. Carrying on where he had left off in this matter during the Willingdon period in Canada, he was highly critical: "It seemed ridiculous too to have an Englishman only a few months in the country going the rounds as a sort of master of ceremonies & 'manufactured sovereign'—'made in Canada' when we who are born Canadians are made to take a second place." King's stand on this question became almost a phobia with him. So strongly did he feel about it that he concluded: "I was right when I spoke of shutting up Govt. Houses for 6 months. This will start a move to abolish them, which should be followed. I think we would be well rid of Govt. House here—the mixing of 'social position', etc, with the business of government is all a mistake. It has led to the wrong people getting control & prevents the right ones having a chance. I am glad I stood out as I have against social frivolity in its relation to public affairs." A few days after this outburst, King brought up the subject with Winston Churchill who was visiting Ottawa by pointing out to him the benefit of changing the system, "how it avoided a breach with the Crown if a mistake made & used Kipling's phrase 'We have our own sulphur & our own matches & can make our own Hell, thank you', in speaking of the wisdom of letting Dominions make their own decisions in a manner which does not reflect on Br. Crown."

Not having anything personal against the Bessboroughs (except when they made the same mistake as their predecessors and asked him to Rideau Hall on a Sunday), King accepted their invitations when possible. Things had changed under the new Governor-General. As remembered by a former A.D.C., 'Lord Bessborough was not a sport. He didn't go in for playing games, either indoors or out. He didn't even care about watching others play them. Bridge was the exception." Since King did not play bridge, what was left to him were the dinner parties and the dances. As to the latter, he was more often to be found 'sitting out' except for duty dances. His host and hostess were unlike the Willingdons; they lacked the colourfulness and dash but were recalled as being 'modest, simple and shy'. This was especially true of the Governor-General. Roberte, Lady Bessborough, the French-born chatelaine of Rideau Hall, was remembered by King as being "one of the most beautiful women I have ever seen. . . . [There was also] that indefinable something called charm, which she had in such measure and which enhanced her loveliness." He echoed these sentiments in writing glowingly that "She looked very beautiful, is really the most beautiful woman in some ways that I have ever seen. . . . She had fascinatingly beautiful eyes, a face full of laughter and sunshine and radiance."

Back in 1925, in the course of a quiet and amicable talk with Byng one evening after dinner, the conversation turned to who might possibly succeed him in the following year. King had then put forward the name of John Buchan, a suggestion that had come to him from Sir Campbell Stuart, a Canadian who held several British directorships including one at the London Times. This would be popular with influential Canadians in Britain and it appealed to Byng who was a personal friend of Buchan. King had met Buchan some years earlier through Violet Markham, and was immediately impressed by his personality and his 'delightful quiet English manner'. In 1924, when John Buchan and his wife, Susan, visited Canada, they were King's guests at Kingsmere overnight and his assessment of Buchan was glowing in the extreme. "I know no man I would rather have as a friend, a beautiful, noble soul, kindly & generous in thought & word & act, informed as few men in this world have ever been, modest, humble, true, man after God's own heart." King did not record any discussion with Buchan as to his feelings about being considered a possible Governor-General but efforts went on behind the scenes. With Violet Markham acting as 'an unofficial postbox' in England, King's views on Buchan as a candidate were passed on to members of the British Government and to the Colonial Office, but Buchan himself was lukewarm to the notion and would not actively seek the appointment. As time went on and the King-Byng crisis developed, Buchan was reportedly quite happy to be passed over in favour of Lord Willingdon in 1926. He had Byng's side of the story and, as well, he had a letter from Lady Byng that likely did not help:

> *My dear John, . . . we really have had a far far more hellish time than any of you at home can realize or believe . . . what a scurvy cad M. K. is and always has been. . . . Power is his watch-word—the power of M. K. . . . A true Judas Iscariot. . . . That he should have dared behave as he did, even I, who always despised and knew him, hardly expected, and God knows I expected a goodish deal of filth, once his power was in danger.*

A decade and two Governors-General later, Buchan's name came up again for discussion. In a letter to Violet Markham in April 1935, King informed her that

> *to permit of the Bessboroughs' getting back to England this fall, Bennett was obliged not only to confer with me about a successor, if the appointment were to be made before a general election, but to have someone who would be acceptable to me. He let me make my own nomination, and I suggested the names of Buchan and Spender. . . . [H]e accepted Buchan saying that he regarded mention of his name as an inspiration.*

Buchan, however, was still not certain that he wanted the post. A great list-maker by habit, he now sat down with one headed 'Against', the other 'For'. In the first he wrote that it would be

> *Too easy a job for a comparatively young man.*
> *A week further away from Mother.*
> *A country and a people without much glamour.*

> On the other side of the coin, he thought that it would be
> *A very easy life for J. B. . . .*
> *The fact that I have been paid the enormous honour of being asked by both Bennett and M. K.*
> *Only five days from England.*
> *Apart from special clothes and uniforms, we could do it on our salary.*

In the end he was persuaded, but when he arrived in Quebec City on 29 November 1935, he was greeted officially by his newly acquired title of Lord Tweedsmuir by all except King. He had earlier told Buchan that "It is as John Buchan, the commoner chosen to represent His Majesty in other spheres, that you will find the warmest welcome and an abiding place in the hearts of Canadians." When the news of the appointment reached King, he had gloried in the fact that "I have broken the precedent of going to the Lords, to the privileged class [for] the King's representative, have had a Commoner selected. . . . It is all quite splendid." Before long, however, rumours spread that Buchan had been offered a peerage, which he felt he could not refuse. Indeed, he did not wish to refuse. In the list of 'Againsts' and 'Fors', one of the latter was that 'an immediate peerage might revive

Lord & Lady Tweedsmuir

Mother' who complained every year when the Honours Lists came out and her son was not mentioned. As soon as she heard of his appointment as Governor-General her reaction was that 'I am sure the King is fortunate to get you' but there had been no word of a peerage and this bothered the elderly and proud lady. "But surely the King cannot go back on that for this appointment. I must say I would like to live to see you a Peer."

Faced with the *fait accompli*, there was little King could do but accept it. He could not, however, resist mentioning the loss of Buchan's 'ancient Scottish name' in a letter of congratulations. He was writing from Kingsmere which, in his own mind, was becoming associated with Buchan and the friendship he hoped would flower in that environment. To this end, he began to set the scene. When the Buchans had visited him in 1924, they had stayed in what he now referred to as the 'vice-regal lodge', the small cottage beside his old one down by the lake. Since then he had moved up to Moorside and had made many improvements to the house and grounds. More were in the planning stage. On reading that Buchan had a Roman ruin on his own grounds at Elsfield House, near Oxford, and that he also had an altar, (actually part of an old temple), King went into action. He had thought of 'ruins' for Kingsmere a year earlier in relation to bringing part of his grandfather Mackenzie's house from Toronto to save it from destruction. He gave up that idea as being too costly and, instead, had a semicircular stone window and stone doorway from an old Ottawa house which was being torn down, erected in the form of a 'ruin' at Moorside. "I think and speak of it as my 'abbey', and to more minds than my own it has brought thoughts of Melrose, and even of the Parthenon!", he wrote to Buchan. "In the construction of this ruin . . . you were constantly in my thoughts. I am looking forward with childish delight to showing it to you when you come." Buchan expressed his pleasure that "like Sir Walter Scott I was bringing 'fragments' of great buildings, etc. to . . .

Kingsmere. What a joy it will be to share the spiritual companionship which Buchan's coming is sure to mean." And what a disappointment to discover that his hopes for a close companionship could not be realized.

As Lord Tweedsmuir, John Buchan came to Canada intent of getting along with his Prime Minister and, on that level, he was largely successful but, on the personal side, the two men were vastly different in temperament. Any chance of real closeness was impossible and not even the recently assembled 'ruins' could make any appreciable difference. They did have some things in common: both had Scottish family backgrounds and both belonged to the Presbyterian Church. Politics was important to each of them, but Buchan's experience in the field fell far short of King's total commitment. As well, both were literary men with King having to his credit books relating to his political and social interests whereas John Buchan was a widely read popular writer. And they both loved their mothers. But it was their differences that got in the way. In *John Buchan*, his official biography written in the 60s, a portrait is drawn of a man who was by nature gentle, intelligent and with plenty of ambition. In those lists of Things to Do which he made up so often, there is no false modesty about what he expected to accomplish. As for becoming Lord Tweedsmuir, he 'frankly enjoyed having a title' but could leave ceremony alone. On his many trips across Canada, he wrote to a friend that "We'll take the red carpet with us because that's what the people like. Then step out, leave them [it?] all behind, and talk to people." Back at Rideau Hall, however, ceremony was strictly observed much to the dismay of his friends who visited from overseas or from the United States.

The picture of King as portrayed in *John Buchan* is not flattering. He is presented as someone whom Buchan 'could not bring himself wholeheartedly to like.' It seemed to him that King was practising a mother cult with pictures of her all around the house; that he was embarrassingly emotional at times; that he was convinced of his own greatness and always had to be first; that he longed to be loved but 'he never put himself out for his friends, or allowed them to make demands upon him'; that his style 'in talks speeches and letters recalled the unctuousness of that type of Scottish Liberal' whom Buchan had reacted against strongly in his youth. Added to all this was the fact that King was a spiritualist who had J.M. Barrie on his reading list and the Governor-General had earlier dismissed much of that author's work as not being cerebral enough. That King was also reading Scott, Lloyd George, Shelley and Wordsworth as well as some of

Buchan's own books did nothing to bring them any nearer to those 'quiet talks' which King had been anticipating.

It was not until after Buchan's death in early 1940 that King learned he was not the only person who found it difficult to relate to the Governor-General. Sir Shuldham Redfern, an A.D.C. at Rideau Hall, told King one day that he "found the Tweedsmuirs very self-centred. Also that he (Redfern) could never get him to enter into a sustained conversation on anything. That he seemed to want to push everything away from himself and go back to his books and papers. . . . There was complete detachment in every way." King was relieved to hear this and "said to R. that I felt he saw himself in terms of *Augustus*—the book that he had written. Of course I think that what, above everything else, governed his every thought and action was his being the King's representative. That was really a religion with him."

Within months of Tweedsmuir's arrival in Canada, King reluctantly had to admit that it had been a shock to him to discover in the Governor-General "a Tory with . . . a super consciousness of his position, a sort of royalty 'complex' which is damnable in my eyes. I cannot abide it, as different from the Willingdons as day from night." One evening at Rideau Hall, King's feelings came tumbling out. He felt slighted by the manner in which he had been greeted that evening and at having been left 'to struggle in [to dinner] as though I were a school boy'. In a talk later that evening, King aired all his grievances. Prominent among them was the fact that, "[having] been friends for twenty years or more, he had never addressed me by my first name or last, but always as Prime Minister . . . [and even] when his staff was not present at no time did he call me either Mackenzie or King, as he had done for so many years." This outburst startled them both and it was a struggle to improve their personal relationship. A few weeks later, a visit by the Tweedsmuirs to Kingsmere turned out to be "a very friendly natural afternoon. If we could have gotten off originally on that foot—the whole present relationship might be quite different. However, today has helped." Yet, despite all their best efforts, a cloud hung over their relationship until near the end of Tweedsmuir's life.

This feeling of estrangement was more easily put aside when they were dealing with official concerns and as 1936 was drawing to a close, they had to face one of major proportions. Gone was any hope that King Edward VIII could ride out the storm that was engulfing his private life. His affair with Mrs. Wallis Simpson, an American, attracted much attention for this seemed to be more serious than any of his other dalliances. When her divorce was finalized in late October, the politicians began to put pressure on the British monarch to renounce Mrs. Simpson. As all the world knows, the end result was the King's abdication in December. Throughout these last few weeks, King and Tweedsmuir worked together on the constitutional implications and found themselves in total agreement. In a letter to Lady Tweedsmuir who was back in England for a visit, the Governor-General wrote "I have had my Prime Minister all afternoon and evening yesterday.... My Prime Minister and I see absolutely eye to eye in the business and I hope we have been of some support to Stanley Baldwin.... We have certainly set the key for the rest of the Empire. I am bound to say my Prime Minister has been extraordinarily wise and sagacious in everything he has done."

In 1939 they were involved in another Royal event, this time a happier one. When King was in London in May 1937, to attend the Coronation of King George VI, he took the opportunity of presenting an invitation to the new Royal couple to visit Canada. The Palace accepted the idea, which had come through the Governor-General, and planning got underway. There were no guidelines to follow for this was the first time a reigning monarch would have visited any Dominion. One stipulation was that the trip must not be too strenuous in order that it might be enjoyable for Their Majesties. That, as well as the protocol of their arrival in Canada, was not an easy matter. Tweedsmuir's feeling was that "I should like to keep as much in the background as possible, and let it be Canada's show. I cease to exist as Viceroy, and retain only a shadowy legal existence as Governor-General in Council." His idea was that he would disappear from the scene except to entertain Their Majesties while they were in Ottawa, but he would greet them on their arrival at Quebec. It was this latter part of the plan that did not appeal to King. He was the Prime Minister of the country and therefore he should be the one to welcome them. Volumes of correspondence crossed the Atlantic before the issue was resolved in King's favour, thus escaping another constitutional crisis.

The plans made, there was some worry lest the visit would be postponed due to the gravity of the European situation. For his part, Tweedsmuir took the stand that the visit must go ahead, that the 'infernal dictators' must not be allowed to interfere with the visit. In early May 1939, the Royal Party sailed only to be delayed by ice off Newfoundland and the Governor-General's cry was 'What induced the North Atlantic suddenly to go Nazi?'

The plans were hastily reshuffled and once underway, the success of the visit surpassed all expectations. The young Royal couple entered easily into the schedule, many of the details having been overseen by King who thought no point too insignificant to be checked personally. After a triumphal tour of Quebec, the visit to Ottawa—three days which were packed with official and social events—Their Majesties left for western Canada with King as Minister in attendance. In this, he had to fight his way past opposition, which he called "another court manoeuvre to euchre me out of this obvious duty", but he made the point that "It was absolutely imperative that someone who could speak with authority should be on board." His duties would include leaving the railway car and, with the King's attendants, be at the platform where the King and Queen would appear on stops across the country. He would then introduce the Lieutenant-Governor of the province and his officials to Their Majesties. So adept did King become at this that the apocryphal story went the rounds that, on the return of Their Majesties to Buckingham Palace, the King looked behind the drapes on occasion to see if his Canadian Prime Minister were there. Tweedsmuir had expected that there might be some comedy before the Canadian trip was over and he was proven right when the press carried stories about an event that happened on the Royal train. It seems that the King's barber who weighed some sixteen stone (about 225 lbs.) fell out of his bunk on top of the Queen's hairdresser, a slight man of only half that weight, and, as the story went, nearly scalped him.

This tour was quite an experience for King who not only went on the entire Canadian trip but he also accompanied Their Majesties on their visit to President and Mrs. Roosevelt in Washington. He was said to look ten years younger at the conclusion and it was with a renewed air of self-confidence that he settled back into the Ottawa routine. He was determined that "I must speak and act more and more on my own, as one with authority and right to do so". And although jokes might be made as to his over-assiduous behaviour during the tour, it pleased him to read that "[The] press generally comments on my having been 'self-effacing' throughout the Royal tour & have come round to praise my having carried out the arrangements."

In September, the European situation boiled over and war was declared with Canada entering the fray on the 10th of the month, a week after Britain's declaration and just long enough later to show that Canada was a sovereign nation. With the outbreak of war, the Governor-General's work changed. "It was, as you know", he wrote to an old friend, "principally educative, travelling everywhere and trying to make the different parts of Canada understand each other. . . . Now I shall have nothing to do except review troops, keep an eye on war charities to prevent waste (I am President of most of them) and hold the hands of Ministers."

The end of Tweedsmuir's time as Governor-General was coming up at the end of September 1940 and King, who was loath to see him go, invited him to stay for the duration of the war, or, at least, for another year but the Governor-General declined. His health, always frail in spite of a spell in a clinic in North Wales (after which it was jokingly said that he looked less like an El Greco and more like a Rubens) and the very restricted diet (which caused him to remark that he was glad he enjoyed his vices when he had them)—these two things made for reason enough to yearn for a quieter life. But there was another element: Lady Tweedsmuir had not wished to come to Canada in the first place. Foremost on her mind was the state of her husband's health, but also her interest in social work in England, especially with Women's Institutes, had become a very satisfying way of life for her. Lady Tweedsmuir was not interested in winter sports but the Governor-General skied until he found he was spending too much time stuck in a snowbank (and was afraid that he might break because he was so lean that he must also be brittle). Self-centred both the Tweedsmuirs may have appeared to their staff at Rideau Hall, but these same critics recognized that "Although deeply influenced by Lord Tweedsmuir and overshadowed by him, she was intensely human . . . [and] had a quiet dignity [but] the requirements of her position . . . [and] now and again the limitations depressed her."

King had his usual problem in getting to know the wife of a Governor-General. At a dinner, which he gave for the Tweedsmuirs soon after their arrival, he noted that he found it very difficult to talk to her because she "is not too responsive and has little to contribute". But what chance did the poor lady have? "It is unfortunate, also, that I had placed to her right Arthur Hardy forgetting that he was so deaf." And while a visit to Kingsmere in the spring of 1936 went very well, he could not help feeling that Lady Tweedsmuir did not like him. It was not until over a year later that things improved when he discovered that "she was interested in having record of dreams & visions . . . we talked a little of [Canon] Streeter, she mentioned some other books she was sending me (re a 'forth' [fourth?] dimension)." Encouraged by that show of interest, King took the Tweedsmuirs into his confidence as to his great interest in spiritualism. At a dinner party at Laurier House, he showed them items of interest to him including what he called 'the dark room' where seances were held on occasion. "[Tweedsmuir] spoke of this as 'muniments' room. I can see that this interested him very much, and will begin, later on, arranging something of the kind at his home at Elsfield." It is doubtful that the Governor-General was any more interested in spiritualism than Violet Markham had been and, in the end, King gave up on them both. A few nights later he had a chat with Lady Tweedsmuir about *Experiment with Time*, a book which she liked because "it dealt with things on a mathematical basis rather than psychical. This [King recorded] is characteristic of those who are blind because they will not see, and who are determined to have their minds conform with the conventions of the time."

On 25 January 1940, the Governor-General opened Parliament and at once granted King dissolution in order to prepare for a general election in March. During the latter part of the day, the two men had a long talk, possibly the last discussion of any length that they were to have. When they turned to the timing of the election call, the Governor-General complimented King on having

> *a greater political flare [sic] than any man he had ever met, not excepting Lloyd George. . . . he was sure [the election] would all come out well. I told him I was quite indifferent to that; that if I won, I would try to go on. . . . As we were coming away, he made some reference to talking over some of his future plans.*

As it turned out, Tweedsmuir was not spared to see the election through or to enjoy a life in retirement. On 6 February, the Governor-General suffered a stroke and died two days later in hospital in Montreal. The funeral services were held in St. Andrew's Presbyterian Church, Ottawa, with King attending to all the details with his usual thoroughness. He could not, in all honesty, say that he was mourning for a friend as had been the case with Harper but it had been an established fact that there was not to be or to seem to be any misunderstanding between himself and the Tweedsmuirs. The title had, indeed, got in the way and Violet Markham was, perhaps, right when she wrote to King that 'J.B.' should have gone to Canada as 'John Buchan'. Would that have helped? Would it even have helped had there been a well-stocked trout stream running through King's property where Tweedsmuir, the enthusiastic angler, could spend some

The Earl of Athlone & H.R.H. Princess Alice

time? If so, it is unlikely to have been a time shared by King who knew very well how to cast for votes but who probably never even held a fishing rod in his hand. There were just too many differences.

In the spring of 1941 it was learned that the Earl of Athlone had been named as the next Governor-General of Canada. The fact that he was married to Princess Alice turned King's mind again to past history. "It would be a fine thing for a grandson of William Lyon Mackenzie to appoint the grand-daughter of Queen Victoria—to have her husband as the King's representative in Canada." That rounding of the circle appealed to King who also took comfort in the feeling that "One thing about them is that they will know their job and make no mistakes." On 22 June, the Athlones reached Halifax after a hazardous crossing of the submarine-infested Atlantic and two days later were in Ottawa. It was the first time that Princess Alice had visited the city but Athlone had been there in 1901 when he accompanied his brother-in-law and sister, later King George V and Queen Mary, on an official visit. It had been an occasion in which King, then a young Deputy Minister, shared. He and Bert Harper turned up for the Procession in frock coats and silk hats that morning in 1901 and the evening scene was one to inspire the diarist in King.

> *[The] illuminations [were] really most beautiful, the finest I have ever seen. The parks & grounds were hung with deep crimson lanterns; the electrical display was magnificent. The outlines of the buildings, windows etc., were one mass of small incandescent lights, and when the whole ablaze, the sight was one never to be forgotten, the flower beds have small lights scattered thro', then the International [the Interprovincial] bridge was illuminated. The effect of the two colours, the diamond-like white & the deep red was most refined and charming. With the music it was like a Persian garden, with the girls there too—a fairy & dream land."*

It was quite a different Ottawa that greeted the new Viceregal couple in 1941. The capital was a much more somber place in wartime and, as soon as the Governor-General was sworn in, his work commenced. Princess Alice, like almost every other chatelaine before her, immediately turned Rideau Hall upside down and pronounced herself satisfied with the results. It was only because there were spending restrictions at the time that some of Lady Willingdon's mauve silk drapes were not replaced but the dye pot came to the rescue. That done, Princess Alice was ready to turn her considerable energies to work relating to the war effort. She accompanied her husband on many visits to plants that turned out war goods but her special interest was in the Women's Divisions of the three Canadian services. Wherever the Athlones went in the line of duty, they were well-received and greatly admired. The same applied to their relations with the staff at Government House. The knowledge that both were members of the Royal family caused a bit of anxiety before their arrival but it soon became evident that, as King had expected, they were 'to the manner born' and they knew their jobs. As it turned out, they were no more royal in behaviour than many of their predecessors and decidedly more pleasant to work with than some others.

As far as King was concerned the Athlone years passed with very little friction between him and the new Rideau Hall tenants. With them, there was none of the high expectations that he had held for a personal friendship as had been the case with Tweedsmuir and their contacts both social and professional were by and large successful. The demands of the war were great on both sides and, as well, King was growing older and becoming more concerned about his own affairs. Although he and the Governor-General were the same age, the years had been less kind to King who had led a solitary life, always struggling to achieve ever higher personal goals. By the early 40s, his thoughts were often on retirement but still he hung on, waiting until the time was right and working out the numbers of days and months he would still have to put in before he beat all others' records. He was often depressed and feeling 'a terrible loneliness at times' but he pressed on to fight and win an election in June 1945, after which he received the congratulations of the Governor-General during a call at Rideau Hall. That was not enough for him, though. In retrospect, he felt slighted that he had not had any written word of congratulations from Athlone and, further, that "Princess Alice, who was in the garden, did not come in to extend her congratulations . . . our relations being as close as they are. The trouble with those people is that their concern lies in what is going best to meet their own convenience. There are few if any wiser sayings than: 'Put not your faith in Princes.' I am beginning more and more to see that the upholding of monarchy is a form of idolatry."

What King had vainly hoped would happen during the Tweedsmuir years became a custom with Athlone who often dropped in at Kingsmere during the summer to have a cup of tea and a chat. Sometimes Princess Alice would accompany him but he was alone in late July 1943, partaking of tea, toast and fresh strawberry jam with King.

> *The Governor [sic] thoroughly enjoyed the jam. Took no less than 3 helpings, [and then proceeded] in an embarrassed sort of way [to ask me] if I had any little cottage I could let him and Princess Alice have for a few days. . . . After canvassing different situations, the Governor asked about the little Farm House here. I at once said: Of course, they would be most welcome here . . . He said in a quite simple way, it is strange, he said; we have wanted to be in that little house.*

It was all part of the 'whirligig of time' in King's mind that "the granddaughter of Queen Victoria would be finding her moment of rest and quiet and peace in the home of [a descendent of William Lyon Mackenzie]" and the coincidence was fortified when King 's mind went to the fact that in the following week he "would be entertaining the President of [the] United States and the Prime Minister of Britain at the Citadel of Quebec (where my father's father's remains lie)."

The Citadel was put on the map, historically, when this meeting, the first Quebec Conference, was held there in August 1943. A little over a year later, the same three allied leaders met there once more and each time the Governor-General and Princess Alice were on hand to extend the hospitality of their summer home which had been turned into a meeting place and guest house for the distinguished visitors. King's own role there had been a matter of some contention, but of one thing he was convinced: he was the overall host. From his diaries, it is evident that he was in his element during these two conferences and much more at ease than when he had been a guest of the Athlones on earlier occasions. He had been there a few months after their arrival in Canada and while he found them thoroughly agreeable as hosts, the formality of Government House life was more tiring to him than a week's hard work. He was also at the Citadel for a two-day visit shortly before the second Conference and was in a weary mood which only resulted in his feeling

> completely ill at ease throughout the whole of the visit. . . . Had I been in prison I could not have felt more constrained. . . . It cannot be helped but here it is. [It had not been] the fault of His Excellency and Her Royal Highness. They did their utmost to make me feel happy and comfortable; it was just a return of the old feeling of revolt at anyone from the Old Country exercising even outwardly any semblance of control over Canada.

In late 1944, King was going through the usual process of considering a successor to Athlone when his term would be up in the following spring. He had been anxious for some time to have a Canadian in the post and put forward General A.G.L. McNaughton's name one day in a chat with Athlone. The idea seems to have met with a favourable reception. "He said nothing about it being any break in the tradition." King's arguments for the change stressed the point "That having gone as high as we could [in the case of the present appointment], our choice would necessarily be limited to someone of lesser rank overseas, and that it was increasingly difficult to secure the right persons for the office." King did not say what had been irritating him greatly: "Government House in Canada and in the provinces has come more and more to stand for a certain Grand Hotel and first class inns at which members of the aristocracy and others in places of privilege from the Old Land are to be entertained on their visits to Canada." The plans to have a Canadian become Governor-General came to a halt, however, when McNaughton decided to try to enter politics. This was a disappointment to King who would not entertain the idea of Vincent Massey for the post but had no other Canadian candidate to put forward. Again, discussion focused on a British successor to Athlone and on 24 July 1945 King received a message from Buckingham Palace to the effect that "the King was much pleased at being given an opportunity to express preference re the Governor-General and giving reasons why he thought Sir Harold Alexander would be preferable."

It was a happy choice as far as King was concerned. "I should have noted a few days ago", he recalled, "that on Saturday last a picture appeared in the Journal showing Sir Harold Alexander and his wife in the garden giving their little boy a swing. As soon as I saw that picture it settled my mind at once as to his being the right person." But it was not only the picture that convinced King that the choice was the right one for the times.

Viscount & Lady Alexander

"Alexander has the qualities of a very wise diplomat. I am sure too the Canadian people will like the appointment, which is particularly appropriate at a time when the country will be filled with returned men, many of whom have served under Alexander." There was also the fact that the appointment of a military man would show that King had no prejudices in this respect despite his problems with Byng.

King had surmised soon after the Alexanders and their family arrived in Ottawa early in April 1946, that he and the new Governor-General would get on well together and so it proved to be. In public as well as in private contacts, the relationship not only with Lord Alexander but also with his wife were possibly the happiest of all King's long relations with the tenants of Rideau Hall. During the first two years of Alexander's term, events crowded the one on the other at a rapid pace and, more and more, it became evident to an aging King, that there would be "some breakdown in my nervous system which I cannot watch too carefully. I dare not combine the social and the strictly disciplined life." Cutting down on social events was no longer enough and in order to save energy for the mammoth task of putting his house in order, King did some arithmetic and found that, as of August 1948, the time was right for him to turn over the leadership of the Liberal Party to Louis St. Laurent. In November of that year, he resigned as Prime Minister and when the 1949 election was fought, he decided not to run. On the night of the opening of the House, King was the guest of the Alexanders at a private dinner party that bridged his entry into the realm of being an elder statesman. The talk around the table and after dinner left him in a reflective mood as he " [viewed] the scene and all it represented from the side lines and yet I can see I would not have been equal to another parliament. . . . If I can only get back my health." It was too late for such a wish to come true and King used what strength he could gather during the winter of 1949-50 in finally getting his will made and in giving some thought to the writing of his memoirs and the life of his grandfather, neither of which was even begun. In June 1950, he made his final move out to Kingsmere and there, a few days later, the Governor-General and Lady Alexander visited him. It was timed to coincide with the prorogation of the Parliament, which King had observed only from the sidelines. Assuredly, the kindness of this visit eased any loneliness he might have felt on the occasion.

A month later, on 22 July, King died in his beloved Kingsmere. He had been close to Rideau Hall and its tenants for a full half century. As a guest, he had crossed the threshold often—too often in his view—but he had to bow to the demands of protocol which, in truth, he did not find too difficult. On the official side, he had made his views known to the various Governors-General on the constitutional matters that arose from time to time, the most notable being the so-called King-Byng affair. When there were 'Royals' at Rideau Hall, he never missed an opportunity to put forth the name of his maternal grandfather and the Rebellion of 1837. And he had seen the role of the Governor-General change during Lord Willingdon's term but in later years, his greatest wish was to have the office belong to a Canadian.

Lord Alexander remained in Ottawa until the winter of 1952 when he was persuaded to return to England and enter the British Cabinet. The choice of a successor became the prerogative of the St. Laurent Government and what King had hoped for over the years became a reality when a Canadian was chosen for the post. The name of Vincent Massey had come up in previous discussions of candidates and had always been dismissed by King who had seen him as 'a place seeker and time server' with whom there had been many contretemps during Massey's days as High Commissioner in London. Had King lived to see this day, one has to wonder if his satisfaction at having a Canadian Governor-General, at last, might have overcome his feelings about Massey.

Rockefeller

"I will not take a business opening, to work for a corporation—however lucrative the offer", was one of the thoughts running through King's mind a few days after his and his Party's defeat at the polls on 21 September 1911. On the one hand, he felt "The sense of relief from the strain of office is almost indescribable. It is the first time for years that I feel as I used to feel when I first came into the civil service." But, being King, he had to rationalize the situation: "I cannot but believe that defeat is all for the best, and that out of this will come opportunities for a fuller & better life." He acknowledged, too, a sense of inadequacy and felt that "I should try in the time immediately ahead to supplement the deficiencies & limitations I have realized while in parliament, particularly as to becoming better informed on Canadian affairs & history." But in all of these rambling thoughts, he still had to face up to the fact that he did not have a job and should consider what paths to pursue. His old, on again, off again, interest in the church as a career had been put aside as something for which he was not temperamentally suited but there was always the possibility of a return to academic work and in its climate he would have time to study and reflect. "A professorship at McGill might prove attractive", he thought, "or the presidency of some college." By the end of the day (which was largely spent in answering letters of condolence on his loss), he had swung around to politics again: "[I]f I can get a seat in parliament, I feel that to be the wise thing to do. With the little I have saved, I could get along on the indemnity, & have time for reading & study, that seems to me the wisest of all courses."

But a return to the House of Commons was not in his immediate future and King entered that period of his life during which he turned his hand to a variety of tasks. This continued to be the situation for almost three years until 1 June 1914, when he received a telegram inviting him to New York to discuss whether or not he might be able to "advise large interests I represent in regard to present labor difficulties and probable far-reaching studies looking toward the future." This telegram was from Jerome D. Greene whom King had known at Harvard and it had been sent on behalf of the Rockefeller Foundation of which Greene was presently secretary. This was the first King even heard of the Foundation's existence but he knew a little about the 'present labor difficulties'—a strike in the Colorado Fuel and Iron Company in which the Rockefellers had a controlling interest. A second telegram from Greene helped clarify what was intended by 'probable far-reaching studies'. It was the Foundation's wish, King was told, to use the strike situation in Colorado as the basis for a study of labour matters in the United States. That was all King knew about it when he went to New York on June 6th. for his first meeting with John D. Rockefeller, Jr. and his advisors. As King later wrote in his diary, Rockefeller told him that

> *When I came to New York on that Saturday morning he had not in mind doing other than getting my advice upon the Colorado situation, and the advisability of instituting a study of the labor problem [but] . . . he was impressed with the manner in which I discussed it with him, and that before the conversation ended he had made up his mind to ask if I would not undertake this work myself.*

Three days later, a telegram from Greene contained a definite proposal of employment for King, employment such as he had never anticipated.

It was not a decision which King could make lightly and during the summer, he sought the advice of personal and political friends, one of them being Violet Markham. In a confidential cable to her he explained the proposal which he felt would be a 'life work' but it would mean giving up Canadian politics. What would she advise? The Rockefellers were not very high in the public opinion polls at this time, being seen as money-grabbing absentee landlords and as such they were the very antithesis of all that Violet and King stood for. Her reply was the soul of reason:

> *You do seem to have come to a stand still in Canada so this unexpected offer of important work elsewhere is not one to cast aside as unthinkable. Frankly I don't like millionaires of the Rockefeller type. One wonders what [he] is after with a proposal of this kind. It is difficult to think a man like that can really care about ideal conditions of labour or*

the higher life of the workers. The first horrid thought which went through my mind was whether this was an attempt to buy you. . . . I couldn't bear the idea that your liberty of thought or action or service should be at the mercy of such a man as Rockefeller—that you should part with one atom of your cherished independence. But, if he is really genuine and sincere in his proposals, if this is a case of honest study & honest work, then I see no reason why you shouldn't accept it.

As to what this move would mean to his political future in Canada, Violet's opinion was: "Why should you not do this job for 10 or 12 years and then come back into Canadian politics?. . . . I am a great believer in fundamental changes at different stages of life. It wakes us up. 'Launch out into the deep and let down the net'." And after weighing the advantages carefully, this was what King did. An agreement was drawn up in early August by which he was named head of the Department of Industrial Relations within the Rockefeller Foundation. Its terms were generous: he was to have $12,000 a year—a princely sum for 1914—and one that would ease his family responsibilities; he would retain his Canadian citizenship and would work out of his apartment in the Roxborough in Ottawa. (A New York office had been assigned to him but he was determined to stay in Canada.). He was also to be given time to engage in Canadian politics when he felt it appropriate. He was not as sure as was Violet that a ten to twelve year absence from Canada would be to his political advantage so the agreement was to be effective for one year at a time.

Having earlier said quite firmly that he would not accept a business opening no matter how good the terms, he was now connected through his employment with one of the wealthiest men in the United States. It was only by reasoning that his work would be for the Foundation where the money was held in trust and not for one of the Rockefeller corporations that he accepted the position. While it looked like a 'Heaven-sent deliverance', he was not sure, at first, that Heaven was on the side of the Rockefellers. What he had known about them up to the time of their first meeting was not very flattering. A mention of their name immediately brought to mind the Standard Oil Companies which were owned by them. Their hands-off policies traditionally resulted in abdicating any responsibility for labour practices and they were opposed to the formation of unions. John D., Sr., had been "described and caricatured for years as a hard man who had reaped where he had not sown and gathered where he had not strawed" and this reputation had also stuck to his son but within months of working together King's opinion of both had changed. By February 1915, he brought Violet up to date regarding his work and his feelings towards John D., Jr. in particular.

> *You will be interested to know . . . that my work . . . is surpassing in interest and satisfaction my most cherished hopes concerning it and that I have found in Mr. John D. Rockefeller, Jr. one of the best of men and most welcome of friends. He is a man of the finest principles and the highest integrity—a man too of quite exceptional ability. It is to me a real inspiration to be associated with him, and the association is becoming a very intimate and delightful one.*

It was to be a friendship between two men who were remarkably similar in their outlook despite their different circumstances in life. They were almost the same age and both were serious about their religious beliefs and their overall expectations of what was needed to make for fulfilling lives. King's friendship with Harper now found expression in this new relationship. It existed in their lofty aims both in the work and the ideals they shared. "I feel a perfect sympathy in all things as we talk together and have felt it since we first met, it is the more extraordinary as it is the last thing I should have expected to experience" was what King reflected after an evening's walk and talk with Rockefeller along the streets of New York at the end of a day's work. "What two men of earnest purpose can accomplish with such an opportunity who can say!"

Since Rockefeller knew little or nothing about King before they first met, it was necessary to fill this gap. One way King chose to accomplish this was to send off a copy of *The Secret of Heroism*, his tribute to Harper, drawing special attention to the last part of the book. There, he emphasized

> *what it means to have the consciousness of another life sharing a like ideal and cooperating towards the realization of it. The letters printed there were written thirteen years ago. Harper and I were beginning then our work for this Dominion. There is so much of similarity in certain aspects of this larger work we have entered upon . . . that it all seems like a new beginning of one vast endeavour.*

King had not taken up his appointment immediately; first there was to be a period of desk-clearing. Ever since his defeat in 1911, he had been speaking and lecturing both in Canada and the United States. When south of the border, he spoke on relations between the two countries or on strike prevention. At home, his topic was on the cause of Liberalism and he was also in charge of the Liberal Information Office, editor of the *Liberal Monthly* and president of the Ontario Reform Association. Before going to work for the Foundation, he had to divest himself of this 'hack work' which was neither financially nor intellectually rewarding. One thing he did not give up was his candidacy for North York, his grandfather's old riding. What these various jobs did ensure was that, although out of active politics, he was still closely associated with the Liberal Party. Thus it was that after war was declared on 4 August 1914 he spent days and nights in conference with Sir Wilfrid Laurier and two other colleagues, drafting Opposition policy. It was not until 1 October that he was free to assume his new responsibilities but during the summer he kept in touch with Rockefeller, giving advice as requested and expressing great anticipation of his work for the Foundation.

> *This frightful war has made me more satisfied than ever with the wisdom of the course I have taken . . . to devote some part of my life to a thorough and far-reaching study of the methods of maintaining and furthering industrial peace. I feel certain . . . that if we can succeed in doing something substantial in this direction we shall also have helped to make a material contribution towards the maintenance of peace in international relations as well.*

And, as seen by one of his early biographers,

> *One finds it difficult to sympathize with those critics who thought Mackenzie King should have abandoned this type of work to become a volunteer in the army. . . . To have taken such a step as this would simply have destroyed an exceptionally useful endeavour to promote industrial peace and hence to accelerate the war effort— in order to obtain the services of an unsuitable and, it must be feared, mechanically inefficient soldier of 44 years of age.**

By early December, King had his work for the Foundation well in hand. Although the Colorado strike had been called off by this time, there

---
*Dawson is incorrect. King was in his 40th year.

was no settlement yet of the miners' grievances. Over seventy companies were involved with most being opposed to any reform but through suggestions passed on over the summer by King to Rockefeller and relayed to the latter's manager in Colorado, there had been a change of attitude. Customarily, American labour disputes of this magnitude had come before the Commission on Industrial Relations with all sides being represented and shortly after King's appointment had been made public, this Commission decided it should take a look at the Colorado dispute. Subpoenas were served on Rockefeller, on Greene and also on King who was then in Ottawa working out his own solution. He was not amused:

> *There seemed to me to be just a little sharp practice or smartness in this. . . . I then drafted a letter . . . which may help to shew the Commission that I know my job, or rather how to go about it, and also that they have laid themselves open to a lesson in courtesy . . . some feeling of jealousy may have prompted it, the intention being to embarrass me if possible.*

There was no avoiding the subpoena and before Rockefeller went on the witness stand in January 1915, King's task was to prepare him for the ordeal. As he saw it, this was an opportunity for the nation's leading industrialist to set out his newly acquired attitude to labour-management relations.

> *[King] did his best to induce him to forsake the traditional Rockefeller attitude of secrecy and extreme caution. He advised, and even preached, in season and out of season, at mealtime, in the office, in walks along New York streets, in the subway, and in the family car.*

It was during this intense 'training period' that King began to appreciate Rockefeller's qualities and he was determined to have him appear before the Commission "as I know him myself, and shall try to have him overcome a natural reticence in the matter of publicly revealing his personality."

During this testimony, King became aware of his protégé's lack of first hand knowledge of conditions at the mines and a trip was planned for March to remedy this. In the end, King had to go alone as Rockefeller's mother died and their joint trip was delayed until September. King's first visit had been something of a whirlwind tour as he

> *went from camp to camp . . . [seeking] information about housing and rents, fencing and gardens, water supply, sanitation facilities, wash houses. . . . He went into the mines and steel mills, workers'*

homes and schools and even into at least one saloon. . . . He talked freely to everyone he came across from [J. F. Welborn] the president [of the Company] to mule-drivers.

It was while visiting the President and Mrs. Welborn one day that he had a break from the strenuous work schedule he had set for himself. Discussions on poetry, religion, art and music made a welcome antidote to the more serious side of his trip. Of this visit to the Welborns, King had an amusing story to relate. His host's farm was his hobby and in showing King around, he

pointed proudly to three young bulls he had recently added to his herd, and then broke it to him that the names he had given them were Mackenzie, Macdougall, and McGregor, in honour, first, of King, and then of his brother and his secretary. . . . 'Some chance now' [King] commented gaily, 'of descendents bearing my name'.

When King and Rockefeller visited Colorado together it was to present an industrial plan which was barely acceptable to Welborn. Obviously some public relations were required to sell it and this King and Rockefeller proceeded to do. Their itinerary was almost a repetition of King's on his earlier visit that now paid off in that he could act as guide and show his employer what the conditions were like. According to Fred McGregor, King's secretary, (and the person for whom one of the Welborn's bulls was named) ,

It was not what could be described as a triumphal tour; neither was it a disappointing one. . . . It was a strenuous fortnight for both travellers, with serious talks together while going from camp to camp. Long evenings were spent in comparing notes. . . . Day after day Rockefeller was his genuine unassuming self. He put questions to individuals and to small groups and won their confidence by his frank answering of their questions to him.

Regularly, dressed in miners' overalls and caps and fitted with headlamps, both men went down the mines and along the shafts where their presence created great interest on the part of the miners. The tour came to an end with a dance in the schoolhouse at one of the camps. Rockefeller was the guest of honor and after he had spoken briefly to the miners and their wives, the dancing began. First on the floor was the honoured guest and to the delight and amazement of the reporters present (who practically ran to the telegraph office to tell the world the great news), he danced, so they said, with every miner's wife, daughter and sweetheart who was there.

It was not until some days later that King had time to write a letter which he admitted was overdue. It was to Mrs. Rockefeller whom he had come to know over the past months. Abby had expressed a lively interest in their trip and King promised himself that he would keep her 'pretty constantly and fully informed.'

> *The truth is, [he wrote her], . . . there has not been for either of us opportunity for more than mere snatches of correspondence. Even the hours that have been devoted to social enjoyment—and there have been many such—have in reality been quite as much in the nature of engagements which related to the purpose of this trip as occasions for change and recreation. . . . Mr. Rockefeller accuses me of having been his manager on this trip, in dictating all kinds of stunts which he has been obliged to perform. To a degree this is quite true, for I will confess that whenever I saw an opportunity of having him reveal a side of his nature which was known to me though unknown to the public and particularly to the miners, I sought to have him take advantage of it.*

He went on to explain that this might account for some of the 'public appearances' of which she would, undoubtedly, have read. The reports of King's contrived 'stunts' would have amused her—the story of the dance in particular. This was something that she would have enjoyed but what a surprise that her husband, that serious, reserved man, had come out of his shell so publicly. Abby Aldrich Rockefeller and her husband were very different in temperament. According to her biographer, Mary Ellen Chase,

> *Perhaps, indeed, no two partners could have been less innately similar than they. He was serious, thoughtful, reserved and inclined to be cautious and slow in his judgments and decisions; she was gay, outgoing, confident and quick in all her reactions. He was perhaps overscrupulous regarding moral and religious percepts . . . [she] sensitive, yet sure . . . intuitive. He logical in his approach to most matters . . . she was often illogical. . . . He was not, like her, whimsical, delighting in fun for its very absurdity . . . he was precise and exact . . . she was likely to throw details to the winds.*

Yet, in spite of these differences, they possessed many similar traits on which they built a marriage that was strong and loving and in which five children were born and nurtured. It was a family into which King was welcomed from his first association with the Foundation and with which he had strong ties until his death over thirty-six years later. King was often their guest both in New York and at Tarrytown, the Rockefeller estate on the Hudson. His first evening in their New York home was a working session but not until after dinner which gave him a chance to meet and talk with Abby and to take note of his surroundings.

> *[The] interior is of a simple classical style, a little smaller than one would expect. . . . At the table the service was of the best, beautiful flowers & fruit but nothing overdone. Mr. Rockefeller, after we were seated asked a blessing . . . in which the sweet relationships of home were remembered, and the 'needy'.*

King was also assessing his host on this occasion and approving what he saw. "Certainly this man is one of the truly noble men of this world, one who lives in the light of a great responsibility and is seeking to fulfill its obligations with modesty and with zeal." On the personal side, King's opinion was that

> *With all his wealth, he lives a life that is exemplary in every particular. Faithful in all his domestic relations, abstemious—neither drinks nor smokes—industrious—at his office at 9.20 & works late, watches details, uses his own judgment and intellect to the best advantage, and stands by his principles.*

Was there no fault in this man? As they worked together over the next few years, King observed that his new friend did, indeed, have feet of clay in some respects. There was his excessive seriousness, his failure to see enough of his family, his aloofness, his inability to relax and the need for him to get away from detail and to deal with major issues. "The truth is", King admitted to his diary, "I see in Mr. R. precisely the same mistakes which I have heard others complain of in myself." And, setting aside his own shortcomings, King proceeded to take Rockefeller to task for his perceived defects. Even before they went to Colorado, King had spoken to John D. Rockefeller, Sr., telling him that "I thought his son should come more in touch with people who were interested in social problems ... that once men came to know him, they would appreciate his spirit and purpose, but that not knowing him, many false impressions would make headway." At about the same time, he spoke out strongly to Rockefeller, himself, about "his own method of living and the degree to which he was becoming immersed in a multitude of obligations, which left him no time for mental rest or spiritual growth." The trip to Colorado had given King an opportunity to show his employer in a new light to the miners but he did not stop there. He could not intrude as far as Rockefeller's family life was concerned but he could and did exert pressure on him where their paths joined. Following the trip west their work drew them into close contact and, by this time, Rockefeller had begun to turn for advice to King whom he regarded in the light of 'the brother I have never had and always wished to have'.

The Plan which they had presented for settling the miners' grievances was accepted in 1916 and, during the spring and early summer of that year, the two men consulted at length on contributions which Rockefeller wished to make to the various camps. 'Does this seem to you wise?' was what was asked of King as suggestions regarding the erection of churches, bandstands and even a dance pavilion were put forward. If there were to be churches (and King naturally favoured the concept),

> *I hope you will be able to persuade the congregation you assist to see that no church is erected without a small tower with a bell in it. . . . The church bell for morning and evening service on Sunday is a pleasant contrast to the mine whistles which are heard on other days of the week, and suggestive of a factor in the life of the people other than their daily toil.*

King almost went so far as to offer to make the bells his own contribution but couched the suggestion with the words 'Were I in a position to do so'. Of all the ideas that Rockefeller had put forward, King preferred the donation of bandstands.

> *Of necessity a band stand must be out of doors. It should be located in what will be the park of the camp and the part reserved for sports and fêtes. In this environment it is suggestive of health, recreation, and to some degree, of art as well, all of which features are apart from work, and therefore phases of the life of the camp with which it is desirable that you should be identified.*

And he had some words of caution—that nothing should be done which would provoke jealousy between the different camps.

It is precisely the same problem as dancing with the miners' wives: if you dance with one, you must dance with all or get into trouble with the rest; and if you dance twice with one, you must dance twice with them all or get into trouble.

Remembering his own problems on the dance floor, he added,

This is a lesson which I ought to learn, but never will; but it is true nevertheless.

While progress was being made in the implementation of the Plan (although it came under criticism for being too paternalistic), King was ready to turn his hand to the writing of that controversial book, *Industry and Humanity*. The Colorado Fuel and Iron Company had served as his laboratory where he experimented with many of the ideas which had been in his mind during years of involvement in industrial relations but putting the results of these tests onto paper proved to be difficult for him. He began to draft the book at the start of 1916 but soon ran into criticism from the Trustees of the Foundation who were concerned because of the direction his work had begun to take. "Mr. King should not get away from our original conception of his task, which was to assemble the experience of the world in different aspects of the industrial problem and set forth the facts . . . as a guide." The trustees might be critical but King had Rockefeller on his side—up to a point which was that he should justify his position. This King proceeded to do citing the problems of continuing with the original plan of work under wartime conditions. As his friend and secretary, Fred McGregor,

J.D. Rockefeller Jr.

wrote, King was discouraged 'but not utterly cast down'. Interruption followed interruption as the demands of the Rockefellers and family concerns took up his attention through 1916. After the death of his father that summer, his problems with the trustees of the Foundation seemed but nothing compared with the deterioration of his own health. On a working trip to New York that October he told Rockefeller how desperate he was to try to get his nerves under control. At once, the suggestion was made that King should go to the Johns Hopkins Hospital in Baltimore where specialists with the finest qualifications would examine him. Extensive tests showed that there was no physical cause for concern and the blame was laid on King's own personality. In his charts, etc., there is a summation to the effect that King was "a genuinely fine man . . . over conscientious, needed to be taught how to live . . . needed a broader philosophy. . . . [The doctor] thought my trouble was due to worrying about myself." The advice given to King was that he should read lighter books—*O Henry* for example—that he should go on a diet and that he should marry soon. It was Rockefeller who sent King to that hospital and it was he who paid the not inconsiderable expenses for the treatment. In writing to King to wish him 'a speedy recovery to your usual vigorous vitality', the offer was made to pick up the tab and after much thought, King accepted having decided that "his motive is one of true friendliness. [Refusing it] would be satisfying a mistaken love of independence for commonsense."

King took up the writing of *Industry and Humanity* with renewed purpose now that he need no longer worry about his health but 1917 proved to be another year of interruptions and family worries. For six months, Fred McGregor was ill and unable to assist King with his work and then in the autumn, Mrs. King who was seriously ill, moved to Ottawa to stay with her son. There was also a political interruption, an election on December 17th in which King ran for North York and was defeated. When we remember that on the following day his mother died, and knowing the important place that she held in his life, it is not to be wondered that he was again unable to write for weeks. When he did have some chapters in hand, he passed them on to Rockefeller for his comments and, in return, received not only disappointing reports from the head of the Foundation but also from Rockefeller, himself. In his opinion

> *the practical people who want concrete programs and definite suggestions as to social policy will be disappointed because the book deals in general*

What Rockefeller expected King to do was to open an office in New York when he took on his new role but, as in 1914, this was not the way King saw it. "I keep my office and residence for the time being in Ottawa," he informed Violet, "and do much of my work by correspondence, visiting the States whenever it is necessary." The only way he would even consider uprooting himself from the friends and familiar surroundings in Ottawa would be if he could, perhaps, find a wife at last and so make a new home for himself but this did not seem to be in the cards for him. The Rockefellers, especially Abby, like other friends before, did their best to make this dream come true. Through them he had met Jean Greer a couple of years earlier and, in February 1918, when he was in New York, he went to call on her and hope surged once more. 'I see in her all that I most wish to find in a woman' was his immediate reaction on seeing her devotion to her aged and ill parents. A long talk by the fireside only served to reinforce his feelings towards her and, on his return to the Harvard Club where he usually stayed when in New York, he sat by the fire in the lounge idealizing her: "Into every relationship of life she seemed to fit—the Church, the State, the rich, the poor—above all the poor . . . together we could give the nation a soul. . . . [It is] all too wonderful." He came down to earth with a vengeance in realizing that he was hungry so ordered some oysters, followed by hot lemonade and cheese 'an awful mixture for which I should have suffered'. The suffering came later when he discovered that Miss Greer was not really interested in him as a prospective husband and despite following up on this meeting by writing to her, sending flowers and even a copy of *The Secret of Heroism*, he made no progress in his pursuit. While King was advisor to Rockefeller on matters concerning industrial affairs, in affairs of the heart it was the other way around. In April of that year, Rockefeller was visiting Ottawa and the talk turned naturally to Miss Greer.

> *He seemed to think she had no thoughts of marriage. He spoke of her as being his age, & of the critical period of life it was for a woman & the greater wisdom of a marriage which would make possible the having children. He felt I was inclined to interpret her actions in accordance with my own feelings & wishes. That women preferred to be pleasant & agreeable. . . . He advised my going slowly—treating her only as a friend and await developments.*

By this time, King had begun to have some self-doubts and he wondered, in the face of no response at all from her, 'whether I am looked upon as an adventurer or what'. Had he but known it at the time, Miss Greer did not tell him that he was not her only suitor. It was not until a year later that a letter from Rockefeller made it clear "why she has held you at arms length. This very day [23 July 1919] Miss Greer has been married to a man whom she says she has known for years and who with her has waited a long time until their union might be possible." Two years later, the Rockefellers' hopes for King rose once more as Abby wrote:

> *We went to the opera last night . . . where we met a most charming girl from the West. . . . I warn you that my husband thinks he has at last found the right person for you, and I feel inclined to agree with him. If the position is still vacant, shall we consider means of bringing about a meeting?*

A few weeks later she had to concede defeat.

> *Fate seems to be against introducing you to that very charming girl, or perhaps the Lord does not mean me to be a matchmaker. . . . I am sure it is better for men to choose their own wives, although at times they do make extra-ordinary choices and they do pass by some of the very best material.*

Rockefeller's visit to Ottawa in April 1918 was in response to an invitation to speak to the Canadian Club there. During his time in town he was King's guest in his apartment at The Roxborough, accepting to stay there only

> *If I will not incommode you, and if you will treat me with the same indifference and neglect with which Mrs. Rockefeller avers I always treat you when you are our guest, I shall be happy to cast in my lot with you. You know I am entirely sincere when I ask you not to make company of me.*

They had not made 'company' of King from the time they first met and this pattern continued over the years. After King re-entered Canadian politics in 1919, he was often prevented by pressure of work from accepting their frequent invitations to visit them in whichever of their homes they happened to be. He could sometimes take a break over the Easter recess and go to New York or to Williamsburg, Virginia, if they were staying in either of these two places. In the summers, he tried to get a few days with the family at Seal Harbor, Maine, and he sometimes caught up with them at Tarrytown where not only Rockefeller and his father had houses but where other family members also lived on the large estate. One summer, King managed to be with them in New York, Tarrytown and Seal Harbor, all in the course of a few days.

> *It was a particular happiness to me, [he said in his bread-and-butter note], to see you and Mrs. Rockefeller the centre of your own home circle at Seal Harbor, and an equal delight to be seated at the same table with you both and Mr. Rockefeller, Sr., at Tarrytown. No pictures of home or family life could be lovelier than those which I have carried away in memory from both places, and they will always be a much cherished possession.*

After the family meals and games of Authors, perhaps, with the children, there was always a little time set aside for more serious matters. When Rockefeller wrote King to congratulate him on being chosen leader of the Liberal Party of Canada in August 1919, it was a letter tinged with some regret and the acknowledgment that

> *I have been human enough and weak enough to realize how serious a blow to me and to the responsibilities which are upon me is the termination of that close, helpful and delightful relationship with you which has existed since we first met.... I have relied so completely and leaned so heavily upon you as guide, philosopher and friend ... that I have found myself more or less a prey to a real sense of depression.*

But there was a flip-side to this in that King had assured him that he would still be standing by in time of need.

> *Your generous proffer of assistance in every way, [was Rockefeller's response], consistent with the other obligations resting upon you, and your desire to have me turn to you as heretofore for advice and counsel, and to send people to you for conference whenever I feel so disposed is deeply appreciated.*

And King's offer of help was taken up from time to time whether on the question of further strikes in the Colorado mines or on the interpretation of proposed new labour legislation in the United States and other labour-related issues. For each and every bit of advice, Rockefeller was most thankful writing that "It is always gratifying to have your opinion on these matters, for it is the result of so much longer and richer experience than mine."

King's attitude had always been that "I am indeed glad to do anything for Mr. R. or his family & it makes me proud & happy to think that I can be of help." He had just received a letter from Rockefeller asking for guidance of a more personal nature. David, the Rockefellers' youngest son, was soon to graduate from Harvard where he had majored in economics but like many before him, he was not sure what he wanted to do next. The question was put to King that

> Because of the interest which you have so kindly taken in our children . . . and, because, as I have told him, I know of no wiser counsellor than you, I have suggested to David that he write you to see whether you could take the time to see him . . . during his Easter vacation.

King's reply was, naturally, in the affirmative, and in late March 1936, David went to Ottawa for a short visit after which his father wrote to express his thanks.

> [David] has written a full and most enthusiastic letter telling us of his interesting, helpful talks with you, of his great enjoyment of the privilege of being with you . . . .and for showing him the attention you have in so gracious a manner.

There was no indication at the time* that David Rockefeller's visit to King influenced his further studies but he returned to Harvard with memories of a personal nature which were passed on to his host.

> May I quote the following sentence from David's letter: "I heartily agree with you in your great admiration and respect for Mr. King. . . . Of all the things which we did I think I was most impressed by the completely simple and natural way in which he talked with everyone. For example, we were walking along the platform of the station as I was leaving. All the conductors and engineers spoke to him as a revered friend and he in turn chatted with them about local affairs as though he had been one of their fellows."

*In a letter to the author on 8 July 1996, David Rockefeller wrote "On the basis of that visit I took my Ph.D. in Economics, studying at Harvard, the London School of Economics and University of Chicago, in reverse order from what Mr. King had done many years earlier. I have always felt his advice was very good."

On occasion, Abby, too, turned to King for advice on one or other of the various projects with which she was deeply involved. The welfare of others was an obligation that she had a genuine desire to meet and this was accomplished in part by her active work for the Y. W. C. A. There, in 1919, she took the lead in discussions as to how the Association could best

> *meet the needs of the industrial girl. . . . You are so awfully good about helping us [she wrote King], that I know I am trespassing but I also know that you want, in any way that you can, to help on the cause of a better understanding among various types of people . . . if it is not asking too much we would greatly appreciate having your criticism [of a draft paper on the subject].*

Later, it was for guidance about a house that she planned to have built near a Standard Oil Company housing development. This house, 'The Seedling', would be used by many concerned with the welfare of women and children but "The great question in my mind" (she confided to King) "is who shall stand behind the enterprise? Financially in so far as it seems wise, I intend to myself." The management of this house still baffled her but she knew that "I particularly do not want it to be a Company thing, because I refuse to be bossed by the directors of the Standard Oil Company, and I also do not wish the Committee of the house to be bossed by me. . . . If you do come down here we can talk it over."

In late October 1946, King was visiting the Rockefellers at Tarrytown and while there he talked with Abby about having her husband's portrait painted. This had been on her mind for a time but she had not succeeded in convincing him of the merit of this idea. In enlisting King's help, she told him, in effect: 'You can do so much more with him than we can'. King took up the challenge as a "mission to see that this chance in not lost . . . . I want those who are to follow on", he wrote to Rockefeller, "to know your spirit as I know it, to gain from a glimpse at your portrait something of the secret of your life and the source of its accomplishments." He had earlier spoken to Abby of Frank Salisbury, an English artist friend, who had done a portrait of Mrs. King, as well as of King, himself. The Rockefellers were sent photographs of both these paintings as evidence of Salisbury's talents and in the spring of 1947 the artist went to the Rockefellers' home in Williamsburg to carry out the desired commission, painting not only Rockefeller, himself, but also Abby. After the work was completed, King, the force behind the project, was invited to dinner and, as Rockefeller put it, "What an exciting time we will have when you inspect the portraits! Mr. Salisbury and I expect to stand cowering in the corner waiting to see whether the king's thumb will be turned up or down."

A year later, just as King was leaving to fly back to Ottawa from Williamsburg where he had been taking a few days rest, he received the news of Abby's death in New York. As soon as he reached home, King sent off a message of condolence to be followed a day or two later by a hand-written letter—one of the few he wrote in his latter years. In it, he expressed "how different each day's existence is certain to be without the consciousness of her visible presence at your side [and of] the 34 years which have slipped so quickly away since we first met." This gave him a chance to mention something which he had noted during those years: "You have heard me speak of resemblances she bore to my own dear Mother in the silvery whiteness of her hair and above the forehead, and above all in her tender Nature, and loveliness of Spirit. A little later on, you must let me come and share some quiet moments with you where we can talk together of her and of the many memories we all shared."

That opportunity did not come until August when King went to spend the better part of a week at Seal Harbor. Hours were spent there in dedication to Abby's memory, many of them in her famous Chinese garden which had been inspired by a trip which she and her husband had taken to the Orient many years previously.

> *It was about 11 when we went out together; as the day was very warm, we took one of the cars to drive to the gate of the garden. . . . I was amazed when I saw the beauty of it. The bricks of the wall and the tiling and the stone monuments representative of poets and authors, scholars etc. Buddhas set in enclosures; steps leading to them, just as they are in China.*

In this ambience, the two sat and talked and, as King later recorded,

> *I felt the atmosphere of it all very strongly. I did feel very much the presence of her spirit. . . . I have never enjoyed a morning more nor felt a closer communion of soul, with another man. . . . Our talk, of course, was mostly of immortality and the evidence of it.*

Before going out into the garden, Rockefeller showed King the Salisbury painting of Abby, a copy of which was hung prominently in the house. Even though his friend had done the work, King could not but be critical of it in some aspects. "To me it lacks something of the sparkle—a little firm around the mouth. The eyes a little sterner. . . . I can see what it is that Mrs. R. herself would have liked a little differently. It has less the touch of a mother about it than she would have wished." On the whole, however, he had to agree that 'the likeness is exceedingly good' and, as for Rockefeller who "turned to me and said that he could never say what he owed me for persuading him to have Salisbury paint these pictures", there was no admitting that the work was less than perfect. One evening they drove to the top of the mountain on the property to a spot where the Rockefellers 'used to go together and sit in the evenings, alone, watching the day close and the moon rise'. There the two men had a picnic supper which did not include Oysters Rockefeller but was simply two ham and cheese sandwiches each along with some coffee.

On the first morning of the visit, as King was enjoying a cup of tea and his host was performing the duties of a valet by unpacking his guest's suitcase, the question of King's own future came up. Just before King went down to Maine there had been a Liberal Party convention in Ottawa at which time he had resigned as leader of the party, being succeeded by Louis St. Laurent. Now, Rockefeller wanted to know, what was King's next move?

> *He asked me whether I would be free to withdraw at any time if I felt tired, or would I be bound for a definite period. I explained that I would be free to leave but could hardly do so without political questions arising. Withdrawing could be construed as some difficulty with colleagues. . . . I did say, however, that I thought I would like in a way to stay on for another year or two because of the income I would derive and [thus] making easier the transition from being head of govt. to being a private citizen.*

As he pointed out, before that time came he still had many things to take care of—there was the disposition of his properties in Ottawa and at Kingsmere; his multitudinous papers had to be put in some order and he had not, to date, made a will despite the urging of close friends. "I felt", he went on, "as one got older, too, one did not know at what moment one might find one's strength failing or sight, etc. It was well to get all things cleaned up while one's memory was still intact."

This was all part and parcel of a question that had been raised with King some five years earlier. On a visit to the Rockefeller home in New York, the conversation was brought around to the very points that King was now raising in 1948 at Seal Harbor.

> *I have been thinking a good deal over your life and work [was how Rockefeller hesitantly began in December 1943] and what you would be doing when you leave office. You and I should have another 10 years to live. You have been giving your life so completely to public affairs that it may be quite a change for you when you take up the quiet, retreat life.*

Of particular concern to Rockefeller was the news that King would not have a pension on his retirement and that led him to propose some financial help.

> *If I sent you a cheque for you to deposit for yourself, would that give rise to any difficulty, as between you and me, there is nothing that either of us could be influenced by in any way, nor could either of us be under any obligation to the other for anything. What I would like to do would be to just give you a little assistance as time goes along from time to time.*

It was an offer that was made in a voice choked with emotion as he spoke of what King had meant to him over the years.

> *You have done more for me than anyone.... You have meant everything to me at a time when I needed guidance in many matters and your whole outlook and attitude has helped me tremendously... at every step [you] had known what course to take, and it was the right one.*

After a few disclaimers from King as to what he, in turn, owed to Rockefeller, the topic was dropped as they turned the conversation to less embarrassing matters.

In subsequent years, cheques arrived regularly from Rockefeller, sometimes around the time of King's birthday and his thanks was always fulsome but never more so than in early December 1948. On his seventy-fourth birthday when he opened Rockefeller's letter, its enclosure informed him that he was to receive stock in the amount of $100,000. It took him a couple of days to restrain his emotions sufficiently to write his letter of thanks in which he spoke of 'the wholly new vista of life' which this gift implied.

> *It will take me some time to realize just all that your magnificent gift, coming at this particular moment, is going to mean to me. At 74, one cannot fail to see the evening shadows are already beginning to lengthen and that life is bound to become, as the years go by, increasingly difficult. For me you have removed completely the greatest of all fears; the dread of insecurity, as one nears the close. . . . I shall now be able . . . to carry on the work that might otherwise fail altogether of accomplishment and to enjoy friends, books, my home in the city and the countryside with a feeling that these joys have not only been legitimately earned but that the title deed to their enjoyment has been given to me as a trust from the hand of a devoted and dearly beloved lifelong friend. For all this and much more I can only thank you.*

In this letter, King also wrote that

> *I can now see where, if given the years and the strength equal to the task, I should be able to carry out a long cherished ambition to write something that may encourage younger men to take a part in public life and to realize that in public service they will find what Mr. Gladstone called 'an elevated and lofty destiny'. I have never doubted that the way [for this] would open up; but I have never expected it would open up so soon nor that the vista would be so wide and the distant view so entrancing.*

For years, too, it had been his wish to write his memoirs and, at last, the way seemed cleared. While he had tried without success to convince Rockefeller to have someone write his own life story ('when a thing was done he was through with it . . . he could not see that there was any contribution that he had made in a large way that would be of interest to others'), the reverse applied to King and the writing of his own memoirs. Early in 1949, he received a phone call one day from Rockefeller who wished to discuss the subject. There was a new President of the Foundation, King was told, who was of the opinion that some way should be found for the financing of this work and that it should be put into motion soon so as to have the benefit of King's input. The Foundation was now proposing that they should provide any necessary assistance and Rockefeller agreed, telling them that 'he had himself undertaken to give me assistance towards that end'. King was of the opinion that he already received this with the income which the stocks, his birthday gift of 1948, would provide. Rockefeller, however, was at pains to point out

> *that the assistance he wished me to have from him should be for my own life and security through my remaining years, and that he would prefer that none of it should be used for the Memoirs which he regarded as a public service which should be met apart from the means that I, myself, possessed.*

When King demurred saying that he felt he could well finance the writing himself now, it was time for the man of business to put on the advisor's hat. Don't make it difficult for the Foundation to extend a helping hand, King was told, and there was more practical advice as well. Rockefeller pointed out to King that he had had little experience, to date, in running two households and that he would be surprised when he became a private citizen how often and how deeply his hand would go to his pocket. In correspondence soon after this, King had expressed his gratitude to Rockefeller for his part in the proposed help only to be told "But you give me credit that I do not deserve because it was not I who first raised the question of some help but another of your friends, whose name I will perhaps some day tell you." But despite the assistance that he could draw on, 'tremendously generous proposal re Memoirs, something quite beyond belief', it was as King had recently predicted—the evening shadows were already beginning to lengthen.

> *I am tired now & feel myself losing a certain interest in whatever happens, which is quite wrong & may be fatigue. I am sure the one right thing to do is to go ahead with the task that has [to] be performed now or never—the making of a will, disposition of papers & outline of Memoirs.*

It was easier said than done and the Memoirs, in particular, were often put on the back burner as their chief architect was distracted by day to day issues. In August 1949, he went back to Seal Harbor for a holiday and there he confided in his host, telling him of the enormity of the task which he faced. It did not need words to express this—the fatigue and care which outlined King's face told the whole story and Rockefeller, while wishing to see the story recorded in some way, cautioned King against any feeling of obligation about it. "He was sure, in the long run,

I would do better work if I were completely rested and would get a joy out of it," wrote King as he put himself in the hands of his host whose prescription for the holiday was to have his guest relax. One time, in the Colorado days, it had been King who was the ringmaster as he put Rockefeller through his paces in order to show his true nature. Now, it was Rockefeller's turn. Earlier in the spring he had advised more gaiety in King's life, telling him that he should see more people both young and old and that he might even plan a few parties to this end. His words fell on deaf ears but, as host, he could now see to it that King's name was on the invitation cards that came in and it was he who rang up Mathilde's daughter, Mary Warlick, and arranged for King to go over for dinner with her and her husband. It was an evening that King regarded as 'one of the happiest events of this present trip'.

It was not all socializing, however. Much of the time was spent as it usually was when the two men were together at Seal Harbor. King had some work to do with Edouard Handy, his private secretary, and Rockefeller had his own concerns but "Mr. R. and I meet at luncheon which we have together", King wrote to his friend, Joan Patteson, in Ottawa. "During the afternoon each of us takes a rest and later go for a drive either in the motor car or with horses. Mr R. owns a good part of the island and his drives extend for several miles." In the evenings, if they were free, they read aloud to each other and, in keeping with the desire for relaxation, their reading material was light: *Cheaper by the Dozen* was one of their choices. And they talked. They talked about Abby whose biography was being written and which they were reading chapter by chapter as it became available. The matter of the Rockefeller riches and how much a part of the book they should be drew from King the opinion that "I thought the real greatness of his life and of Mrs. R's was not the possession of wealth but what they had accomplished in spite of wealth." Perhaps the long discussion on what Abby had done to help others, particularly through financial support to the Young Women's Christian Association, reminded King of his own finances and

> *I then got a chance to tell Mr. R. what I have been wanting to tell him right along, that I had really found that I possessed more in the way of income than I believed I had at the time I received the gift he made to me.*

As a man of money, Rockefeller congratulated his friend on the management of his personal funds and only wished that it might have been twenty times the amount.

As the holiday drew to a close and the two sat together at the breakfast table,

> *Mr. R. said to me: I am going to be very lonely when you go. I like to see you sitting at the end of the table opposite. It is like talking with Mrs. R. We can talk or be quiet, as we please. I said to him it made me feel that there was a communion between us, wherever we might be.*

The invitation was extended to be Rockefeller's guest at Williamsburg any time he wished or to stay with him when in New York where "[You could] feel free to do exactly as you like; go anywhere or see anyone. I shall do the same. We should spend such odd hours and odd times together as would be free, with each other."

This warm invitation could not be accepted nor did King get back to Seal Harbor again. By January 1950, his deteriorating health forced him to write that "You may be sure that in the quiet of Kingsmere, as the summer days go by, my thoughts will be greatly enriched by the memories of the hours spent together at Seal Harbor in bygone years." In 1943, Rockefeller's prediction was that they should each have ten more years to live. This did not hold true for King but Rockefeller lived on until 1960 without the one whom he had spoken of as being his closest friend.

Joan Patteson

And then, finally and notably among King's friends, there was Joan Patteson, who was by his side for over thirty years. As had been the case with Marjorie Herridge, he was drawn to those who had less than fulfilling marriages and who were in need of companionship as much as he, himself, was. Other relationships that were carried on over a distance by means of letters and the occasional visits did not create those emotional dilemmas which fill so many of the pages of his diaries, but with both Marjorie and Joan it was a different matter. They each had their homes in small-town Ottawa near King and, in summer, Kingsmere was where Marjorie and Joan (although in different periods) spent their holidays. Given the need on the part of the participants and the close proximity of their daily lives, it is small wonder that at times they found themselves treading on dangerous ground.

In 1918 when Joan Patteson is first mentioned in King's diary it was in connection with the completion of his book, *Industry and Humanity*. In September of that year, the writing was finally finished with the exception of some revisions. The ink on the pages was scarcely dry before he called in his Kingsmere neighbours, the Jenkins, to have dinner and to listen as he read portions of the book to them. Those people go down in history as being "most appreciative, very delightful people, talented, artistic & good." A more formal recognition was paid the book when in early October, King invited some friends to dine with him at the Golf Club, 'as a sort of celebration'. Among the guests were Joan Patteson and her husband, Godfroy, who were King's neighbours at the Roxborough. After the dinner "Mr. and Mrs. Pattison [sic] came into my rooms and spent an hour there. It was quite a happy evening." He does not say whether or not he sought Joan's opinion of the book that evening but, in the following thirty years, her judgment was something that he prized greatly in all facets of his life.

King's thoughts on having finished writing *Industry and Humanity* were that

> the book meant a dividing line in my life, that it was my life & work up to date so to speak. . . . I looked up to the little clock on the cottage shelf & to my surprise saw both hands exactly over the hour twelve.* I exclaimed aloud over the significance of the fact, then went to my little room & knelt by the side of the little bed in which dear mother suffered so patiently & so long.

It was by then almost a year since his mother had died and this, along with the almost total estrangement from Marjorie, left a large gap in his life. It was a gap which was soon to be filled by Joan Patteson as King set out on what he saw as the next phase of his life 'under the conception of the presence of God in all things'.

This new woman in King's life is remembered by acquaintances as having been 'a darling', 'pretty', 'a woman of great charm and dignity as well as beauty even when in her seventies.' Walter Turnbull, who worked for King for many years, saw her from a different angle. Before going to work in the Prime Minister's Office in 1936 he was warned "very carefully to be nice to Mrs. Patteson because she had a great influence with the Prime Minister", and while he took this advice to heart, he found it quite easy to follow. "I was nice to her because I liked her," he said. "I really genuinely liked her. She was a lady in every sense of the word." One of King's biographers presented Joan as having been "an unusually discreet and sympathetic woman; . . . widely read, a woman of good taste, sensitive and perceptive." The writer of a psychobiography of King concluded that Joan was a mother substitute in his life but that, as well,

> She embodied most of the virtues which had marked earlier friendships but had less of their disadvantages. The key dimension . . . was that it was not demanding on King. . . . Only in Joan Patteson's care and admiration could King find a mirror that reflected the true self of his self-image.

What one might have learned of another writer's views about Joan

---

*The hands of the clock being in conjunction or at some particular angle meant to him that the spirits were near.

Joan Patteson

have been lost to us through King's intervention. In early January 1949, he read through a manuscript and found it "on the whole good when on public issues, I do not like the personal incident side." What bothered him was a "most objectional reference to friendship with Joan, not that it is not nicely written, but to single her out by name to exclusion of all others, is most unchivalrous and will cause her with a sensitive nature to be greatly embarrassed." This book by a member of the press did not escape the stubby little pencils which were once a King trademark as the offending parts of the manuscript were excised.

Although this friendship escaped the book's pages, it was not a secret nor was it carried on in a clandestine manner. It began to develop along the same lines and as naturally as had his association with Marjorie. This time it was even more convenient: he had only to walk along the hall at the Roxborough and knock on the Pattesons' door to be welcomed. Godfroy's position as manager of the Ottawa branch of Molson's Bank gave them entrée into local social life but their horizons were widened by this burgeoning friendship with King who moved only in the highest circles. He soon formed the habit of dropping in on them regularly, often late in the evening. Sometimes it was after a dinner party elsewhere or following an evening service at St. Andrew's Church or when he got back after a late sitting of the House. "After dinner [I] spent the evening with Mrs. Patteson. Some music and mostly conversation", he wrote. And, "Music before and after service with Mrs. Patteson." Or, "Spent the evening with Mrs. Patteson. Stayed and talked till after 1.30." From the very beginning it was evident that it was Joan, not Godfroy, who was the drawing card and his diaries did nothing to hide this. It almost sounded as if Godfroy were not there but it is simply a fact that he and King had little in common.

Almost concurrent with King's new-found attachment there were other changes in his life. His work with the Rockefeller Foundation was finished but he had been offered the chance of spending several months abroad with Fred McGregor as his secretary to study post-war problems facing industries. Given his relationship with the Rockefellers, this was a tempting offer. So, too, was another surprising opportunity which was offered to him by Mrs. Andrew Carnegie. The position of Director of the Carnegie Corporation in New York was his if he chose to accept it. The terms were generous: $25,000 a year with side benefits and, as he told Mrs. Carnegie, "[It] would take all the spiritual courage at my command to make a wise decision." But the third option was the one that held the day. "I would rather serve my own country than any other land. . . . To change to another country at my age is not to enjoy the peace of mind and heart which a political career in Canada would afford."

His mind was made up: Canadian politics it was to be and not in any minor role. His ambition and past accomplishments dictated to him that he should aim for the leadership of the Liberal Party but, while waiting for the right moment, he continued to carry out some commissions for the Rockefeller Foundation. As it turned out, he did not have long to wait. In mid-February 1919, he was on a working trip in Ohio when he heard that Laurier had suffered a paralytic stroke and, fearing the worst, King decided to return to Ottawa at once. It was when changing trains at Buffalo that he picked up a newspaper in which he learned of Sir Wilfrid's death. During the rest of his homeward trip, King's mind was full of thoughts of his long association with Laurier and the recognition that "In his death I lose a political father as well as a great leader." On the other hand, he was comforted by the recollection that "I am glad that before his death Sir Wilfrid on three different occasions made plain to me his desire to have me succeed him in the leadership." Laurier had not, however, made his wishes widely known and there was the expected rivalry amongst the different candidates but, in early August, at a convention in Ottawa, King was chosen as leader. "This begins a new chapter in my life, a chapter of great responsibilities and I believe great opportunities." These words which he had written on the way home from Ohio had a personal caveat which was "To go into politics without marrying would be folly. I cannot live that cruel life without a home and someone to love and be loved by. . . . Marry then I must." But, at the same time, in the back of his mind was the nagging fear that "what is needed for politics and married life would terrify me out of both were I to stop and contemplate them." There was not, of course, to be a marriage and of the two things which might have terrified him had he thought too much about either, politics easily won out. On the other hand, he was not quite alone. There was Joan and there would *always* be Joan. She was there for him from the start of this 'new chapter' in his life until the very end of his days.

As early as the spring of 1920, one could easily substitute the name 'Joan' for that of 'Marjorie' and the story that developed would need hardly any changing. King was again drifting into a close relationship and, while he could see what was happening, he was reluctant to do anything about it. It was all so convenient, so comforting and seemed to be so undemanding. Some credit can be given him for seeing that "It is apparent to me that I am sitting up too late in these visits to the Pattesons. . . . I am very fond of Mrs. Patteson, but I realize it is not in the best interest of my work, and perhaps it is better for each of us to see less of each other." But, on the debit side, he had apparently learned nothing from his association with Marjorie which ran its stormy course for years and he was about to repeat the same emotional roller-coaster ride with Joan until they both came to a *modus vivendi*. Until that day, the going was sometimes rough.

It seems to have been particularly so just after Labour Day, 1920. The Pattesons were King's guests at Kingsmere that weekend and such closeness appears to have taken its toll. The result was that King felt the need of censoring his diary, actually going to the extent of cutting out the better part of a week's entries after their visit. It had all seemed to be going along quite calmly but something, we shall never know what, happened and when they were back in Ottawa where he and Joan could speak in private, an entry which King did <u>not</u> cut out tells us that

> *It seems so hard to overcome oneself. . . . These storms of passion—for that is what they are, are madness and wrong. They 'rock the mind' and must cease. We both have strength enough to see that, and we will help each other to what is best for each, hard as the struggle may be.*

'Nearly desperation' was King's phrase for what they were going through at this time but, a few days later, a diary entry that could have been written during the 'Marjorie years', tells of their pledging their lives to 'united effort and service'.

> *Joan and I talked in front of an open fire in the [Patteson's] living room . . . I read aloud to her Wordsworth's 'Ode to Duty', and 'the Happy Warrior'. We spoke of the fight we would make together for what is best for both of us. . . . It was one of the happiest evenings we have ever shared together.*

While King may not have realized that he was repeating his actions with Marjorie, he did become aware of another parallel experience when he went to see *Parsifal*, the Wagnerian opera that has as its theme the spiritual redemption of man. This happened during an Easter holiday in New York in 1921 and it opened his eyes, he said, to

> *the meaning of Good and Evil in love as never before. The reality of it. . . . I wished so much Joan had been with me. It was <u>our</u> play. The Holy Grail. I was amazed to see how unconsciously we had hit upon the central theme in life. The play of dual personality is very real in this great production.*

When King said it was their play, his and Joan's, it was because he could compare his situation with that of one of the characters, Amfortas, King of the Knights of the Holy Grail, who had been lured away from his company by Kundry, a sorceress, and had been badly wounded in a confrontation. "I wondered if I could be as Amfortas," King mused, "stricken with a wound that will not heal." So intense were his feelings as he compared himself with the characters in the opera and related it to his situation with Joan that he was impatient to get back to Ottawa to discuss the opera's message with her. He had bought the libretto and for two consecutive evenings they read it aloud, pondering its meaning for them.

> *We came to one passage which suggested a train of thought that immediately changed our whole evening. . . . It was very sudden, very unexpected. . . . Joan was quite frank & honest about its effect upon her and by speaking the truth openly we were able to face the question before us. This problem is increasingly difficult to solve but we are determined to solve it.*

The difficulties implicit in bringing about a change in their relationship made for some bad moments, some sleepless nights and prayers for 'strength to overcome all temptations'. In the early summer of 1921, they reassessed the uphill battle that they had been fighting.

> *[Joan] spoke of her fondness for me, & of having to give me up. . . . She feels that a great struggle has been come thro' successfully—she said she felt she had nursed me thro' a great illness for wh. she had been partly responsible. How true. She spoke of the anxiety she has suffered for months. Her sorrow & tears were a reaction now that the struggle was over.*

It should not surprise anyone to learn that the struggle was not, in fact, over, that there were frequent lapses to the end of King's life. While he, himself, made resolutions better than he kept them, there remained an inter-dependency which neither one could ever give up. But what of Godfroy? He appears to have been remarkably long-suffering and patient, much more compliant than Dr. Herridge had been. There was not to be any locked door for Joan as there had been for Marjorie nor was there to be any incoherent confrontation between King and Godfroy as there had been with the Reverend. There was surely provocation enough to have expected that there would be some reaction from Godfroy who, from 1918 on, could scarcely call his home his own. What must he have thought of those late-night visits by King who stayed on talking with Joan until 1.30 or later? What of the increasingly numerous times he found King a guest at table? What, in particular, could have been his mood on Sunday, 6 November 1921, when King returned from an electioneering trip to the Maritimes and practically collapsed in the Pattesons' apartment for the whole day? In King's own words, he was

> *Glad, oh so glad to reach Ottawa again this morning, to speak with Joan over the phone and later at 11 to have breakfast with her and Godfroy. I was very tired all day, almost exhausted in fact but Joan let me rest quietly and we had a few hymns together, a little wine, some food later on, a very happy day. . . . We were very happy together.*

What were Godfroy's feelings when King came back from New York at Easter and, having failed to find the right gift there for Joan, presented her with "an emerald ring (symbolic of immortality) from a collection that belonged to Mother. Gave it in a box with cover Dante & Beatrice—all to symbolize the highest & best & finest love." Or, on the day of the election in 1921 when he gave her a bracelet with the inscription

J. P. from W. L. M. K.
A strength was in us from the vision
The Campaign of 1921

It was a very expensive bracelet, $125, which was a lot of money at that time, much more than Godfroy with his banker's salary could have afforded to spend on a gift for his wife. Had King been tactful he might have given them a joint gift to express his gratitude for all the help he had received in their home, especially during the stress and strain of the election, but he did not. The inscription on the bracelet tells it all. It was taken from one of his favourite poems, The Holy Grail, and this, of course, was full of significance to Joan and him ever since the *Parsifal* experience. All in all, is it any wonder that Godfroy often went off to bed while King and Joan were burning the midnight oil or that he found reasons to get out of the apartment for a while when King was monopolizing both his home and his wife? Mathilde's husband, George Barchet, gentle man that he was, found that he could tolerate King's usurpation of his wife's affections by making little teasing jokes about it; Dr. Herridge reacted violently and Godfroy sometimes depended overly on a bottle to see him through.

Had King been consulting a medium or sitting at the 'little table' in the late autumn of 1921, he might have learned that there was to be a move in his future, one that may not have bothered Godfroy as much as it did Joan. King was to leave the Roxborough and move into Laurier House as it had been left to him by Lady Laurier. He was out of town when she died on 1 November 1921, just as he had been away when Sir Wilfrid died. This time he was in Guelph, campaigning, when he had a phone call informing him of her death and that he had been remembered in her will. "I took this to mean her house, which she once said she wd. give me as a wedding gift if I married." Scheduled political meetings were cancelled and he returned to Ottawa, going directly from the train to have breakfast with Joan where 'everything [was] as comfortable and happy as could be'. After a few minutes' talk with her he went over to Laurier House to take up his position with the other pallbearers. On the way to the church where funeral services were conducted, he was told just what he expected to hear, that Lady Laurier had, indeed, left him the house and he was given a letter which verified this. When he later saw Joan and showed her the disposition, *she felt quite badly—thought of what it meant of separation from the Roxborough. I felt sorry for the express'n of grief which I saw come to her life. She spoke of it meaning necessarily my marriage. Her heart is very tender. She was however very brave and splendid.*

A few weeks after learning of the bequest, King dined at Laurier House with Sir Wilfrid's nephew, Robert Laurier, and his wife and had a chance to take a critical look at his future home. He was not impressed. "It is a bleak, bare place in size & furnishings, not at all to my liking in any particular." By the autumn he was happier about it as he could see that it was turning out 'very fine', thanks to the efforts—and financial contributions—of friends including Peter Larkin, the wealthy tea merchant, who was soon to turn up as Canadian High Commissioner in London as thanks for his special generosity.

When King wrote up his diary for 12 January 1923, it was to say that

Am writing for the first time in my new library at Laurier House and spending the first night beneath my own roof. . . . I came up after having had dinner with Joan & Godfroy. . . . Joan was quite sad at the thought of my going. . . . I shall miss her & Godfroy greatly but perhaps it is all for the best for my life & work.

In actual fact, the move made very little, if any difference to how often they were together at one house or the other. The late night visits, the invitations to dine or to have tea, went on as they had for the past few years. And King's dependence on Joan increased. Not only did he still rely on her to be there for him when he needed tea and sympathy but from the moment he moved into Laurier House he sought her advice on how to organize his new household. For years, he and his reliable valet, Nicol, had managed for themselves, but now the size of his household was a challenge. Help, however, was only a phone call away and Joan was often called in to try to establish some order. When King began to entertain at Laurier House, she went in to arrange the flowers throughout the house and, surely, to check on the staff to see that they all knew their duties. If the Pattesons were guests at a party, they stayed on to do a post mortem; if they were not among the invitees, they went over to have a chat after the last guests had departed. At Easter, 1923, the Pattesons and King were in New York and he took advantage of Joan's presence there to help him choose picture frames and small artifacts which would add some colour to his rooms. Joan, it seems, was only too willing to help in whatever way she could. If sorting and putting away his many, many Christmas cards, for example, was on his mind and he could not get around to doing this task, she took charge. She was of enormous help in many little familial ways. As well, when King had to be out of town for any length of time, the Pattesons just moved in to Laurier House and kept an eye on things. There really was no cause for Joan's earlier concern that King's moving out of the Roxborough would mean any distancing from each other.

In fact, from 1924 on, King and the Pattesons saw more of each other than ever before. Godfroy and Joan had been renting a summer house at Kingsmere but Joan had earlier been eager to buy property there and build on it. King thought this a good idea and spent some time designing a house with her just as he had done with Marjorie. It was only the location that worried him since it was opposite his own property and thus was 'too conspicuous'. A solution was found when he bought the Herridge property in 1924 and the Pattesons became his tenants in the house that had witnessed so many emotional scenes between him and Marjorie. One might have thought this ill-befitting but King felt calm, secure, in the sure knowledge that

> *Mrs. Herridge's spirit, free from all the pains and sorrows & limitations of her terrible infirmity, is now in the presence of God. It is as if there had been restored all the near communion of soul, which I knew years ago but which for about a decade has been gradually being obliterated.*

With Marjorie's soul thus at peace, he had no fear of any envious or bitter ghost haunting the house and disturbing the Pattesons. The cottage became their summer home for four years until King decided to carry out extensive renovations and moved there himself. In the meantime, he had purchased Shady Hill, a small cottage nearby, and Joan and Godfroy occupied this even for a few years after King's death.

He could change the name of Marjorie's house; he could see Joan and Godfroy put their own stamp on both the house and the garden but, possibly, he was too optimistic if he thought that the spirit of the former chatelaine was entirely banished. By the end of the 1924 season it was clear that, while the players had changed, the play still went on with many of the same pressures as before. In a diary entry which is reminiscent of the Herridge days, King wrote that in late September, he *took a number of different photos of Joan over different parts of the moor and woodside, both of us seemed to be at high tension—nervous strain—the breaking up of the season, I suppose. I always find Joan difficult at partings or endings.*

While the 'mad storms of passion' of a few years previous were, seemingly, under control, there would always be other strains in the King-Joan relationship. From the time the Pattesons took up summer residence at Kingsmere, the nearness of their daily lives, summer and winter, brought its own rewards, its own punishments. The rewards were obvious. Joan was at King's beck and call whenever he needed someone to talk to, read with, share a meal or take a walk around his newly expanded property. She was his companion now on an almost constant basis. This dependency was also reciprocal and it was to King she turned when she had need of a sympathetic ear.

On the down side was the fact that there was no cooling-off period for any tensions that surfaced. What was upsetting in their relationship when they were both in Ottawa was just packed up with the cottage supplies and taken to Kingsmere and vice versa. Much of the blame must be laid at King's door and, especially when he began to see Joan in the light of someone who would have made a 'good life's partner'. He may not have told Joan of this feeling but it would have made a difference in his attitude to her in that, more than ever, he looked to her as a stand-in wife. For her part, whatever her feelings for King were at this juncture, Joan displayed many of the characteristics of a demanding companion. If King did not drop by to see her for an evening, she made it clear that she felt neglected. There are reports of little spats over nothing in particular and, as King saw it, Joan could be 'very sharp and very selfish' at times. The phone would be hung up but apologies would follow later in the evening and thus it went on. When King's schedule was full to the brim and he did not have time to talk with Joan, things got worse. "When we share we have to be alone briefly and when we are apart the world seems to get in between with its causes of jealousy and friction."

Despite little contretemps from time to time, an accommodation was worked out with King taking the line that they could 'each do much for the other'. He was assured of Joan's help in domestic matters (which was more than generous considering that she had her own household to run) but she was of great assistance to King in other ways too. It had become a habit for him to take drafts of speeches over to the Pattesons for their reaction. It seems to have been Joan who was mainly involved in this and there are many tributes to her for her contributions. In the summer of 1925, the Rotary Club of Kitchener presented a portrait of King to be hung in the city hall there and King took his draft speech

> up to 'Moorside' and read [it] aloud to Joan & Godfroy who were both deeply touched by it. . . . Joan was helpful in one or two suggestions, and correction of some quotations. Indeed I owe to her the idea of the address itself. She has been most helpful to me on my speeches.

Later that same year, they worked together on choosing a suitable inscription for the large bell in the Carillon of the Peace Tower. The wording that appealed most to them was:

> To commemorate the peace of 1918 and to keep in remembrance the service and sacrifice of Canada in the Great War—erected by authority of prlt. AD 1926—with the words 'Glory to God in the Highest, on earth Peace and Good-will to Man' around the rim of the bell at the base. This latter inscription Joan came across in my Hinchey [?] Bible . . . .it was her idea to put it around the base. The words 'to keep in remembrance' are hers—the rest is mine.

His speech on this occasion, along with others of a non-political nature which were delivered during the Jubilee festivities, appeared in his book, *The Message of the Carillon* which was published in November, 1927. Joan, who had checked for grammatical errors and faulty construction in the preface, received the first copy of the book as her birthday gift that year. The inscription read "To Joan, with love and best wishes for many happy returns of the day from her devoted friend, Rex."

King also highly approved of material provided by Joan when he was preparing a speech for broadcast to Britain in June 1941. "It had the inspirational and emotional note which I feel is what is most needed now. Her material seemed to me to be away ahead of what had come from other sources." But that did not sit well with those 'sources' who, at that time, were Jack Pickersgill, Leonard Brockington and Walter Turnbull. As a result of their combined efforts, some of Joan's thoughts were deleted and King noted that they had partial success in inserting something about Canada's war effort and aid to Britain. At an earlier date, when another speech was being mulled over, Joan got up early one morning and was 'inspired' to jot down some ideas for King. "The material with which she had supplied me was of real assistance, and the speech is as nearly the composition of the two combined—the meeting of two minds—as anything can be." Diverting his attention for a moment was the reflection that

> *Maybe that is the manner in which Nature sublimates—denied one avenue of expression—the physical,—it seeks a higher—the mental—denied both—or perfected through both, it seeks & finds yet another, the spiritual. That would seem to be the course of evolution.*

Joan and King may have enjoyed this great meeting of minds and she was often credited with being 'devotion itself' but, on occasion, this otherwise admirable attribute of hers became an intrusion. On one July morning King was walking around his garden at Kingsmere, looking at the flowers and singing to himself '0 God of Bethel', and 'Fight the Good Fight' before going back to the cottage verandah to write up his diary for the past few days. "[As I was] writing, Joan came down. I told her I must work now, my only thought must be my work, she must help me in that, not take me from it." This was in 1926 during the King-Byng crisis and he was in a testy mood anyway as he later wrote in his diary words that are, again, reminiscent of his problems with Marjorie. It was only when she was out of town, he said, that he got any work done. He had fought battles with various Governors-General to try to save Sundays for himself and he had to wage war with Joan for the same thing. One Sunday, "Joan tried to have me come in to tea, she has tried it in different ways, evidently not wanting a break in any Sundays from a visit." It took a few more years for King to get it all in perspective and by then it was too late. Twenty years after the Pattesons first appeared in his diary, he had reached a point where, after another episode that he found to indicate selfishness on Joan's part, he spelled things out to himself.

> *Something tells me that to develop the personality I require for my work and the purpose of my life, I must do things more and more for myself, and not to seek too greatly to share everything, to read more to myself, to work alone more, to decide things, even re gardens, dinners, etc., alone and carry them out and [be] wholly free from unnecessary contacts or consideration of personal relations with Joan*

& Godfroy. Each going our own way more & more will be better in the end, with days or hours shared now & then.

This was near the end of April 1938, and he had other things on his mind just then. Of great moment was the question as to whether or not he was mediumistic and, in his own mind, the answer was 'Yes'. "I have a feeling, it is a belief, that I am . . . that I take on quickly epochs, or environments, or atmospheres." He was also convinced that Joan, too, possessed this ability. Her involvement in spiritualism began only in 1932 but King's interest in psychic phenomena went back many years, back to his student days. "I have been groping in this direction for some time in the past", he wrote in 1899, "for some years, in fact." His forays into this field began when he went with other University of Toronto students to visit a 'phrenologist-mesmerist, etc.' who put him to sleep for half an hour and told him of his weaknesses. With a classmate, too, he later went to call on a fortune teller who, for $1, told him exactly what he already knew about himself and how he was about to shape his career. The price was right, as well, when he went in to the London Phrenological Institute in 1900 "as a sort of joke to take advantage of the rate offered to persons of limited means." This time he came away with the conclusion that "All that [the phrenologist] said as to faults, as to acceptance of beliefs, facts, opposition, desire to lead and impress men, etc., I think is true."

There was, evidently, plenty of choice for someone who was interested in dabbling in this field and King tried them all. It was not until 1925, however, that he took a more definite step along the road to spiritualism. A Mrs. Bleaney from Kingston was in Ottawa and King invited her to Laurier House where "She gave me a reading in the drawing room this afternoon, a truly remarkable experience. . . . She is the one who told my fortune in a remarkable way 4 years ago." So impressed was King with what Mrs. Bleaney told him this time that he sent at once for Joan and Godfroy to come to meet her and have tea. Then, Joan, too, had a reading that was, it seems, equally amazing in its accuracy. Although she continued to be somewhat sceptical, her interest had been aroused and after another reading in 1929, the die was cast. There is no doubt, of course, that King was the leader with Joan interested enough to follow him. It was a busy trail he laid down for her. His need of contact with the ones who had departed this life was constant but never more so than at times of crisis. During pre-election jitters or in stressful political situations, he was to be found seeking assurance through Mrs. Bleaney until, in the early 30s, he began to consult Mrs. Emma Wriedt, a well-known medium from Detroit. King had met her in Brockville at the home of the late Senator George Fulford in early 1932. Scandal was then staring the Liberal Party in the face and when Mrs. Fulford invited him to meet this medium whom she had personally consulted for over twenty years, King accepted eagerly. Four seances with her in two days convinced him of her abilities and she was invited to come to Ottawa where Joan joined him for more adventures of a remarkable nature. While the drawing room at Laurier House had been adequate for fortune telling, it would not do for seances, especially since Mrs. Wriedt used the direct voice method and some of the messages came through rather loudly. In order to keep as far away from the servants as possible, a small room at the top of the house was cleared of office staff and there Mrs. Wriedt, King and Joan had a series of 'conversations' which left them convinced of 'the wonder of it all'.

A few weeks later, when Joan and Godfroy were dining with King one evening and encouraged by the seances, no doubt, all three decided to see what they could do in this direction on their own. "We tried sitting alone in the dark for half an hour to see if [we] could secure evidence of psychical phenomena, but did not, tho' I believe we shall later on." They were much more successful when they learned how to use the 'little table' and although Godfroy's interest was not sufficiently keen for him to get involved, King and Joan took it up with fervour. It was on a Saturday night in late November 1933 that

> *Joan and I started to see if we could get results from placing our hands on the small table. It had spelled out the word 'Godfroy'... later we got quite a number of messages. . . . It was <u>our</u> first experience of 'table wrapping' [sic] and was amazingly successful. I was delighted to find Joan & I had the power.*

Having discovered this, there were many Saturday and Sunday nights over the next few years when they went to the 'little table' seeking and finding confirmation on a variety of topics. Depending on what they wanted to know, they were able to call up the appropriate persons to get the matter settled. In the summer at Kingsmere, the tempo increased and to accommodate this, King had a special room set up at Moorside as he had earlier done at Laurier House.

Sometimes these sittings were pleasing to them, but on other occasions they began to have doubts as to the veracity of what they were told. It was Joan's opinion that

> *the mediums [were] the best way to get information as they were usually ignorant people—their minds a blank—that with our minds so strong & feelings, etc. entering as we wrote . . . we were not getting the right source, we were either using our own subconscious thoughts, or an evil spirit was creeping in. . . . She believed what we got thro Mrs. Wreidt—but had to careful about 'opening the door'.*

King admitted that there was a danger "in trying to interpret to suit ones own preconceived plan or wish to make things work out in accordance with ones desires." While Joan was inclined towards mediums as being preferable to the 'little table', King was of the opinion that true guidance was only to be found in the Bible. And further, "I see no record in the bible of 'table-wrappings' [sic] tho' many accounts of spirits evil as well as good manifesting in divers ways." Along with the doubts which both had at this time, King was finding that he was very tired. He did all the writing of what transpired at the 'little table' and sometimes this took him well into the night before he was finished.

Joan's expressed preference for the use of mediums may have been because of her concern for King's fatigue. One thing he could not do, however, was to put any of the blame for this on those who 'spoke' with Joan and himself. When a session lasted too long, the advice he received, often from his parents, was 'Go to bed now. Get some rest'. One night John King was 'speaking' and King asked his father: "Do you think the table tires me, or why am I so fatigued at times?" The reply was that "The table is exhausting. It might be well to stop it for a time." Once again, King did not heed this fatherly advice and for a period in the 1930s, he and Joan very often turned to the 'little table'. In 1937 King recorded a total of 75 conversations, including visions which he believed to be truly genuine and in which he interested Joan to the point where she wrote out her own dreams/visions. Their interest in psychic phenomena continued for the rest of his life in varying degrees of intensity. The 'little table' was not relegated to a cupboard in the 'muniments room', as Buchan had called it, at Laurier House nor in the secret room at Moorside. As late as 1949,

King and Joan, he in his 75th year, she five years older, could at times be found, side by side, at the 'little table', still receiving messages from family and friends as well as from political figures whom King had known or admired.

Although Godfroy kept his distance from these experiences except for some initial show of interest, he did succumb to a seance with Mrs. Wreidt in early 1938. Possibly it was because he was basically an unbeliever in the whole process but as King noted, "The power was not strong—none of the voices very loud." While Godfroy did not have the psychic powers that King and Joan felt they possessed, they had other company around the 'little table' in the 30s. King had an Irish Terrier, a gift from the Pattesons in 1924, and for some time he had suspected that this little dog was no ordinary animal. Confirmation of this came while at the 'table' one night in 1937. Gladstone had come to talk with them on this occasion and King recorded the following conversation.

> *King: (Pat comes in and whines, looks at me and lies at my feet).*
> *Gladstone: The dog is very psychic.*
> *He knows we are talking together.*
> *The dog is a good medium.*
> *He will speak to you of many things.*

This just verified what King had thought as early as 1931 when Pat was ill one time and was being so patient. "[He] reminds me of dear Mother. Little Pat has her spirit of love and faithfulness. His eyes never leave me. She may have sent him to be a guide and guard for me." There had been other times when King was convinced that Pat was in sympathy with his own feelings and that he had, indeed, been sent by 'dear Mother'. One Sunday evening, he went to dinner with Joan & Godfroy and

> *Took little Pat with me. After dinner Joan played the piano,—beautifully. When we came to hymns and I asked for 'Lead Kindly Light'—Mother's hymn, Pat got up off the floor, came up on the sofa and rubbed his little head on my trouser legs. . . . I feel more and more he is a little spirit dog, revealing dear Mother's continued presence to me.*

Pat's place in King's life was thus very special. Derry, 'his little brudder', as King once called him, was the Pattesons' dog from the same litter. In 1940, Derry became ill and was put to sleep but Pat lived on until the summer of 1941 when he was seventeen years old and in very poor health. King was out of town when Pat's condition worsened in early July but as soon as he was back, he went directly to Kingsmere for an emotional farewell to his little friend. The next two days were very traumatic and King did not make matters easier for himself by drawing comparisons between his mother's death in 1917 and that of Pat, his 'little spirit dog'. He was too late for the former and almost too late, also, to share Pat's last hours. Early in the morning of 15 July 1941 Pat died and that evening a remarkable burial service was held for him. Joan, who had been at King's side almost constantly during those last two days, comforting both master and dog, was with King for this service as were Godfroy and members of King's household staff. From The Farm where King was then living, they drove past Moorside to the Temple Ruins and, there, Pat's body was placed in a grave just beside Derry's. "I stood just above Derry's grave and Joan and Godfroy at the foot of both," and, to complete the tie with 'Mother', the grave was marked with vases of flowers in one of which "was a rose, with maiden hair fern which I took from a vase on the bedroom mantle near dear Mother's picture."

The following night, around the 'little table' John King passed on the news that

> *Pat is here beside me. . . .*
> *He runs all over the place like a young dog. . . .*
> *He talks to Derry about Kingsmere.*
> *They think they own the place.*
> *They love to go off on hunts together.*
> *They know where the groundhog holes are.*
> *They know all about hunting rabbits and squirrels.*

At this point Joan joined in the conversation by remarking that

> *I hope there are no cats in heaven, it would be hell if there were.*

For this she was roundly reproved by John King who said

> *Joan is quite facetious.*
> *The dogs are in their natural home here.*
> *God loves everything He has created.*

By October, King had another dog, Pat II, also a gift from the Pattesons, and while he could soon say that 'I like him a lot', there was no replacing the first Pat. In 1947, this dog died and he, too, found a burial spot in Kingsmere, near the Bethel Stone.*

Joan's support at the time of Pat 1's death and her companionship in psychic matters aside, her nature had not changed as she grew older; she was still prone to bouts of selfishness and jealousy where King was concerned. She seems to have felt very threatened whenever another woman crossed King's path and he found this irritating.

> *I had a difficult time with Joan over the phone. It was a jealousy on her part over Madeline Coldwell coming to dinner. She cannot see it is better to have others at times. It is very trying, that sort of thing.*

Joan had no reason for harbouring any such feelings about this dinner guest of King's but, if she had known how he felt about Julia Grant in the 30s, the green-eyed monster of jealousy would certainly have raised its ugly head. Julia was the granddaughter of the American President, Ulysses S. Grant and King had met her in Newport in 1899 during his graduate year at Harvard. She was then engaged to Prince Michael Cantacuzene, a Lieutenant in the Russian guards cavalry. King's impression of the Prince was that he 'seemed a poor affair' and evidently Julia later came to feel the same way about him when, in 1934, she divorced him on the grounds that he 'failed to show any interest in matrimonial duties'. King and Julia seldom met again until about the time of her divorce but, in the years just before and after this event, they carried on an intense correspondence and met whenever possible. The relationship that developed threatened to get out of hand at times and King came very close to letting his emotions really take over for once. What stopped him was that he felt guilty about "not having Joan fully in my confidence or Julia fully in my confidence re Joan. Still I do not take aught away from either and both are friends and devoted friends. There can surely be nothing wrong in [such a] friendship." It took the reading of I Samuel XXV to clear King's thinking about those two women in his life.

> *I was rejoiced to read of Abigail in the morning bible reading, a*

---

*The exact location of the dogs' graves is not clear but it is in the vicinity of the ruins. After Pat II died, King was given another Irish Terrier, Pat III as a gift from the family of J. Edouard Handy, his private secretary.

woman of good understanding and beautiful countenance, that is Joan surely. Now she restrains David from carrying out a wrong interest and held him to the highest. That is Joan's purpose and mission in my life.

Julia, on the other hand, was variously seen by him as a Delilah, a Salome or a Queen of Sheba—in any case, a temptress and, as such, she was fated to lose out to the one who played Abigail in King's life. It is a moot point just how much Joan knew about King's feelings for Julia. He did his best to keep her in the dark about the depth of his emotions but, knowing him as long and as well as she had, it would be surprising had she not sensed that he was going through a very difficult period. If so, Julia's visit to Kingsmere in the summer of 1939 would have been quite a strain on Joan but, as far as King could see (or wanted to see), it all went off rather well. "The last few days have been a little trying for [Joan] but she has risen above all feelings that were natural enough. I would not let her be hurt for worlds—and she has not been—in thought or word or deed."

There was no such threat or tension when Violet Markham visited King. Her visits, the one just two weeks after Julia left and, again, in the summer of 1949, were the uncomplicated meetings of old and dear friends with none of the sexual overtones that ultimately changed the direction of the King-Julia association. There was absolutely nothing for Joan to fear from Violet and, as it turned out, the two women quickly established a common bond in their concern for King and his future. With the world on the brink of war in 1939, King had little time to devote to his English guest and this resulted in Joan and Violet being left to their own resources. That being the case, they were able to talk over what they felt was wisest for King to do now that he was approaching his 65th birthday. When Violet went back home, it was left to Joan to be the day-to-day catalyst over the years from 1939 onwards, but they kept in touch by letters.

In October 1945, King sailed on the Queen Mary for a month's visit to England, taking with him a letter to Violet from Joan. In her reply, Violet wrote of her deep concern

at his appearance when we met a few days ago. . . . I have never seen a more tired man, or one more utterly weary. . . . I do wish he would lay down the burthen of the Premiership. . . . He spoke of his wish to retire but I know full well the right moment never comes to men in his position. . . . Perhaps I have exaggerated in my own mind the impression of fatigue he made on me but after an interval of some years naturally I saw a change which would not strike so forcibly those who meet him daily.

Joan had similar concerns about King's heavy workload and declining health, but three more years were to pass before he was persuaded to first give up the leadership of the Liberal Party and then, a few months later, to resign as Prime Minister.

But both Violet and Joan continued to worry about King as he entered retirement. On one of his regular morning walks with Joan at Kingsmere in the late summer of 1948, he "discussed with her pretty freely the pros and cons . . . [of dropping] out of the govt. altogether . . . regardless of the embarrassment that might be created through a drop thereby of some $14,000. in salary." Neither Joan nor Violet had any knowledge of King's financial situation and they feared he might have to pinch pennies in his old age. It was with this in mind that later in the year, Violet offered him the 'legacy' that was never collected. In fact, King, himself, was not aware at this time that he was really a wealthy man* and he, too, had some worry as to how he might manage. At one time he even considered "an offer to read articles for Funk and Wagnall's enclyclopedia [sic]. Would have brought in some income."

Of equal importance was the question of trying to make some progress sorting out papers, especially those of a private nature, which were in his vast accumulation. What he could now handle physically without too much strain were bundles of old letters and he often called Joan over to Laurier House to read extracts from these to her. On a Saturday night in April 1950, he was taking another trip back down memory lane with Joan. The letters he read that evening were from the early 1920s, days that had

---

*In his diary on 31 March 1949, King wrote that "to my amazement I found that my investments had been so carefully husbanded that they were really about double of what I had believed them to be. I have been so careful not to touch the savings section, kept against the day of being out of office, and adding where I could here & there from such sources as I could e.g. Sir Wm. Mulock's gift of $50,000, that I had not realized that my investments mostly in Dominion Bonds & a few private Co shares had reached proportions that would not be understood by the public. With Mr. R's additional gift I now have a new problem to face. I can honestly say I would almost prefer to be without more than a mere subsistence, could I be sure of this to the end of my life. I would not like my life's record of service to be overshadowed by anything savouring of wealth, and that is now what I have come to possess, believing the fact, that I was none too well off or one being out of office, and a calling of any kind.

special significance for both of them when their relationship was in danger of pulling them into deep waters. That evening he also read aloud parts of a will which he had made in the 1920-21 period. It would have come as a surprise to Joan to hear that in it

> *I had willed to her all my property at Kingsmere for her lifetime but with the understanding that it would be, after her death, used as a sort of community property for girls in the civil service, shops, etc. where they might have a chance for rest and recreation.*

It was thirty years since the making of this will and the intervening time had seen many changes in King's holdings at Kingsmere. No longer was his estate comprised of only the small original cottage by the lake with its wharf, boat and bathing house. By 1950 it was a vast country estate of some 575 acres and there were now five houses and their outbuildings as well as large tracts of parkland. All of this did not happen by accident. In his last will, King wrote that

> *I had not been long in office before I conceived the idea of acquiring sufficient land to make Kingsmere properties into a park which would be worthy of its location in the immediate vicinity of Ottawa, and which some day I might present to the country as a thank-offering for the opportunities of public service which the people of Canada have given me.*

This disposition did not mean that Joan was forgotten in King's final will. He was aware of the struggles she, by then in her late seventies, was facing in trying to care for Godfroy who was almost an invalid. Without putting the offer in so many words, he sought to reassure her by saying "she could always count on my being at her side to help her meet every situation." Clearly, she was not to inherit the waterfront property but neither was she to be excluded from Kingsmere. A clause in King's will stipulated that

> *Inasmuch as relatives and friends of mine have spent their summers, or part of them, at Kingsmere as my guests or tenants . . . I would therefore ask that the Government should authorize my Trustees to provide that, for a period of three years after my death, the cottages . . . shall be available, rent-free, for use [by members of family and friends]*

There was a further and specific request in that

> *I direct my Trustees to pay to my friends, Mr. and Mrs. Godfroy B. Patteson, of Ottawa, Ontario, jointly during their lives, the sum of Twenty-Five Hundred Dollars per annum . . . to be continued to the survivor during his or her life.*

Although this seems a rather insignificant sum now, it was not at the time, being then the equivalent of a year's salary for many.

'It breaks my heart to think that the Summer of '49 is over' were the words that came to mind at the end of August that year. So many summers had come and gone at Kingsmere, some of them having been very traumatic when dealing with his relationship with either Marjorie or Joan but this one was to be his last full summer there. He felt that his health had improved a little but all he could hope for was 'God grant me power to keep cheerful and to press on'. Indeed, it was almost impossible to do either to any degree. Despite Joan's presence whenever she could take time away from Godfroy and his needs, King had felt very much alone after his retirement. Public life was now a thing of the past and even the spirits of the departed were not a comfort to him as they had been when he could summon them around the 'little table'. In his last few years, this means of communication was seldom used, possibly because he did not have the physical strength that it seemed to demand. This loss of contact was painful to him and, in April 1950, he admitted that

> *What I have regretted most is my feeling of remoteness from those I love who have passed away. I do not seem to have been able to feel their nearness, though I have a curious feeling when I am suffering or feeling distressed that my Mother either shared or is sharing with me.*

In late June 1950, King went once more to Kingsmere, agreeing to 'take a night nurse for a day or two just to get settled but more to please Joan who thinks it wise'. Since the beginning of the year he had been under constant medical care, and although he felt that he was stronger than he had been for some months and that a summer in the country would prove to be the best medicine, such was not the case. Realistically, he felt that "A month or two will tell what the length of time is likely to be and may remain. I have felt off and on of late that the time might be quite short." And, indeed, it was; he did not even have one month. His days were as they had been at Laurier House of late—rising around noon and then a nap in the afternoon. The other constant was Joan's evening visits. She went over to see him at least once a day and, when he was able, they read together or took a short walk around the grounds. His relationship with Joan was free, at last, from any of the old jealousies and his ultimate tribute to her was that "She has been amazingly kind. . . . So helpful and cheerful. Godfroy equally so. I can never repay all their kindness." There was one even higher accolade: "She has filled the place of my mother in my heart over the years."

As King's strength waned over the last year or so, he had sometimes thought of diary-keeping as being a waste of time but he still continued to dictate each day's events even if he recognized that what he had to say mainly related to his health. In early July 1950, he dictated the final record for that most remarkable of diaries, his last words being "Very, very sorry to have kept Lafleur all that time." When the diary was resumed the following day it was written up by the said Lafleur, one of King's secretaries, who noted that

> *After luncheon [on the 20th] Mr. King decided to sit in the sun on the verandah. While there admired the beauty of the countryside. Then decided to go up for a rest, and as he did not seem to be feeling very well, asked Camille [Cleroux, his chauffeur] to 'look in every fifteen minutes or so'. This was shortly after 3. At 20 past 5 Mr. King got up for a moment, but felt a severe chill which culminated into a serious heart attack. . . . From then on Mr. King entered into a coma.*

On Dominion Day, 1950, King had dictated what was to be his last letter to Violet Markham and, as chance would have it, her reply was the last piece of personal correspondence he read. Joan, who had been keeping Violet informed of his condition after the heart attack, passed on this bit of news in a telegram along with the information that "Rex's life drawing rapidly to close." It was several days after King's death on July 22nd before Joan felt up to writing to Violet to tell her that King had sent for her soon after the attack and that during the rest of the time that he was conscious,

> *he was so sweet kept praying that God would let him live to finish his work, thanked me for what I had done, but I don't think he realized that it was the very final attack. . . . Godfroy went up the hill and climbed the stairs to bid him good bye but he broke down*

and could not stay longer. . . . At 9.42 Saturday night it was over and we were alone. It was a lovely evening but just at the moment he died thunder and lightning and torrents of rain came without any warning. So many have remarked it—for the rain fell only at Kingsmere—not Ottawa even. The rest you know. The country took charge and he was out of our care.

Just as King had paid Joan the compliment of saying that she had filled the place of his mother in his heart, so too Joan had her own tribute to pay. In her letter to Violet, she wrote "Godfroy and I are like two creatures of stone . . . for the one who gave us the very essence of our life, has been taken from us."

Acknowledgements

After completing a book, the author has the pleasure of saying 'Thank you' to all those who have helped along the way. I should like to start by acknowledging the receipt of a grant from the Explorations Programme of the Canada Council. This was of great assistance in my research for the necessary material.

Many hours were spent in Library and Archives Canada in Ottawa where the staff of the Reading Room were ever helpful as I delved into Mackenzie King's legacy of his diaries and letters. I consulted at different times with Maureen Hoogenraad, the archivist handling Prime Ministers' Records, and benefitted from her help.

This particular look at Mackenzie King was undertaken with the full cooperation of his nephews and nieces who were interested in learning so much more than they expected about their uncle. They were generous, too, in sharing memories of him.

I wish to thank Dr. H. Blair Neatby and also Lee d'Anjou, my editor for *Agnes: The Biography of Lady Macdonald,* who read an early draft of the book and each gave me good advice. This draft was read, as well, by Dwight Fulford, Mackenzie King's godson, who, naturally, knew something of him (but he also learned something more).

As well as reading letters from King's friends, it was wonderful to be in touch with some of their families. A letter from a great-niece of Violet Markham (written in Moon Green, Kent, England) made my day as did one from David Rockefeller who wrote of the close friendship between his father and Mackenzie King.

My friends were generous in their support and I particularly wish to thank Helen Small, Valerie Knowles, John Hilliker and the late Harry Carter for practical support. In Comox, British Columbia, where I now live, I was fortunate in having the help of David Dalton who did the layout and cover design for the book.

Most importantly of all, my thanks to all of my family on both sides of the Atlantic for seeing me through this exercise. I am most appreciative of their support and understanding. I called on them for help in everything from spell-checks to computer problems and they were there for me. Thank you so much.

Sources

There is no richer source for anyone wishing to write about Mackenzie King's personal life than can be found in his own diaries. These were begun in 1893 and continued until shortly before his death in July, 1950. They are in the Library and Archives Canada in Ottawa and have been fully open to the public since 1973 when microfiche copies were made available through the University of Toronto Press. Also the period from 1939 to 1948 was covered in four volumes of edited excerpts from the diaries. These constitute *The Mackenzie King Record*, the first volume having been prepared by J. W. Pickersgill. The remaining three volumes were done with the assistance of D. F. Forster of the University of Toronto.

The Archives also contain the voluminous correspondence between Mackenzie King, his family and friends. All of these sources are in the Mackenzie King Papers in the Archives. Wherever letters are quoted the writers are identified in the text. Since this is not an academic work it was decided to not clutter up the text with numerals. However, specific questions about any sources may be sent to the author in care of Trafford Publishing.

Much of the background material for *Mackenzie King: Friends and Lovers* was drawn from the above noted sources. As well previously printed materials were accessed and these are listed in the following chapter notes.

Preface:
Canadian Issues, a Publication of the Association of Canadian Studies, vol. 1, no.2, spring, 1977.
Bruce Hutcheson, *The Incredible Canadian*, Longmans Canada, 1970 ed.
C. P. Stacey, *A Very Double Life*, Macmillan of Canada, 1977 ed.
Michael Bliss, *Right Honourable Men*, HarperCollins Publishers, 1994.

Introduction:
From *Alligator Pie* (Macmillan of Canada, 1974; Key Porter books, 2001). Copyright © 1974 Dennis Lee. With permission of the author.
H. Reginald Hardy, *Mackenzie King of Canada* by OUP, 1949.

William Kilbourn, *The Firebrand, William Lyon Mackenzie and the Rebellion of Upper Canada*, Clarke Irwin, Toronto, 1956.

Chapter One: Mathilde Grossert.
This was based entirely on diary entries and letters.

Chapter Two: Bert Harper.
W.L.Mackenzie King, *The Secret of Heroism: A Memoir of Henry Albert Harper*, The Ontario Publishing Co., Ltd. Toronto, 1919 ed.
R. MacGregor Dawson, *William Lyon Mackenzie King, A Political Biography, 1874-1923*, University of Toronto Press, 1958.
Henry Ferns and Bernard Ostry, *The Age of Mackenzie King*, Lorimer, 1976.
Violet Markham, *Friendship's Harvest*, Max Reinhardt, London, 1956.

Chapter Three: Marjorie Herridge.
M. R. D. Foot and H. C. G. Matthew, *The Gladstone Diaries*, Oxford, 1974.

Chapter Four: Violet Markham:
Violet Markham, *Friendship's Harvest*, op.cit.
Violet Markham, *Return Passage*, OUP, London, 1953.
F .A. McGregor, *The Fall & Rise of Mackenzie King, 1911-1919*, Macmillan, Toronto, 1962.
See also: *A Very Double Life* by C. P. Stacey, op.cit.

Chapter Five: The Governors-General.
Sandra Gwyn, *The Private Capital*, McClelland and Stewart Ltd., Toronto, 1984.
R. MacGregor Dawson, op.cit.
Jeffery Williams, *Byng of Vimy*, Secker and Warburg, London, 1983.
See also: H. Blair Neatby, *William Lyon Mackenzie King, The Lonely Heights*, University of Toronto Press, 1963 ; J. L. Granatstein, *Mackenzie King, His Life and World*, McGraw-Hill Ryerson Ltd., 1977; R. MacGregor Dawson, op.cit. ; Roger Graham, *Arthur Meighen, Vol. 2,* Clarke, Irwin & Co., Ltd., Toronto, 1963; Eugene A. Forsey, *The Royal Power of Dissolution of Parliament in the British Commonwealth*, OUP, 1943 and 1968.
R. H. Hubbard, *Rideau Hall*, McGill-Queen's University Press, Montreal and London, 1977.

H. Willis-O'Connor and Madge Macbeth, *Inside Government House*, Ryerson Press, Toronto, 1954.
Janet Adam Smith, *John Buchan, A Biography*, OUP, 1985.
Lawrence Martin, *The Presidents and the Prime Ministers*, Doubleday, 1982.

Chapter Six: Rockefeller
F. A. McGregor, op.cit.
R. MacGregor Dawson, op.cit.
Mary Ellen Chase, *Abby Aldrich Rockefeller*, Macmillan, N. Y., 1950.

Chapter Seven: Joan Patteson
Florence Bird, *Anne Francis, An Autobiography*, Clarke, Irwin, 1974.
Joy E. Esberey, *Knight of the Holy Spirit*, University of Toronto Press, 1980.
H. Blair Neatby, *William Lyon Mackenzie King, Vol. 3*, University of Toronto Press, 1976.

Care has been taken to trace the ownership of copyright material used in this book. The author would appreciate any information enabling her to rectify any references or credits in subsequent editions.

Photo Credits

All photos are from the Library and Archives Canada and used with their kind permission. The respective reference number follows the photo description.

xxi - (Four King Children) C7352

xxiv - (King with his parents) C46521

xxxi - (King in 1910) PA 25970

p. 02 - (Mathilde Grossert) C 79189

p. 26 - (Bert Harper) PA 126941

p. 52 - (Marjorie Herridge) PA 141392

p. 75 - (Violet Markham) C 14179

p.101 - (Countess of Aberdeen) PA 27917

p.103 - (Earl of Minto) C51950

p.104 - (Earl & Countess Grey) C 30723

p.107 - (Duke of Devonshire) C1013

p.108 - (Duke of Connaught) C 59

p.110 - (Lord & Lady Byng) C 33995

p.117 - (Viscount & Lady Willingdon) PA 148544

p.122 - (Earl of Bessborough) C 1018

p.126 - (Lord & Lady Tweedsmuir) PA 148539

p.133 - (Earl of Athlone & Princess Alice) PA 148533

p.136 - (Viscount & Lady Alexander) PA 148542

p.151 - (J.D.Rockefeller Jr.) C 2127

p.171 - (Joan Patteson) PA 126156

INDEX

A

Aberdeen, Lady, 99-101.
Aberdeen, Lord, 99-101.
Addams, Jane, 31.
Alexander, Sir Harold, 136-8.
Alexander, Lady, 138.
Arnold, Matthew, 37, 50, 51, 58, 68, 69.
Athlone, Countess of, 133-135.
Athlone, Earl of, 133-136.

B

Baltimore, 16, 17.
Barchet, George, 13-15, 17, 176.
Barchet, Mary, 14-19, 165.
Barchet, Mathilde. See Grossert, Mathilde.
Barchet, Nellie, 14.
Barchet, Stephanie, 14,15.
Barchet, Stephen, 14,15.
Barrie, xxvii, 23, 24, 26, 27, 29, 32.
Barrie Collegiate, 26.
Belfield, 15-17, 19, 20.
Berlin, (now Kitchener, Ontario), xxi, xxiii, xxiv, 19, 26.
Bessborough, Lord, 122, 123, 125.
Bessborough, Roberte, Lady, 122-125.
Bishop Strachan School, 26.
Blair, Bessie, 23, 24.
Bleaney, Mrs., 182, 183.
Bliss, Michael, xvi.
Brockington, L. W., xii, 180.
Buchan, John, xxxii, 92, 124-129, 131, 184.
Buchan, Susan, 124-129, 131, 132.
Burbidge, Henry, 'Burb', 38, 41, 48.
Byng, Lady, 109-117, 124.
Byng, Lord, 109-118, 124, 137, 138, 181.

C

Campbell, Wilfred, 69, 91.
Carlyle, Thomas, 37.
Carnegie, Mrs. Andrew, 172.
Carruthers, James, 82, 83, 89.
Castine, Maine, 18, 19.
Chelsea, 39, 49, 50, 55.
Chesterfield, Settlement, 71, 72.
Chicago, 1-4, 8, 10, 12, 13, 20, 31, 32, 45, 72, 99, 158.
Chicago, University of, 1, 30.
Churchill, Winston, 123.
Clark, Gregory, xii.
Corot, 68.
Connaught, Duchess of, 109
Connaught, Duke of, 105-107.

D

Dafoe, J. W., xii.
Dawson, R. McGregor, xiii.
Denver, Colorado, xxvii, 15.
Department of Labour, 37.
Devonshire, Duchess of, 109.
Devonshire, Duke of, 107, 109, .
Diamond Jubilee of Confederation, 118.
Dufferin, Lord, 120.
Duncan, Emily, 40, 49-51, 61.
Duncan, George, 61.

E

Edgmoor, 59, 67.
Edward VII, 104.
Elliot, Lady Ruby, 102-104, 109.
Esberey, Dr., Joy E., xv, xvi.

F

Falconbridge, Jack, 28.
Ferns, H. S., xiv.

G

Gatineau, xxii, 23, 39.
George, John, 4, 10, 11.
Gerry, Bob, 48, 78.
Gladstone, W. E., 59, 100, 102, 163, 185.
Glee Club, xxiv.
Goethe, 1.
Government House, 23, 72, 105-111, 116, 122, 134-136.
Granatstein, J. L., xvi.
Grand Opera House, Toronto, 26.
Grant, Julia, 187, 188.
Greer, Jean, 155, 156.
Grenfell Mission, 60.
Grey, Lady, 71, 104, 106, 109.
Grey, Lord, 43, 71, 103-105.
Grossert, Mathilde, xix, xxx, 1-21, 24, 33, 40, 41, 52, 53, 56, 61, 64, 72, 73, 79, 84, 165, 176.

H

Hardy, H. Reginald, xii, xiv, xv.
Harper, Henry Albert 'Bert', xxxi, xxxiii, 4, 14, 16, 23-45, 49-55, 58, 59, 60, 102, 105, 132, 133, 144.
Harvard, xxvi, 2-4, 6, 9, 11, 12, 14, 19, 33-35, 48, 55, 78, 142, 155, 158, 187.
Herridge, Marjorie, xxxi, 39, 40, 45, 47-69, 72, 103, 105, 169-171, 173-175, 178, 181, 191.
Herridge, Dr. William Thomas, 39, 47-67, 175, 176.
Herridge, William, 'Bill' 61, 62, 66.
Holmes, Oliver Wendell, 28.
Hull House, 3.
Hutchison, Bruce, xii.

I

Industry and Humanity, 151-154, 169, 170.

J

(*no subjects*)

K

Kappa Alpha, 28, 44.
King, Arthur, xxvii.
King, Dougall Macdougall, 'Max', xxi, xxii, xxvii, 15, 53.
King, Isabel Grace, xxii, xxiv, xxv, xxviii, xxx, 5, 7, 40, 53, 54, 105, 152.
King, Isabel, 'Bella', xxi, xxv, xxvi, 58, 84, 92.
King, Janet, 'Jennie', xxi, xxvi, xxvii, 5, 6, 26, 58, 77.
King, John, xxi, xxii, xxiv, xxv, xxix, xxx, 7, 58, 84, 99, 186.
King, William Lyon Mackenzie 11, xxvii.
King Mountain, 49.
Kingsmere, xxii, xxvii, 16, 39, 49, 50, 58, 59, 61, 66-68, 84, 91, 92, 124, 126, 128, 131, 135, 138, 161, 166, 169, 173, 178, 179, 181, 183, 186-190, 191, 193.
Kingswood, 58, 59.
Knudson, Dr., 10.

L

Labour Gazette, 34-36, 41.
Lamb, W. K., xiii.
Lay, H. M. 'Harry', xxvii.
Lay, Harry (son), xxvii.
Lay, Jean, xxvii.
Lay, John, xxvii.
Lay, Nelson, xxvii.
Lay, Rosabelle, xxvii.
Laurier House, xxvii, 94, 110, 115, 132, 176-178, 182-184, 189.
Laurier, Lady, 53, 176, 177.
Laurier, Sir Wilfrid, 16, 62, 105, 118, 145, 172, 176.
Leacock, Stephen, 104.
Lee, Dennis, xix.
London Advertiser, 30.
Ludwig, Emil, xii, xiv.

M

Mackenzie, William Lyon, 'The Rebel', xiii, xxvii- xxix, 5, 126, 133.
Markham, Violet, xxi, 44, 71-96, 105, 124, 125, 132, 142, 143,

153, 155, 188, 189, 192, 193.
Massey, Vincent, 112,136, 138.
May Court Club, 104, 108.
McCook, Martha, 78.
McGregor, Fred, xiii, xv, 96, 147, 151, 152, 154, 172.
McMinn, Mrs., 39, 49, 50, 55.
McNaughton, Gen. A. G. L., 136.
Meighen, Arthur, 88, 89, 111, 112.
Minto, Lady, 23, 109.
Minto, Lord, 23, 99-104.
Moon Green, 88, 89, 91, 96.
Moorside, 65, 126, 180, 183, 184.
Mulock, Sir William, xxviii, 30, 34, 49, 60, 189.
Muskoka, 12, 49.

N

Neatby, H. Blair, xiii.
Nesbitt, Violet, 13, 440, 41.

O

Osgoode Hall, xxvi.
Ostry, Bernard, xiv.
Ottawa, xxv.
Ottawa Canoe Club, 34.
Ottawa Press Gallery, xx, 30, 34.
Ottawa Rowing Club, 34.
Oxford, 6.

P

Parsifal, 174, 176.
Passmore Edwards House, 72
Pat 1, 16, 91, 117, 185-187.
Patricia, H.R.H., Princess, 106.
Patteson, Godfroy, xxiv, 67, 169, 171, 175-183, 185, 188, 190-193.
Patteson, Joan, xxiv, xxxi, 67, 91, 95, 165, 169, 170, 171, 173-193.
Pickersgill, J. W., xiii, 180.

Prince of Wales, later King Edward VIII., 107, 108, 118-120.
Prince George, later King George VI., 118.

Q

Quebec Conference of 1943, 135.

R

Rebellion of 1837, xxviii.
Reform Club, 24.
Rexy!, xvi.
Rideau Club, 43.
Rideau Hall, xxxi, 71, 99. See also Government House.
Ritchie, Charles, xi.
Robertson, Heather, xvi.
Robertson, Norman, xiii.
Rockefeller, Abby, 148, 149, 155-157, 159-161, 165, 166.
Rockefeller, David, 158.
Rockefeller, John D. R., Sr.,142, 143, 149, 157.
Rockefeller, John D. R., Jr., xiv, xv, xxxi, 17, 18, 142-166, 172, 189.
Rockefeller Foundation, xv, xxxi, 16, 64, 66, 106, 107, 172.
Roosevelt, President Franklin D., 17, 130.
Russell House, 34.

S

St. Andrew's Presbyterian Church, Ottawa, 39, 46, 56, 57, 132.
St. Laurent, Louis, 137.
St. Luke's Hospital, 1, 13, 18.
Salisbury, Frank, 159-161.
Sandford, Eva, 113-115.
Sandwell, B. K., xii, 44.
Seal Harbor, Maine, 18.
Shakespeare, 58.
Stacey, Charles, xii, xv, xx.

T

Tennyson, 37.

Toynbee, Arnold, 31, 104.
Toynbee Hall, 3.
Turnbull, Walter, 170, 180.
Tweedsmuir, Lady, see Buchan, Susan.
Tweedsmuir, Lord, see Buchan, John.

U

US Naval Academy, 15.
University College, Toronto, 26, 27.

V

Versailles, Peace of, 86.
Victoria College, 100.

W

Warlick, Mary. See Barchet, Mary.
Warlick, Walter, 17, 18.
Washington, 15, 17, 130.
Waterloo, University of, xi, xiii, xvi.
Watt, George Frederick, 42.
Williamsburg, 17.
Willingdon, Lady, 117-121, 123.
Willingdon, Lord, 117-121.
Woodside, xxi-xxiii, xxv.
Wreidt, Emma, 183-185.

X, Y, Z.

(*no subjects*)

ISBN 1-41205985-2